U.S. History-Based Writing Lessons

Implementing the Structure and Style® Writing Method

Teacher's Manual

by Lori Verstegen

Illustrated by Laura Holmes

Second Edition © November 2019
Institute for Excellence in Writing, L.L.C.

Also by Lori Verstegen

Advanced U.S. History-Based Writing Lessons
All Things Fun and Fascinating Writing Lessons
Ancient History-Based Writing Lessons
Bible Heroes Writing Lessons

Dress-Ups, Decorations, and Delightful Diversions
Medieval History-Based Writing Lessons
U.S. History-Based Writing Lessons
Modern World History-Based Writing Lessons

The purchase of this book allows its owner access to PDF downloads that accompany *U.S. History-Based Writing Lessons*. See blue page for details and download instructions. Our duplicating/copying policy for these resources is specified on the copyright page for each of these downloads.

Additional copies of this Teacher's Manual may be purchased from IEW.com/USH-T

Institute for Excellence in Writing (IEW®)
8799 N. 387 Road
Locust Grove, OK 74352
800.856.5815
info@IEW.com
IEW.com

Printed in the United States of America

IEW® and Structure and Style® are registered trademarks of the Institute for Excellence in Writing, L.L.C.

These lessons are not intended as a history curriculum replacement, but rather their purpose is to broaden subject knowledge while students learn to write.

Accessing Your Downloads
Teacher's Manual

The purchase of this book allows its owner access to PDF downloads of the following:

- the optional *U.S. History-Based Writing Lesson Reproducible Checklists* (32 pages)
- the optional *U.S. History-Based Writing Lessons Simplified Source Texts*
- the optional *U.S. History-Based Writing Lessons Advanced Additions*
- the optional *U.S. History-Based Writing Lessons Exemplars*

To download these e-resources, please follow the directions below:

1. Go to our website: IEW.com

2. Log in to your online customer account. If you do not have an account, you will need to create one.

3. After you are logged in, type this link into your address bar: IEW.com/USH-TE

4. Click the checkboxes next to the names of the files you wish to place in your account.

5. Click the "Add to my files" button.

6. To access your files now and in the future, click on "Your Account" and click on the "Files" tab (one of the gray tabs).

7. Click on each file name to download the files onto your computer.

Please note: You may download and print these e-books as needed for use within *your immediate family*. However, this information is proprietary, and we are trusting you to be on your honor not to share it with anyone. Please see the copyright page for further details.

If you have any difficulty receiving these downloads after going through the steps above, please call 800.856.5815.

Institute for Excellence in Writing
8799 N. 387 Road
Locust Grove, OK 74352

Contents

UNIT 1: NOTE MAKING AND OUTLINES

UNIT 2: WRITING FROM NOTES

UNIT 3: RETELLING NARRATIVE STORIES

UNIT 4: SUMMARIZING A REFERENCE

UNIT 5: WRITING FROM PICTURES

UNIT 6: SUMMARIZING MULTIPLE REFERENCES

UNIT 7: INVENTIVE WRITING

UNIT 8: FORMAL ESSAY MODELS

UNIT 9: FORMAL CRITIQUE AND RESPONSE TO LITERATURE

Appendices

Welcome to *U.S. History-Based Writing Lessons.* This Teacher's Manual shows reduced copies of the Student Book pages along with instructions to teachers and sample key word outlines. Please be aware that this manual is not an answer key. The samples provided in this book are simply possibilities of what you and your students could create.

Lesson instructions are directed to the student, but teachers should read them over with their students and help as necessary, especially with outlining and structure and style practice. It is assumed that teachers have viewed and have access to IEW's *Teaching Writing: Structure and Style* video course and own the *Seminar Workbook.* Before each new unit, teachers should review the appropriate information in that workbook and video. You can find references to the *Teaching Writing: Structure and Style* course in the teacher's notes for each new unit.

Introduction

The lessons in this book teach Structure and Style® in writing. As they move through various American History themes and topics, they incrementally introduce and review the models of structure and elements of style found in the Institute for Excellence in Writing's *Teaching Writing: Structure and Style®.*

It is important to note that these lessons are not intended as history curriculum replacement, but rather their purpose is to broaden subject knowledge while students learn to write. The primary purpose is for students to learn structure and style in writing.

Student Book Contents

- **Scope and Sequence Chart** (pages 8–9)

- **The Lesson Pages**
  This is the majority of the text. It contains the instructions, source texts, worksheets, and checklists you will need for each lesson.

- **Appendix I: Modified MLA Format**

- **Appendix II: Magnum Opus Notebook and Keepsake**
  This appendix explains the Magnum Opus Notebook and includes a checklist.

- **Appendix III: Mechanics**
  This appendix contains a compilation of the correct mechanics of writing numbers, punctuating dates, referencing individuals, etc. that is found in many of the lessons. Well-written compositions are not only written with structure and style, but they also contain correctly spelled words and proper punctuation.

- **Appendix IV: Critique Thesaurus**
  This appendix provides a list of literary terms and their synonyms that are often used when critiquing various forms of literature. This page will be used in Unit 9.

- **Appendix V: Adding Literature**
  This appendix suggests various American novels to be read or listened to. It also includes templates of literature-response pages for you to use if your teacher assigns such pages. Teachers should read the books before assigning them to their students.

- **Appendix VI: Vocabulary Chart and Quizzes** (Cards in Student Book only)
  This appendix provides a list of the vocabulary words and their definitions organized by lesson as well as quizzes to take periodically. Twenty lessons include new vocabulary words to cut out, study, and learn. Every lesson includes vocabulary practice. The goal is that these great words will become part of your natural writing vocabulary.

Customizing the Checklist

The total point value of each assignment is indicated at the bottom of each checklist. This total reflects only the basic items and does not include the vocabulary words. If this is used, add the appropriate amount of points and write the new total on the custom total line.

Important: Teachers and parents should remember IEW's EZ+1 Rule when introducing IEW stylistic techniques. The checklist should include only those elements of style that have become easy plus one new element. If students are not yet ready for a basic element on the checklist, simply have them cross it out. Subtract its point value from the total possible and write the new total on the custom total line at the bottom. If you would like to add elements to the checklist, assign each a point value and add these points to the total possible, placing the new total on the custom total line.

Reproducible checklists are available. See the blue page for download information.

Checklists

Each lesson includes a checklist that details all the requirements of the assignment. Tear the checklist out of the book so that you can use it while writing. Check off each element when you are sure it is included in your paper. With each assignment, turn in the checklist to be used by the teacher for grading. Reproducible checklists are available. See the blue page for download information.

Teacher's Manual

The Teacher's Manual includes all of the Student Book contents (except the vocabulary cards) with added instructions for teachers, including sample key word outlines and style practice ideas. Teachers may teach directly from this manual without the need of their own copy of the Student Book.

Teaching Writing: Structure and Style

Along with the accompanying Teacher's Manual for this Student Book, it is required that the teacher of this course has access to *Teaching Writing: Structure and Style*. This product is available in DVD format or online streaming. For more information, please visit IEW.com/TWSS

Adapting the Schedule

Groups who follow a schedule with fewer than thirty-one weeks will have to omit some lessons. Because there are several lessons for each of the nine IEW units, this is not a problem. Teach lessons that introduce new concepts and omit some of those that do not.

Grading with the Checklist

To use the checklists for grading, do not try to add all the points earned. Instead, if an element is present, put a check in the blank across from it. If an element is missing, write the negative point value on its line or box. Total the negative points and subtract them from the total possible (or your custom total).

Note: Students should have checked the boxes in front of each element they completed.

Encourage students to bring a thesaurus to class. Most students enjoy using an electronic thesaurus, but for those who prefer books, IEW offers a unique one entitled *A Word Write Now*.

This schedule is provided to emphasize to parents and students, particularly in a class setting, that teachers and students should not expect to complete an entire lesson in one day. Spreading work throughout the week will produce much better writing with much less stress. Parents teaching their own children at home should follow a similar schedule.

Suggested Weekly Schedule

All of the instructions for what to do each week are included in the Assignment Schedule located on the first page of each lesson. While there may be slight variations, most lessons are organized as follows:

Day 1

1. Review vocabulary words or past lesson concepts.

2. Learn a new structural model and/or writing concepts.

3. Read the source text, write a key word outline (KWO), and tell back the meaning of each line of notes.

Day 2

1. Review the key word outline from Day 1.

2. Learn a new stylistic technique and complete practice exercises.

3. Study the vocabulary words for the current lesson and complete vocabulary exercises.

4. Begin the rough draft using the KWO. Follow the checklist.

Day 3

1. Review vocabulary words.

2. Finish writing your composition and check each item on the checklist.

3. Submit your composition to an editor with completed checklist attached.

Day 4

1. Write or type a final draft making any corrections your editor asked you to make.

2. Paperclip the checklist, final draft, rough draft, and KWO together. Hand them in.

The lessons are organized in such a way that all new concepts regarding structure are introduced on day 1, and new style concepts and vocabulary words are introduced on day 2.

Students will benefit from learning new structure and style concepts with a teacher. In addition, students should plan to read the source text and begin KWOs with a teacher. These instructions are also found on day 1.

The instructions on day 3 and day 4 may be completed by students more independently. However, teachers and/or parents should be available to help and to edit.

Scope and Sequence

Lesson	Subject and Structure	Style (First Introduced)	Vocabulary Words	Literature Suggestions
Unit 1 1	Native Americans Meet Christopher Columbus introduction to structure	introduction to style	reverently presume transfixed, hostile	*Squanto, Friend of the Pilgrims* by Clyde Robert Bulla
Unit 2 2	Spanish Explorers Arrive in America	-ly adverb	zealously futilely prosperity, quest	
3	Englishmen Arrive in America		audaciously inevitably endeavor, eerily	Elementary: *A Lion to Guard Us* by Clyde Robert Bulla
4	The *Mayflower* Mishap title rule	*who/which* clause	perilously imprudently subside vehemently	Junior and Senior High: *Night Journeys* by Avi
Unit 3 5	Ambush in the Wilderness		animosity, adroitly onrush, warily	
6	The Boston Massacre	strong verb banned words: *go/went, say/said*	confront, provoke obstinately indignantly	Elementary: *Ben and Me* by Robert Lawson
7	The Boston Tea Party	*because* clause	squander, waver cunningly, venture	Junior and Senior High: *Give Me Liberty* by L.M. Elliot
8	The Shot Heard Round the World		persevere, compel destined, appalled	
Unit 4 9	Benjamin Franklin topic-clincher sentences		draft, diligently acknowledge resolve	
10	George Washington Bonus: Quality Adjective Poem	quality adjective banned words: *good, bad*	exemplary esteemed prominent conceive	Girls: *Tolliver's Secret* by Esther Wood Brady
11	Thomas Jefferson	*www.asia* clause	stirring, affirm tyrant, adept	Boys: *Guns for General Washington* by Seymour Reit
12	The Louisiana Purchase	#2 prepositional opener banned words: *pretty, big, small*	grueling stupendous extensive formidable	
Unit 5 13	The Westward Movement		laden, fathom incessant trepidation	*By the Great Horn Spoon!* by Sid Fleischman
14	The Underground Railroad	#3 -ly adverb opener	deplorable, loom imperative, distraught	

Lesson	Subject and Structure	Style (First Introduced)	Vocabulary Words	Literature Suggestions
15	The Civil War		diminish awestruck, solemn encounter	Elementary: *Mr. Lincoln's Drummer* by G. Clifton Wisler
Unit 6 16	Oklahoma Land Rush of 1889 source and fused outlines			Junior and Senior High: *Behind Rebel Lines* by Seymour Reit
17	Transportation Milestones, Part 1	#6 vss opener		
18	Transportation Milestones, Part 2 bibliography		milestone, thrive innovative profound	*Hattie Big Sky* by Kirby Larson
19	The Sinking of the *Lusitania*			
Unit 7 20	Hopes and Dreams, Part 1 body paragraphs		espouse, adverse aspire, lofty	
21	Hopes and Dreams, Part 2 introduction and conclusion	#5 clausal opener *www.asia.b* clause	enthrall, persistent emblem, elated	
22	The Preamble to the Constitution, Part 1			
23	The Preamble to the Constitution, Part 2			*Journey to Topaz* by Yoshiko Uchida
24	The American Flag	#1 subject opener #4 -ing opener		
Unit 8 25	Transportation Milestones, Part 3		achievement flourish transformation efficient	
26	A Prominent American, Part 1			*Cheaper by the Dozen* by Frank B. Gilbreth Jr. and Ernestine Gilbreth Carey
27	A Prominent American, Part 2			
Unit 9 28	Davy Crockett, Part 1		narrative intrigue recount triumph	
29	Davy Crockett, Part 2			
30	John Henry character analysis			
Bonus	Vocabulary Story			

Lesson 1: Native Americans Meet Christopher Columbus

Structure: Unit 1: Note Making and Outlines

Style: Introduction to Structure and Style

Writing Topic: Native Americans Meet Christopher Columbus

Literature Suggestion: *Squanto, Friend of the Pilgrims* by Clyde Robert Bulla

Teaching Writing: Structure and Style

Watch the sections for Unit 1: Note Making and Outlines. At IEW.com/twss-help reference the TWSS Viewing Guides.

UNIT 1: NOTE MAKING AND OUTLINES

Lesson 1: Native Americans Meet Christopher Columbus

Goals

- to learn the Unit 1 Note Making and Outlines structural model
- to create a key word outline (KWO)
- to retell the content of a source text using just your outline
- to correctly use new vocabulary words: *reverently, presume, transfixed, hostile*

Assignment Schedule

Day 1

1. Read Introduction to Structure and Style and New Structure—Note Making and Outlines.
2. Read "Native Americans Meet Christopher Columbus." Read it again and write a key word outline (KWO).

Day 2

1. Review your KWO from Day 1.
2. Look at the vocabulary cards for Lesson 1. Discuss the words and their definitions and complete Vocabulary Practice.
3. Try to add at least one vocabulary word to your KWO.

Day 3

1. Prepare to give an oral report using your KWO. Read. Think. Look up. Speak. Practice telling back the information one line at a time. Read a line; then, look up and talk about it. Then read the next line, look up, and talk about it. Continue through the outline this way.
2. Practice until the presentation of the paragraph is smooth. It is important to realize that you are not trying to memorize the exact words of the source text. You are trying to remember the ideas and communicate those ideas in your own words.

Day 4

1. Review the vocabulary words.
2. After practicing, use your KWO and give an oral report to a friend or family member as explained on Day 3. If applicable, be prepared to give the oral report in class.

Literature Suggestion

Acquire and begin reading *Squanto, Friend of the Pilgrims* by Clyde Robert Bulla for Lessons 1–2.

Students will benefit from reading the source text and beginning KWOs with a teacher. Teachers should plan to teach New Structure, New Style, and introduce the vocabulary words. These items are always found in Day 1 and Day 2 of the Assignment Schedule.

Beginning the KWO

In a classroom setting, write class ideas on a whiteboard. Students may copy these or use their own ideas. See the sample key word outline (KWO) on page 15.

Vocabulary

Use a student's book. Hold up the page of cards for Lesson 1. Read each definition and ask your student to guess which word it matches by looking at the pictures.

Introduction to Structure and Style

In this book you will learn many ways to make your writing more exciting and more enjoyable to read. You will learn to write with *structure* and with *style*.

Structure

What is structure? The dictionary defines structure as "the arrangement of and relations between the parts or elements of something complex."

What has structure? Think of a ship. What had to happen before the ship was built? Someone had to draw out the plans for the builders to follow. The builders had to follow the plans so that each part was in its proper place. The captain certainly would not want the helm (steering wheel) placed in the hold nor the anchor in his cabin. Each part had to be placed in its own special spot, and each step had to be completed in its proper order, giving the ship its proper structure.

Writing a paper, in some ways, is similar to building a ship. A paper contains many facts and ideas. If you were just to begin writing without planning, your facts and ideas would probably not be arranged in the most logical way. Your composition would not be structured well and would not communicate your thoughts effectively. So, in this course you will "draw plans" for everything before you write. Your "plans" will be outlines, and they will follow a particular model of structure for each type of composition.

Style

What comes to your mind when you hear the word style? Many people think of clothes. Clothes come in a variety of styles. One would dress differently to attend a wedding than to go to a baseball game. That is because formal events require a formal style of clothing, whereas casual settings do not.

Similarly, there are also different styles of language. Below are two sentences that communicate the same information in different styles. Which do you like better?

He hit the ball!

The determined little leaguer firmly smacked the spinning baseball with all his might.

You probably like the second sentence better because it is more descriptive. If it were part of a written story, the second would most likely be better. However, what if you were at the ball game with your friend and the little leaguer was your brother? Which of the above sentences would you be more likely to exclaim? He hit the ball! would be more appropriate in this case. The second would sound silly. Why the difference?

When you are speaking to people, they are with you, experiencing the same scene and event as you are. You do not need to fill in details. When you write, however, you must realize that the readers are not with you and cannot see, hear, or feel what is in your mind. This means that you must fill in the details and paint vivid pictures with your words. Descriptive words will help readers see, hear, feel, and experience the scene you are writing about as the second sentence does. The IEW elements of style will give you the tools you need to do just this.

New Structure

Note Making and Outlines

In Unit 1 you will practice choosing key words to form an outline—a key word outline (KWO). A KWO is one way to take notes. Key words indicate the main idea of a sentence. By writing down these important words, you can remember the main idea of a text.

Read the source text. Then locate two or three important words in each sentence that indicate the main idea. Transfer those words to the KWO. Write the key words for the first fact of the KWO on the Roman numeral line. Write no more than three words on each line.

Symbols, numbers, and abbreviations are "free." Symbols take less time to draw than it would take to write the word. Abbreviations are commonly accepted shortened forms of words. Can you guess what each of the following might stand for?

As you form the KWO, separate key words, symbols, numbers, and abbreviations with commas.

After you have completed the KWO, you must test it to ensure the words you chose will help you remember the main idea of the sentence. For this reason whenever you finish writing a KWO, put the source text aside and use your outline to retell the paragraph line by line, sentence by sentence.

Encourage students to use symbols, numbers, and abbreviations. A symbol is legal if it can be written in less time than it takes to write the word.

Symbols   = people   > = more/after/greater than/larger   = see

Numbers   123 = numbers

Abbreviations   ppl = people   Amer. = America   w/ = with

Source Text

Native Americans Meet Christopher Columbus

In the fifteenth century the people living in the Americas were very different from the people living in Europe. Most of the Native Americans lived very simple lives in small villages. They greatly respected nature and worshiped elements of nature like the sun and the moon. They also did not believe men should own land, so everyone in a tribe shared all the land they lived on. They did not build large cities with shops and roads. Even their boats were just simple, small canoes. Then, in 1492, Native Americans of San Salvador watched in amazement as massive ships from across the ocean neared their shore. Soon light-skinned men in strange clothes stepped onto the land, led by a man named Christopher Columbus. Would they be friendly?

Read and Discuss

Read each source text with your students and ask questions to get them thinking about the information they will be working with. It is also important to make sure students understand words that may be unfamiliar to them in the text.

Locate Key Words

Model how to find key words. Reread the first sentence. Ask your students, "If I want to remember the main idea of that sentence, what three words are key words?" (Underline those words.) Sentence by sentence, repeat the process as the students give key word suggestions.

The KWOs in the Teacher's Manual are only samples. Every class and each student will have unique outlines.

Sample

Key Word Outline

On the lines below, write no more than three key words from each sentence of the source text. Choose words that will best help you remember the meaning of the sentence. Use symbols, numbers, and abbreviations freely. They do not count as words. However, be sure you can remember what they mean.

I.   *15th century, ppl, Amer., different, ppl, Europe*

1.   *simple, lives, -- villages*

2.   *respected, nature, worshiped ☀ ☾*

3.   *X own, land, shared*

4.   *0 ++ cities, w/ shops, roads*

5.   *boats, -- canoes*

6.   *1492, San Salvador, 👁👁 ++ ships*

7.   *strange, 👤 👤, w/ Columbus, stepped*

8.   *friendly?*

Cover the source text and tell the meaning of each line of notes in your own words. If a note is unclear, check the source text and add what you need to in order to make it clear.

Tell Back

Telling back the KWO is an important step in the prewriting process.

Read.
Think.
Look up.
Speak.

Andrew Pudewa teaches, "You may look at your notes, and you may speak to your audience, but you may not do both at the same time."

Vocabulary

Students study vocabulary to become better thinkers, speakers, and writers.

Allow students to use derivatives of words.

Vocabulary Practice

Look at the vocabulary words for Lesson 1. Fill in the blanks with a word that makes sense.

1. Native Americans treated the land and nature _____ *reverently.* _____

2. The Native Americans stood _____ *transfixed* _____ and watched as strange boats approached.

3. The Native Americans hoped the visitors would not be _____ *hostile.* _____

Lesson 2: Spanish Explorers Arrive in America

Structure:	Unit 2: Writing from Notes
Style:	-ly adverb
Writing Topic:	Spanish explorers
Literature Suggestion:	*Squanto, Friend of the Pilgrims* by Clyde Robert Bulla

Teaching Writing: Structure and Style

Watch the sections for Unit 2: Writing from Notes. At IEW.com/twss-help reference the TWSS Viewing Guides.

Lesson 2: Spanish Explorers Arrive in America

UNIT 2: WRITING FROM NOTES

Lesson 2: Spanish Explorers Arrive in America

Goals

- to learn the Unit 2 Writing from Notes structural model
- to create a key word outline (KWO) about Spanish explorers
- to write a paragraph about Spanish explorers from the KWO
- to correctly add a new dress-up: -ly adverb
- to be introduced to the composition checklist
- to correctly use new vocabulary words: *zealously, futilely, prosperity, quest*

Assignment Schedule

Day 1

1. Play No-Noose Hangman. Directions for this game and all other suggested games can be found in the Teacher's Manual.

2. Read Mechanics and New Structure—Writing from Notes.

3. Read "Spanish Explorers Arrive in America." Read it again and write a KWO.

Day 2

1. Review your KWO from Day 1.

2. Learn how to dress-up your writing. Read New Style and complete Style Practice.

3. Look at the vocabulary cards for Lesson 2. Discuss the words and their definitions and complete Vocabulary Practice.

4. Using your KWO as a guide, begin writing a rough draft of your paragraph in your own words.

5. Go over the checklist. You will need to underline one -ly adverb. You may use more than one, but only underline one. Also, label the vocabulary words that you use. Put a check in the box for each requirement on the checklist you have completed.

6. See Appendix I. It explains how to format your papers.

Day 3

1. Review all vocabulary words learned thus far.

2. Finish writing your paragraph using your KWO, your Style Practice, and the checklist to guide you. Try your best not to look back at the source text.

3. Turn in your rough draft to your editor with the completed checklist attached. The back side of all checklists are blank or only have an illustration so that they can be removed from this consumable book.

In Unit 2 students use the KWO to write a summary paragraph. As you model writing from the KWO, stress the importance of writing in your own words. Be sure students understand that they should not try to remember and write the exact words of the source text.

They should use their notes to understand the key ideas and write those ideas in their own words. One note may become two or more sentences, or two notes may become one sentence.

No-Noose Hangman

See Appendix VII for game directions. For this lesson use the following phrases and bonus questions:

MOTIONLESS WITH AMAZEMENT
Bonus: What is the vocabulary word? *transfixed* Can you finish the definition? *or horror*

THREE KEY WORDS
Bonus: In addition to two to three key words, what may you write on each line of a KWO? *symbols, numbers, and abbreviations*

Day 4

1. Write or type a final draft making any corrections your editor asked you to make.

2. Paperclip the checklist, final draft, rough draft, and KWO together. Hand them in.

Study for Vocabulary Quiz 1. It will cover words from Lessons 1–2.

Literature Suggestion

Finish reading *Squanto, Friend of the Pilgrims* by Clyde Robert Bulla.

Acquire *A Lion to Guard Us* by Clyde Robert Bulla (elementary) or *Night Journeys* by Avi (junior/senior high) to read for Lessons 3–5.

Mechanics

Numbers

Occasionally you will incorporate numbers into your writing. Here are rules to keep in mind:

1. Spell out numbers that can be expressed in one or two words.

   twenty, fifty-three, three hundred

2. Use numerals for numbers that are three or more words.

   123, 204

3. Spell out ordinal numbers.

   the seventh city, the first settlement

4. Use numerals with dates. Do not include st, nd, rd, or th.

   January 1, 1400

   December 25 *not* December 25th

5. Never begin a sentence with a numeral.

   1492 is a famous year in history. (incorrect)

   The year 1492 is a famous year in history. (correct)

New Structure

Writing from Notes

In Unit 2 you will use a key word outline (KWO) to write a paragraph. When you write your paragraph using your key word outline, make sure your sentences are complete and make sense.

This is the first sentence of the source text:

> Following the expedition of Christopher Columbus, many Spanish explorers sailed to the New World.

Your key word notes may look something like this:

> I.   Following CC, Spanish ➜ New World

Practice

Using the key word notes, write a sentence that communicates the main idea of the first sentence without using the exact words *following, expedition,* and *sailed.* Use a thesaurus for help. Here is an example:

> Once Christopher Columbus opened the way to a new land, several Spanish explorers set out on their own quests.

After Christopher Columbus succeeded in reaching the New World,

Spain sent several more explorers.

The Editor

Selecting and 'hiring' an editor is key to your writing success. You will need to acquire an editor to complete your assignments in this book. The purpose of the editor is to look over your work to amend anything that is not correct or complete. When you receive your paper back with the corrections marked, you will then rewrite your paper including the changes suggested by your editor. This process is very important because through the editing process you will receive useful feedback from your editor and learn correct spelling, punctuation, and proper grammar usage.

When editing, Andrew Pudewa says, "Hands on structure, hands off content." Make the paper grammatically legal; however, refrain from meddling with content.

For tips on evaluating your students, search at IEW.com for Andrew Pudewa's article "Marking and Grading," available at no cost to you.

Source Text

Spanish Explorers Arrive in America

Following the expedition of Christopher Columbus, many Spanish explorers sailed to the New World. Most wanted fame and fortune and were not friendly toward the natives. Ponce de Leon wanted to find a legendary fountain of youth, which, of course, he never found. However, in his search he became the first man from Spain to reach the mainland of North America. He called the land he reached Florida, most likely because of the many flowers in bloom there. Another explorer, Francisco Coronado, searched for the mythical seven cities of gold. He did not find them, but his men discovered the Grand Canyon. It was the Spanish who established the first permanent European settlement in America: St. Augustine, Florida. This settlement began as a small fort but grew into a city that still exists today.

Sample

Key Word Outline

On the lines below, write no more than three key words from each sentence of the source text. Choose words that will best help you remember the meaning of the sentence.

You may find the symbols and abbreviations below helpful for this outline.

➔ = to go   b/c = because   perm. = permanent

I.   *following, CC, Spanish, ➔, New World*

1.   *👀, fame, fortune, X friendly*

2.   *Ponce de Leon, 👀 X fountain of youth*

3.   *1st, Spanish, mainland, N Amer.*

4.   *named, Florida, b/c, flowers*

5.   *F. Coronado, 👀, 7, cities, gold*

6.   *men, discovered, Grand Canyon*

7.   *Sp., 1st permanent, settlement = St. Augustine, FL*

8.   *1st, sm, fort, city, today*

Cover the source text and tell the meaning of each line of notes in your own words. If a note is unclear, check the source text and add what you need to in order to make it clear.

New Style

Dress-Ups

There are many IEW elements of style. The first element you will be introduced to is called a dress-up because it will help you "dress-up" your writing. The IEW dress-ups are descriptive words, phrases, or clauses that you add to a sentence. You will learn six dress-ups. To indicate that you have added a dress-up to a sentence, you should underline it. Although you may use more than one of a specific type of dress-up in a paragraph, only underline one of each type in each paragraph.

-ly Adverb Dress-Up

In this lesson you will learn the first dress-up: the -ly adverb.

An -ly adverb is an adverb that ends in *-ly*. Adverbs are words that modify verbs, adjectives, or other adverbs. Most often they tell *how* or *when* something is done.

Notice how the meaning of this sentence changes when different -ly adverbs are added:

> The captain gave the order.
>
> The captain gave the order <u>angrily</u>.
>
> The captain gave the order <u>nervously</u>.

Now you choose an -ly adverb.

> The captain gave the order   *rudely*   .

From now on, include an -ly adverb in each paragraph you write. Mark the -ly adverb by underlining it.

-ly Adverbs

angrily

anxiously

boldly

eagerly

evilly

excitedly

fearfully

foolishly

futilely

hopefully

humbly

hysterically

innocently

intrepidly

joyfully

longingly

nervously

rudely

savagely

sheepishly

smugly

stubbornly

suspiciously

tirelessly

woefully

Students benefit from looking at word lists like those listed on this page. A longer list of -ly adverbs can be found on the *Portable Walls for Structure and Style® Students* as well as the IEW Writing Tools App.

From this point forward students should include one -ly adverb in each paragraph they write. Although more than one -ly adverb may be placed in a paragraph, only one should be underlined.

This dress-up now appears on the checklist.

Style Practice

-ly Adverb Dress-Up

You must include an -ly adverb in the paragraph you write for this lesson. Write a few ideas for possible -ly adverbs on the lines below. You may look at the list on the previous page or at a longer list found on the *Portable Walls for Structure and Style® Students* or on the IEW Writing Tools App. Some of your vocabulary words may be helpful as well.

1. What -ly adverbs could express how the Spanish sailed to the New World?

    *boldly, **audaciously**, bravely, hopefully, eagerly, intrepidly*

2. What -ly adverbs could express how the explorers searched for the mythical fountain of youth and seven cities of gold?

    *foolishly, tirelessly, greedily, naively, relentlessly, **futilely***

Note: A vocabulary word that is an -ly adverb may count as both an -ly adverb and a vocabulary word.

> Suggested answers in bold indicate the word is a vocabulary word.

Vocabulary Practice

Look at the vocabulary words for Lesson 2. Fill in the blanks with a word that makes sense.

1. The explorers were on a _____*quest*_____ to find _____*prosperity.*_____

2. Ponce de Leon searched _____*futilely*_____ for a fountain that did not exist.

Which of the vocabulary words from Lesson 1 might work in the following sentences?

1. The Spanish _____*presumed*_____ (ed) they would find gold in the New World.

2. Many Spanish explorers were _____*hostile*_____ toward the natives.

Note: Derivatives of a vocabulary word may be used. For example, you may add an *-ed* or *-ing* to a basic vocabulary word.

Before students begin to write, preview the checklist. This ensures that the students understand expectations.

Unit 2 Composition Checklist
Lesson 2: Spanish Explorers Arrive in America

Writing from Notes

IEW Institute for Excellence in Writing
Listen. Speak. Read. Write. Think!

Name: _____

STRUCTURE

☐ MLA format (see Appendix I)	_____	6 pts
☐ title centered	_____	5 pts
☐ checklist on top, final draft, rough draft, key word outline	_____	5 pts

STYLE

¶1 Dress-Ups (underline one of each)   (5 pts each)

☐ -ly adverb	_____	5 pts

MECHANICS

☐ capitalization	_____	1 pt
☐ end marks and punctuation	_____	1 pt
☐ complete sentences (Does it make sense?)	_____	1 pt
☐ correct spelling	_____	1 pt

VOCABULARY

☐ vocabulary words - label *(voc)* in left margin or after sentence		

Total:	_____	25	pts
Custom Total:	_____		pts

If your students are handwriting their assignments, disregard the MLA requirement on the checklist.

In each lesson students are directed to give their editors their rough draft with the completed checklist attached. The back side of all checklists are blank or only have an illustration so that they can be removed from this consumable book.

Teachers are free to adjust a checklist by requiring only the stylistic techniques that have become easy, plus one new one. EZ+1

Instruct the students to tear the checklist out of the book so that they can use it while writing. Train students to "check what you do and do what you check."

UNIT 2: WRITING FROM NOTES

Intentionally blank so the checklist can be removed.

Lesson 3: Englishmen Arrive in America

Structure:	Unit 2: Writing from Notes
Style:	no new style
Writing Topic:	Englishmen in America
Literature Suggestion:	Elementary: *A Lion to Guard Us* by Clyde Robert Bulla
	Junior and Senior High: *Night Journeys by Avi*

Lesson 3: Englishmen Arrive in America

UNIT 2: WRITING FROM NOTES

Lesson 3: Englishmen Arrive in America

Goals

- to practice the Units 1 and 2 structural models
- to create a 1-paragraph KWO
- to write a 1-paragraph summary about Englishmen in America
- to take Vocabulary Quiz 1
- to correctly use new vocabulary words: *audaciously, inevitably, endeavor, eerily*

Assignment Schedule

Day 1

1. Play Around the World.
2. Take Vocabulary Quiz 1.
3. Read "Englishmen Arrive in America." Read it again and write a KWO.

Day 2

1. Review your KWO from Day 1.
2. Complete Style Practice.
3. Look at the vocabulary cards for Lesson 3. Discuss the words and their definitions and complete Vocabulary Practice.
4. Using your KWO as a guide, begin writing a rough draft in your own words.
5. Go over the checklist. Put a check in the box for each requirement you have completed.

Day 3

1. Review all vocabulary words learned thus far.
2. Finish writing your paragraph. Try your best not to look back at the source text.
3. Turn in your rough draft to your editor with the completed checklist attached.

Day 4

1. Write or type a final draft making any corrections your editor asked you to make.
2. Paperclip the checklist, final draft, rough draft, and KWO together. Hand them in.

Literature Suggestion

Begin reading *A Lion to Guard Us* by Clyde Robert Bulla or *Night Journeys* by Avi.

Around the World

See Appendix VII for game directions. Use the vocabulary chart on page 322, Lessons 1–2. Because there are only eight words, it is fine to repeat. You are helping students prepare for the quiz.

When students turn in their final drafts, read some of their compositions aloud. Clap for them! It is very motivating for writers to hear their pieces being read aloud. This is why we write—for an audience.

Source Text

Englishmen Arrive in America

Beginning in 1497, England began sending explorers to America. However, many years passed before they attempted to establish colonies. One of the first attempts was by a group led by John White. In 1587 they landed on Roanoke Island, near what is now North Carolina. White left over a hundred settlers there, but when he returned in 1590, the entire settlement was gone! Because of its strange disappearance, this settlement is known as the Lost Colony. It was not until 1607 that a group of Englishmen were successful in beginning a permanent settlement. These men landed in Virginia and named their settlement Jamestown after King James. The settlers experienced many hardships, but over time Jamestown became a prosperous city.

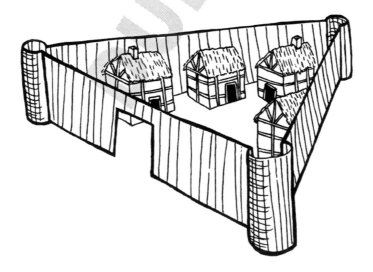

Mechanics _____

John White is used in the third sentence, but only *White* is used after that. Names of adults are referenced by their first and last name the first time they are mentioned. After the first time, they are only referenced by their last name.

Institute for Excellence in Writing

Sample

Key Word Outline

On the lines below, write no more than three key words from each sentence of the source text. Choose words that will best help you remember the meaning of the sentence.

I.   *1497, England, explorers, ➜ America*

1.   *++ yrs., X try, colonies*

2.   *1, 1st, attempts, led, John White*

3.   *1587, Roanoke Island, NC*

4.   *White, left, >100 ppl, rtn, 1590, gone*

5.   *b/c disappeared, "Lost Colony"*

6.   *1607, English, 1st permanent, settlement*

7.   *Virginia, Jamestown, after* 👑

8.   *hardships, time, prosperous*

Cover the source text and tell the meaning of each line of notes in your own words. If a note is unclear, check the source text and add what you need to in order to make it clear.

Style Practice

-ly Adverb Dress-Up

You must include an -ly adverb in the paragraph you write for this lesson. Use a thesaurus or your vocabulary words. Write a few ideas on the lines below each sentence.
Choose your favorite to write on the blank in the sentence.

1. The settlement at Roanoke had _____ _____ ***eerily*** _____ disappeared.

    -ly adverbs *mysteriously, **eerily**, untraceably, strangely*

2. The men who reached Jamestown _____ *eventually* _____ established a permanent settlement.

    -ly adverbs ***audaciously**, painstakingly, laboriously, eventually*

3. The Englishmen _____ ***reverently*** _____ named their settlement after their king.

    -ly adverbs *affectionately, **reverently**, dutifully, respectfully, immediately*

Vocabulary Practice

Look at the vocabulary words for Lesson 3. Fill in the blanks with a word that makes sense.

1. _____ *Inevitably or Audaciously* _____ the English ventured to America too.

2. Though the settlers at Roanoke _____ *endeavored* _____ (ed) to establish

    a permanent settlement, they unexplainably failed.

Remember that derivatives of a vocabulary word may be used. At the end of the source text, did you notice a derivative of the word *prosperity*? What is it?

prosperous

Look at the vocabulary chart on page 322. Try to use words from Lessons 1–3 in sentences or phrases that could be in your summary about the English in America. Write at least one idea below.

*The English **presumed** they could settle the New World too.*

*John White must have stood **transfixed** at the sight of the Lost Colony.*

Unit 2 Composition Checklist
Lesson 3: Englishmen Arrive in America

Writing
from
Notes

IEW Institute for Excellence in Writing

Name: _____

STRUCTURE

☐ MLA format (see Appendix I) _____ 6 pts

☐ title centered _____ 5 pts

☐ checklist on top, final draft, rough draft, key word outline _____ 5 pts

STYLE

¶1 **Dress-Ups** (underline one of each)   (5 pts each)

☐ -ly adverb _____ 5 pts

MECHANICS

☐ capitalization _____ 1 pt

☐ end marks and punctuation _____ 1 pt

☐ complete sentences (Does it make sense?) _____ 1 pt

☐ correct spelling _____ 1 pt

VOCABULARY

☐ vocabulary words - label *(voc)* in left margin or after sentence

Total: _____ 25 pts

Custom Total: _____ pts

If your students are handwriting their assignments, disregard the MLA requirement on the checklist.

Teachers are free to adjust a checklist by requiring only the stylistic techniques that have become easy, plus one new one. EZ+1

Intentionally blank so the checklist can be removed.

Lesson 4: The *Mayflower* Mishap

Structure:	Unit 2: Writing from Notes
	title rule
Style:	*who/which* clause
Writing Topic:	*Mayflower*
Literature Suggestion:	Elementary: *A Lion to Guard Us* by Clyde Robert Bulla
	Junior and Senior High: *Night Journeys by Avi*

Lesson 4: The *Mayflower* Mishap

UNIT 2: WRITING FROM NOTES

Lesson 4: The *Mayflower* Mishap

Goals

- to practice the Units 1 and 2 structural models
- to create a 2-paragraph KWO
- to write a 2-paragraph summary about the *Mayflower*
- to correctly add a new dress-up: *who/which* clause
- to correctly create a title
- to correctly use new vocabulary words: *perilously, imprudently, subside, vehemently*

Assignment Schedule

Day 1

1. Read "The *Mayflower* Mishap." Read it again and write a KWO.
2. Read New Structure—Titles.

Day 2

1. Review your KWO from Day 1.
2. Learn a new dress-up, the *who/which* clause. Read New Style and complete Style Practice.
3. Look at the vocabulary cards for Lesson 4. Discuss the words and their definitions and complete Vocabulary Practice.
4. Using your KWO and Style Practice to guide you, begin writing a rough draft in your own words.
5. Go over the checklist. Put a check in the box for each requirement you have completed.

Day 3

1. Review all vocabulary words learned thus far.
2. Finish writing your 2-paragraph summary. Include an -ly adverb dress-up and a *who/which* clause dress-up in each paragraph. Italicize *Mayflower*. (Underline if you are handwriting.)
3. Turn in your rough draft to your editor with the completed checklist attached.

Day 4

1. Write or type a final draft making any corrections your editor asked you to make.
2. Paperclip the checklist, final draft, rough draft, and KWO together. Hand them in.
3. If you are making a Magnum Opus Notebook, revise your Spanish Explorers summary from Lesson 2. (See Appendix II.)

Point out that the source text for this lesson has two paragraphs. Each Roman numeral on the KWO represents one of those paragraphs.

Day 4 encourages students to revise their Spanish Explorers summary from Lesson 2 to begin a Magnum Opus Notebook. If your students are creating a Magnum Opus Notebook, take time to look at Appendix 2.

Literature Suggestion

Continue reading *A Lion to Guard Us* by Clyde Robert Bulla or *Night Journeys* by Avi.

Source Text

The *Mayflower* Mishap

In 1620 Goodman John Howland boarded an old, creaky merchant ship called the *Mayflower* with a group of Englishmen seeking religious freedom. They ventured across the vast Atlantic Ocean toward America. During the trip there was a terrible storm. Lightning flashed, thunder crashed, wind roared, and massive waves violently rocked the boat. The passengers stayed below in the gun deck, hoping the ship would not sink. It was crowded, and they were wet, cold, and scared.

Goodman Howland did not like being cooped up, so he climbed to the upper deck. Without warning the ship rolled, and he fell into the ocean. As he fell, he grabbed a hanging rope. As he dangled over the ocean, he screamed frantically for help. Luckily, the sailors had seen what had happened. They were able to grab him with a boat hook. He was relieved and grateful to be back on the boat. However, Goodman Howland knew that this journey to the New World would be a long and difficult one.

Mechanics _____

Mayflower is italicized. Names of ships, aircraft, and spacecraft are italicized. If a report is handwritten, the names of these vessels are underlined.

Sample

Key Word Outline

Each Roman numeral represents one paragraph.

I.   *1620, Goodman Howland, Mayflower*

1.   *cross, Atlantic ➜ America*

2.   *during, trip, storm*

3.   *⚡ thunder, wind, ∿∿ rocked*

4.   *passengers ➜ gun deck*

5.   *wet, cold, scared*

II.   *G. Howland, ☹ ➜ upper deck*

1.   *ship, rolled, GH, ocean*

2.   *grabbed, rope*

3.   *dangled, screamed, help*

4.   *sailors, 👀*

5.   *saved, w/ boat hook*

6.   *relieved, grateful*

7.   *knew, difficult, journey*

Cover the source text and tell the meaning of each line of notes in your own words. If a note is unclear, check the source text and add what you need to in order to make it clear.

New Structure

Titles

An interesting title grabs a reader's attention. To make an intriguing title, repeat one to three key words from the final sentence.

> The last sentence of "Spanish Explorers Arrive in America" (Lesson 2 source text) says, "This settlement began as a small fort but grew into a city that still exists today." An intriguing title might be "The Fort That Became a City."
>
> The last sentence from "Englishmen Arrive in America" (Lesson 3 source text) states, "The settlers experienced many hardships, but over time Jamestown became a prosperous city." An intriguing title might be "A Prosperous City."

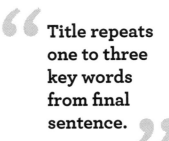

Title repeats one to three key words from final sentence.

Titles have simple rules for capitalization:

> Capitalize the first word and the last word.
>
> Capitalize all other words except articles (a, an, the), coordinating conjunctions (for, and, nor, but, or, yet, so), and prepositions (such as in, over, on, without).

Practice

You do not know what your final sentence for this writing assignment will be. However, you can practice forming titles using the source text. The final sentence of the source text with key words in bold is below. Create an intriguing title that includes one to three of these words. Write two or three ideas.

> However, **Goodman Howland** knew that this **journey** to the **New World** would be a **long** and **difficult** one.

A Long and Difficult Journey

Goodman Howland's Unforgettable Journey

Close Call on the Journey to the New World

From now on, make a title for your compositions by repeating one to three key words from the final sentence. If you develop your title first, ensure you follow the title rule by incorporating key words from the title into your final sentence.

To form a title, key words in a last sentence sometimes need to be changed. That is fine. If students ask, offer suggestions.

Institute for Excellence in Writing

New Style

Who/Which **Clause Dress-Up**

In this lesson you will learn another dress-up: *who/which* clause.

A *who/which* clause is a clause that provides description or additional information.

> The sailors, <u>who</u> heard John's screams, grabbed a boat hook.
>
> The waves, <u>which</u> leapt from the sea, tossed the ship.

Notice:

1. A *who/which* clause begins with the word *who* or *which*.

   Use *who* when referring to people and *which* when referring to things.

   To indicate a *who/which* clause, underline only the first word of the clause: *who* or *which*.

2. The *who/which* clause gives information about a noun—a person, place, thing, or idea.

   > The *sailors*, <u>who</u> heard John's screams, grabbed a boat hook.
   >
   > The *waves*, <u>which</u> leapt from the sea, tossed the ship.

3. The *who/which* clause is added to a sentence that is already complete.

   If you remove the *who/which* clause, a sentence must remain.

   > The sailors, <u>who</u> heard John's screams, *grabbed a boat hook.* (sentence)

   If you only insert the word *who* or *which*, you will have a fragment.

   > The sailors, who heard John's screams (fragment)

❜ A nonessential *who/which* clause is set off with commas; an essential clause has no commas.

   > John, <u>who</u> climbed up the deck, fell into the ocean. (nonessential, commas)
   >
   > Passengers <u>who</u> sought religious freedom trusted God. (essential, no commas)

Practice

Add a *who/which* clause to each sentence. Place a comma at the end of each *who/which* clause.

1. The Englishmen, <u>who</u> *desired a new life in the New World,* _____
   _____ hoped the ship was safe.

2. The thunder, <u>which</u> *boomed incessantly,* _____
   _____ shook the tiny ship.

✎ From now on, include a *who/which* clause in each paragraph you write.
Mark the *who/which* clause by underlining the word *who* or *which*.

U.S. History-Based Writing Lessons: Student Book   37

Two dress-ups now appear on the checklist.

Who/which clauses are set off with commas if they are nonessential but take no commas if they are essential.

Passengers <u>who</u> sought religious freedom trusted God.

Not all passengers trusted God. The *who* clause is essential to the sentence.

For younger students simply encourage them to place commas around all *who/which* clauses and only later teach essential and nonessential *who/which* clauses.

Read the sentences and orally fill in the blanks several times. When students understand the pattern of the *who/which* clause, direct them to write.

Style Practice

Who/Which Clause Dress-Up

Add a *who/which* clause to each sentence. Place a comma at the end of each nonessential *who/which* clause unless it is at the end of a sentence. Underline the word *who* or *which*.

1. A massive wave, which *leapt over the rail,*

    _____ swept Goodman Howland from the deck.

2. The sailors rescued Goodman Howland, who *then collapsed onto the deck.*

    _____

-ly Adverb Dress-Up

You must also continue to include an -ly adverb in each paragraph you write. Write a few ideas on the lines below each sentence. Choose your favorite to write on the blank in the sentence.

1. The hostile waves beat _____ *relentlessly* _____ upon the helpless ship.

    -ly adverbs *violently, **vehemently**, relentlessly, mercilessly, savagely*

2. Goodman Howland _____ ***imprudently*** _____ climbed to the upper deck.

    -ly adverbs *foolishly, naively, **imprudently**, grumpily, **audaciously***

Vocabulary Practice

Look at the vocabulary words for Lesson 4. Fill in the blanks with a word that makes sense.

1. The passengers hoped that the storm would _____ *subside.*

2. Goodman Howland dangled _____ *perilously* _____ over the sea.

Look at the vocabulary chart on page 322. Try to use words from Lessons 1–4 in sentences or phrases that could be in your summary about the *Mayflower*. Write at least two ideas below.

*They were on an **audacious quest** for religious freedom.*

*Howland gripped the rope **vehemently** as he **endeavored** to hold on.*

Unit 2 Composition Checklist
Lesson 4: The *Mayflower* Mishap

Writing
from
Notes

Institute for Excellence in Writing

Name: _____

STRUCTURE

☐ MLA format (see Appendix I) _____ 6 pts

☐ title centered and repeats 1–3 key words from final sentence _____ 5 pts

☐ checklist on top, final draft, rough draft, key word outline _____ 5 pts

STYLE

¶1 ¶2 **Dress-Ups** (underline one of each)   (5 pts each)

☐ ☐ -ly adverb _____ 10 pts

☐ ☐ *who/which* clause _____ 10 pts

MECHANICS

☐ ☐ capitalization _____ 1 pt

☐ ☐ end marks and punctuation _____ 1 pt

☐ ☐ complete sentences (Does it make sense?) _____ 1 pt

☐ ☐ correct spelling _____ 1 pt

VOCABULARY

☐ vocabulary words - label *(voc)* in left margin **or** after sentence

Total: _____ 40 pts

Custom Total: _____ pts

The two boxes under style indicate two paragraphs. Students should include and mark an -ly adverb and a *who/which* clause in each paragraph.

Remind students to italicize the name of the ship, *Mayflower*. Suggest that they add this to their checklist so they do not forget.

Teachers are free to adjust a checklist by requiring only the stylistic techniques that have become easy, plus one new one. EZ+1

Intentionally blank so the checklist can be removed.

Lesson 5: Ambush in the Wilderness

Teaching Writing: Structure and Style

Structure:	Unit 3: Retelling Narrative Stories
Style:	no new style
Writing Topic:	The French and Indian War
Literature Suggestion:	Elementary: *A Lion to Guard Us* by Clyde Robert Bulla
	Junior and Senior High: *Night Journeys* by Avi

Watch the sections for Unit 3: Retelling Narrative Stories.
At <u>IEW.com/twss-help</u> reference the TWSS Viewing Guides.

Lesson 5: Ambush in the Wilderness

UNIT 3: RETELLING NARRATIVE STORIES

Lesson 5: Ambush in the Wilderness

Goals

- to learn the Unit 3 Retelling Narrative Stories structural model
- to create a 3-paragraph KWO using the Unit 3 Story Sequence Chart
- to write a 3-paragraph story about the French and Indian War
- to correctly use new vocabulary words: *animosity, adroitly, onrush, warily*

Assignment Schedule

Day 1

1. Complete the Review.

2. Read Historical Information.

3. Read New Structure—Retelling Narrative Stories.

4. Read "Ambush in the Wilderness." Then write a KWO by answering the Story Sequence Chart questions. As you answer each question, place two or three key words on each line of the KWO. Use symbols, numbers, and abbreviations when possible. Each Roman numeral on the KWO represents a paragraph, so your completed story will be three paragraphs in length.

5. Cover the source text and tell the meaning of each line of notes in your own words. If a note is unclear, add what you need to in order to make it clear.

Day 2

1. Review your KWO from Day 1.

2. Complete Developing the Setting.

3. Complete Style Practice.

4. Look at the vocabulary cards for Lesson 5. Discuss the words and their definitions and complete Vocabulary Practice.

5. Using your KWO as a guide, begin writing a rough draft in your own words.

6. Go over the checklist. Put a check in the box for each requirement you have completed. There are three boxes for both dress-ups because all three paragraphs should include both dress-ups.

In this new unit students begin by reading a story. No longer are key words taken from each sentence; rather, key words are now found in developing key ideas.

Key ideas are formed by answering questions related to the Story Sequence Chart. For example, you will ask, "Who are the characters?" Form key words from the answer.

The same outlining rules apply: three key words per line; symbols, numbers, and abbreviations are free.

Day 3

1. Review all vocabulary words learned thus far.

2. Finish writing your 3-paragraph story.

3. Turn in your rough draft to your editor with the completed checklist attached.

Day 4

1. Write or type a final draft making any corrections your editor asked you to make.

2. Paperclip the checklist, final draft, rough draft, and KWO together. Hand them in.

3. If you are making a Magnum Opus Notebook, revise your Englishmen Arrive in America summary from Lesson 3.

Literature Suggestion

Finish reading *A Lion to Guard Us* by Clyde Robert Bulla or *Night Journeys* by Avi.

Acquire *Ben and Me: An Astonishing Life of Benjamin Franklin by His Good Mouse Amos* by Robert Lawson (elementary) or *Give Me Liberty* by L.M. Elliot (junior/senior high) to read for Lessons 6–9.

Review

Play No-Noose Hangman.

How should you create an intriguing title?

Read the title of your *Mayflower* story.

Read one of the sentences with a *who/which* clause in your *Mayflower* story.

Historical Information

In the 1700s Spain, Britain, and France, who were bitter enemies, each had claims in North America. Hostilities between the British and the French grew when both desired to control the Ohio River Valley. The British colonists believed the territory belonged to them, but the French built forts, such as Fort Duquesne, to keep them out. Conflicts erupted that led to a declaration of war. The war became known as the French and Indian War because many Indians fought alongside the French. France won most of the early battles, but Britain eventually won the war and, thus, controlled almost half of North America, chiefly the Atlantic Coast and the land east of the Mississippi River. The story in this lesson is an account of one of the battles in the conflict between the British and the French and Indians in North America.

Review

Title repeats one to three key words from final sentence.

No-Noose Hangman

For this lesson use the following phrases and bonus questions:

TITLE FROM FINAL SENTENCE

Bonus: Explain the title rule. *The title must repeat 1–3 words from the final sentence.*

TO BECOME LESS VIOLENT

Bonus: What is the vocabulary word? *subside*

TO MAKE A MAJOR EFFORT

Bonus: What is the vocabulary word? *endeavor*

New Structure

Retelling Narrative Stories

In Unit 3 you will focus on story writing. Every story, regardless of how long it is, contains the same basic elements: characters and setting, conflict or problem, climax and resolution. As a result, you will use a new method of note taking. To create an outline for a story, you will not choose words from each sentence like you did in Units 1 and 2. Instead, you will choose key words by asking questions about a story using the Story Sequence Chart.

The Story Sequence Chart

The Story Sequence Chart has three Roman numerals. That is because the assignments in Unit 3 are each three paragraphs long. Each paragraph has a distinct purpose. The first paragraph tells about the people or animals in the story and when and where they live. The second paragraph tells about the conflict or problem that occurs within the story. The third paragraph begins with the climax, the turning point in the story, and ends with the resolution, the events that occur after the climax.

I.   Characters and Setting

Who is in the story?
What are they like?
When does it happen?
Where do they live/go?

II.   Conflict or Problem

What do they need/want?
What do they think?
What do they say and do?

III.   Climax and Resolution

How is the problem/need resolved?
What happens after?
What is learned?

Read the source text and then use the Story Sequence Chart to analyze the story. Begin with the characters and setting. Ask the questions within each section in any order. For example, in Section I it does not matter whether you introduce the characters or the setting first.

The answers to the questions become the details for the outline. As you answer a question, write two or three key words on the KWO. Use symbols, numbers, and abbreviations when possible. You do not have to answer every question. You may need more than one line to answer one question, or you may be able to answer two questions on one line. Keep your answers brief. You can add more details when you write your own version of the story.

Source Text

Ambush in the Wilderness

It was a hot summer day in 1755, but the forest of the Ohio River Valley seemed dark, gloomy, and eerily quiet. The British army trudged on, led by General Edward Braddock. Braddock was a well-trained, experienced officer; however, his training and experience had been on the vast, open fields of England, not in the dense wilderness of America. Additionally, he knew little of the ways of the Native American warriors.

A young American officer was at his side. His name was George Washington. Washington knew the terrain of the land well. He had spent much time in the woods. He also had already been involved in battles with the French and Indian forces, so he knew their tactics.

The objective of the British army was to capture Fort Duquesne. The French had built this fort to keep the British out of the Ohio River Valley. This particular land was very valuable because it had several rivers needed for trading goods. The British believed the land belonged to them.

The soldiers were now just ten miles from the fort, hoping for a quick victory. Suddenly, shots and shouts rang out. Fierce Indians and ruthless French soldiers charged at the British from all sides. They quickly killed many of the officers, including General Braddock. The soldiers panicked.

Washington soon took control. He fought hard. Two horses were shot out from under him. Musket balls and arrows whizzed by him, and four shots tore right through his coat. Still, he was able to lead many of the survivors to safety. They escaped with their lives, and George Washington was hailed a hero. This ambush in the wilderness was just one of the many battles of the French and Indian War that lasted from 1754 to 1763.

Before completing the KWO, remind students that this is a new unit and that key words are found differently. Key words are no longer found by looking at each sentence. Key words are found by using the Story Sequence Chart to ask and answer questions. Not all of the questions on this page need to be answered. Within each section, questions may be asked in any order that helps the story flow.

The KWOs in the Teacher's Manual are only samples. Every class and each student will have unique outlines.

Sample

Lesson 5: Ambush in the Wilderness

Key Word Outline—Story Sequence Chart

Characters and Setting

When does the story happen?

Who is in the story?

What are they like?

Where do they live or go?

I. summer, 1755, forest, Ohio R. Valley
1. Gen. Braddock, w/ Brit. army
2. well-trained, fields, X forests
3. Washington, young, aid
4. knew, forests
(5.) experienced, Fr + Ind, tactics

I. Characters and Setting

In this paragraph answer questions about when and where the story takes place, General Braddock, and George Washington.

Conflict or Problem

What does the main character want or need?

What do the main characters do, say, think, and feel?

What happens before the climax?

II. desired, capture, Ft Duquesne
1. fort, Brit, off, land
2. Brits, believed, owned
3. 10 mi, shots, shouts
4. Fr + Ind, attacked, XX, Gen. Braddock
(5.) soldiers, panicked

II. Conflict or Problem

In this paragraph answer questions about the big problem, which is the ambush. First tell what the main characters hope to accomplish and why the problem occurs.

Climax and Resolution

What leads to the conflict being solved (the climax)?

What happens as a result?

What is learned? (message, moral)

III. Washington, took, control
1. 2 horses, shot, under
2. ➔ ➔, 4 musket balls, coat
3. led, men, safety
4. X fort
(5.) Washington, hero, Fr + Ind war

III. Climax and Resolution

In this paragraph begin with the climax, which is Washington taking control. Tell what happens once he does; then, tell how the conflict is resolved. (Do the English capture the fort? What happens to Washington?)

Title repeats 1–3 key words from final sentence.   _XX = dead_

Each Roman numeral indicates a different paragraph. Encourage students to use the KWO to tell back the story in complete sentences. Model the process as needed.

Developing the Setting

Remember that the job of the first paragraph of your story is to describe the setting and the characters. One goal of describing the setting is to make your readers feel as if they are there—to draw them into the story. A way to accomplish this is to describe the setting in a way that helps the readers see, hear, and feel things by creating strong images and feeling. Another goal of describing the setting is to create a mood for the story. For example, a happy story might begin with the sun shining and birds singing whereas a sad story might begin with a dreary, cloudy day. As you begin your story, look for places to provide details that create strong images and feeling.

1. What is the day like? Consider the temperature (*warm, hot, mild, ...*), the sky (*blue, gray, cloudy, clear, bright, ...*), the sun (*bright, scorching, hidden, covered, blaring, blistering, blazing, ...*), the air (*still, heavy, moist, dank, sweltering, sultry, ...*), the wind (*howling, still, rustling leaves, blowing gently, ...*).

   Example: *The sky was gray, and the air was hot and damp around the river.*

   Describe the day in a way that helps the readers see, hear, and feel things.

   The blazing sun beat down on the tired men, and the hot, still air seemed to suffocate them.

   _____

   _____

2. What is the forest like, and what was its effect on the men? Consider what the soldiers would see (*river, trees, rocks, mud*), hear (*rattling of supplies, river, horses*), and feel (*flies, mosquitoes, hot, damp air*). What do you picture in your mind?

   Example: *The trees seemed endless. The only sounds were the rattling of supplies and the buzzing of flies.*

   Describe the forest and its effect on the men.

   The narrow, rocky, winding path made it difficult to maneuver through the dense forest,

   but the men continued on warily. Only an occasional snort of a horse or snap of a twig

   could be heard.

Style Practice

Who/Which Clause Dress-Up

Add a *who/which* clause to each sentence. End each non-essential clause with a comma and underline the word *who* or *which*.

1. General Braddock, <u>who</u> *had traveled from England,* _____

   _____ had never fought in the dense wilderness of America.

2. Fort Duquesne, <u>which</u> *served to deter English settlers,* _____

   _____ had to be captured.

3. George Washington, <u>who</u> *had taken charge and saved many lives,* _____

   _____ was declared a hero.

-ly Adverb Dress-Up

Write a few ideas for an -ly adverb dress-up on the line below each sentence. Choose your favorite to write on the blank in the sentence.

1. The soldiers plodded on __*warily.*_____

   -ly adverbs *confidently, **warily**, determinedly, wearily, **indignantly**_____

2. The French and Indians attacked *ruthlessly.*_____

   -ly adverbs *mercilessly, suddenly, ruthlessly, unexpectedly*_____

3. George Washington fought *heroically.*_____

   -ly adverbs *bravely, tenaciously, boldly, **adroitly**, heroically*_____

Vocabulary Practice

Look at the vocabulary words for Lesson 5. Fill in the blanks with a word that makes sense.

1. There was much _____ *animosity* _____ between the French and the British.

2. Suddenly, there was an _____ *onrush* _____ of French and Indians.

Look at the vocabulary chart on pages 322–323. Try to use words from Lessons 1–5 in sentences or phrases that could be in your story. Write at least two ideas below.

The French and Indians charged **vehemently**. _____

Washington fought **adroitly** *and* **audaciously**. _____

Vocabulary

The sample sentences are only suggestions. If students ask for help, offer an idea. Listen as they read their sentences aloud.

Unit 3 Composition Checklist

Lesson 5: Ambush in the Wilderness

Retelling
Narrative
Stories

IEW Institute for
Excellence in
Writing
Listen. Speak. Read. Write. Think.

Name: _____

STRUCTURE

☐ MLA format (see Appendix I) _____ 5 pts

☐ title centered and repeats 1–3 key words from final sentence _____ 5 pts

☐ story follows Story Sequence Chart _____ 6 pts

☐ each paragraph contains at least four sentences _____ 6 pts

☐ checklist on top, final draft, rough draft, key word outline _____ 5 pts

STYLE

¶1 ¶2 ¶3 **Dress-Ups** (underline one of each) (3 pts each)

☐ ☐ ☐ -ly adverb _____ 9 pts

☐ ☐ ☐ *who/which* clause _____ 9 pts

MECHANICS

☐ capitalization _____ 1 pt

☐ end marks and punctuation _____ 1 pt

☐ complete sentences (Does it make sense?) _____ 1 pt

☐ correct spelling _____ 2 pts

VOCABULARY

☐ vocabulary words - label *(voc)* in left margin or after sentence

Total: _____ 50 pts

Custom Total: _____ pts

Because positive reinforcement is a wonderful motivator, consider incorporating a ticket system as described on page 337. When you return graded papers, give a ticket for each vocabulary word used.

Teachers are free to adjust a checklist by requiring only the stylistic techniques that have become easy, plus one new one. EZ+1

Intentionally blank so the checklist can be removed.

Lesson 6: The Boston Massacre

Structure:	Unit 3: Retelling Narrative Stories
Style:	strong verb, banned words: *go/went, say/said*
Writing Topic:	The Boston Massacre
Literature Suggestion:	Elementary: *Ben and Me* by Robert Lawson
	Junior and Senior High: *Give Me Liberty* by L.M. Elliot

UNIT 3: RETELLING NARRATIVE STORIES

Lesson 6: The Boston Massacre

Goals

- to practice the Unit 3 structural model
- to create a 3-paragraph KWO using the Unit 3 Story Sequence Chart
- to write a 3-paragraph story about the Boston Massacre
- to correctly add a new dress-up: strong verb
- to ban weak verbs: *go/went, say/said*
- to correctly use new vocabulary words: *confront, provoke, obstinately, indignantly*

Assignment Schedule

Day 1

1. Complete the Review.
2. Read Historical Information.
3. Read Mechanics.
4. Read "The Boston Massacre." Then write a KWO by answering the Story Sequence Chart questions with two or three key words per line.
5. Cover the source text and tell the meaning of each line of notes in your own words. If a note is unclear, add what you need to in order to make it clear.

Day 2

1. Review your KWO from Day 1.
2. Complete Developing the Setting and Characters.
3. Learn a new dress-up, the strong verb. Read New Style and complete Style Practice.
4. Look at the vocabulary cards for Lesson 6. Discuss the words and their definitions and complete Vocabulary Practice.
5. Using your KWO as a guide, begin writing a rough draft in your own words.
6. Go over the checklist. Put a check in the box for each requirement you have completed.

Day 3

1. Review all vocabulary words learned thus far.
2. Finish writing your 3-paragraph story.
3. Turn in your rough draft to your editor with the completed checklist attached.

Day 4

1. Write or type a final draft making any corrections your editor asked you to make.

2. Paperclip the checklist, final draft, rough draft, and KWO together. Hand them in.

3. If you are making a Magnum Opus Notebook, revise your *Mayflower* Mishap summary from Lesson 4.

> Study for Vocabulary Quiz 2. It will cover words from Lessons 1–6.

Literature Suggestion

Begin reading *Ben and Me* by Robert Lawson or *Give Me Liberty* by L.M. Elliot.

Review

Play a vocabulary game from the Teacher's Manual.

The first paragraph of your story includes what two things?

Read your description of the setting in your story from Lesson 5.

The second paragraph of your story identifies what?

The third paragraph of your story begins with the climax. What is a climax?

Historical Information

The French and Indian War had been expensive for Britain. In order to recover the cost, the King of England placed many taxes on American colonists. They became resentful because America did not have any representation in the British Parliament. In addition, some colonists did not want to be ruled by a king so far away. To keep law and order, the king sent soldiers to America. The colonists did not like that either. The following story takes place when tensions were rising between the king's soldiers (the redcoats) and the colonists.

Games

Around the World and Elimination are quick games. If you have more time, play Vocabulary Find the Card.

Review

The first paragraph includes characters and setting.

The second paragraph identifies the problem.

The climax is the turning point in the story.

Mechanics

Notice the words in quotation marks in the source text. When characters talk in a story, use quotation marks to indicate the exact words that the characters say.

> The Patriots rushed at White yelling, "Kill him! Kill him!"

Separate the speaking verb (*yelling*) from the direct quote with a comma. If the direct quote is an exclamation or question, follow it with an exclamation mark or question mark. Follow the patterns:

speaking verb, "quote."	speaking verb, "quote!"	speaking verb, "quote?"
"quote," speaking verb	"quote!" speaking verb	"quote?" speaking verb

Commas and periods always go inside the closing quotations. Exclamation marks and question marks go inside closing quotations when they are part of the material quoted; otherwise, they go outside.

Source Text

The Boston Massacre

It was an unusually cold, bleak March night in Boston. The year was 1770. Private Hugh White was standing guard on King Street. He was a British soldier, a redcoat. At the moment, all was quiet, but Private White was anxious. Many colonists who were out that night were Patriots. They were angry at King George for his unfair laws and taxes. They resented his soldiers being there, and they had been stirring up trouble all over. Private White nervously watched the streets.

It wasn't long before a group of young Patriots saw some redcoats. A teen among them hurled insults at an officer. Private White insisted that the boy be more respectful to the officer, but the teen only threw out more insults. White eventually became so angry that he struck the boy in the face with the butt of his gun. The boy gathered his fellow Patriots, and they rushed at White yelling, "Kill him! Kill him!" White called for backup help.

Captain Preston rode over with several soldiers. The additional redcoats angered the mob more. The Patriots began throwing ice chunks, sticks, and stones. They spit at the soldiers. They dared the soldiers to fire. Things were out of control.

Eventually a redcoat was hit and knocked over by a chunk of ice, which caused his musket to fire. The mob pressed in more, and some soldiers panicked. They fired into the crowd. Several colonists were hit. Five of the men who were hit died. More trouble was sure to follow this bloody event.

On the left are the story sequence questions that students ask about the story as they create the KWO. Use the helpful hints to guide students to answer the questions. Within each section, ask the questions in any order to help the story make sense.

Sample

Key Word Outline—Story Sequence Chart

Characters and Setting

| When does the story happen? |
| Who is in the story? |
| What are they like? |
| Where do they live or go? |

I. _cold, ☾, Boston, 1770_

1. _Pr. Hugh White, redcoat_
2. _guarding, King St, anxious_
3. _patriots, ☹, resented, soldiers_
4. _street, quiet, now_
(5.) _____

I. Characters and Setting

In this paragraph, answer the questions about when and where the story happens. Tell about Private White.

Conflict or Problem

| What does the main character want or need? |
| What do the main characters do, say, think, and feel? |
| What happens before the climax? |

II. _yg, patriot, insulted, officer_

1. _White, confronted, respect_
2. _➜ fight, face, w/ gun_
3. _patriots, rushed, "Kill"_
4. _White, called, help_
(5.) _____

II. Conflict or Problem

In this paragraph answer questions about the big problem that began when Private White confronted the Patriot. Explain how it began and why it escalated.

Climax and Resolution

| What leads to the conflict being solved (the climax)? |
| What happens as a result? |
| What is learned? (message, moral) |

III. _Capt. Preston, w/ soldiers_

1. _mob, + ☺_
2. _ice, sticks, stones_
3. _spit, dared, fire_
4. _redcoats, panicked, fired_
(5.) _patriots XX, ➜ more, trouble_

III. Climax and Resolution

In the final paragraph begin with the climax, which begins when backup redcoats come. This leads to a fight, panic, and death. Trouble would follow.

Title repeats 1–3 key words from final sentence.

Developing the Setting and Characters

The source text is historical fiction, which means it is based on a real event in history. You may add descriptive details to the setting as long as you do not change the basic historical facts. You may also describe the characters in more detail. As you begin your story, look for places to provide details that create strong images and feeling.

1. What is the night like? Consider the temperature (*cool, cold, frigid, ...*), the sky (*gray, cloudy, clear, starry, ...*), the moon (*bright, hidden, covered, reflecting off the snow, ...*), the air (*still, heavy, moist, icy, ...*), the wind (*howling, whistling, still, ...*). Is it raining, sleeting, or snowing? What do you picture in your mind?

    Example: *It was a frigid night, and the streets were dotted with patches of snow and ice.*

    Describe the night in a way that helps the readers see, hear, and feel things.

    The night was hazy and gray, so the moonlight was dim. The wind whistled,

    and sleet slapped Private White's cheeks. He could hear distant laughing and

    the crunch of ice as he paced to keep himself warm.

2. What is Private White like? Consider how he would be dressed (look at pictures of redcoat uniforms), how he was standing (*stiff, tense, rocking, pacing, ...*), his age (*thirty*), his mood (*wary, anxious, smug, ...*), his thoughts (*Will there be trouble? Those insolent Patriots need to be put in their place*). How do you picture Private White in your mind?

    Example: *Private White stood erect and alert, watching suspiciously. He did not trust the Patriots; in fact, he despised them.*

    Describe Private White.

    Private White stood tall and tried to look confident in his red uniform,

    but still he glanced from side to side nervously.

New Style

Strong Verb Dress-Up

In this lesson you will learn another dress-up: strong verb.

Every sentence has a verb, but not all verbs are strong verbs. Strong verbs show action. The strongest verbs show action that is easy to picture. They help a reader picture what someone or something is doing. Here is the verb test. If a word fits in one of the blanks, it is a verb.

I will _____   Yesterday, I _____

Use the verb test. Underline the word if it is a verb.

table   <u>bolted</u>   teacher   <u>glide</u>   <u>sing</u>   <u>devour</u>

Banned Words

Boring verbs should be avoided in writing. For this reason you will not be allowed to use certain verbs in the writing you do for this class. These will be called *banned words*.

"Help! Help me, please!" the girl *said*.

Does the word *said* help you imagine the excitement? What strong verbs might be more descriptive than *said*? On the line below, add to the list of synonyms for *say/said*.

Synonyms for *say/said*   *cried, shouted, pleaded , shrieked, sobbed*

Here is another example of a boring verb:

After months at sea, the passengers *went* onto the land.

Does the word *went* help you imagine the emotion? What strong verbs might be more descriptive than *went*? On the line below, add to the list of synonyms for *go/went*. Notice how changing the verb changes what you imagine when you read the sentence.

Synonyms for *go/went*   *rushed, stumbled, trudged , shuffled, hurried*

From now on in these lessons, the words *say/said* and *go/went* are banned. To help yourself avoid these banned words, use a thesaurus or your vocabulary words or look at the lists of substitutes on the *Portable Walls for Structure and Style Students* or the IEW Writing Tools App.

> From now on, include a strong verb in each paragraph you write.
> Mark the strong verb by underlining it.

⊘ BANNED WORDS   VERBS: SAY/SAID, GO/WENT

This is the third dress-up introduced in this book. This means three dress-ups now appear on the checklist, and three dress-ups should be underlined in each paragraph written for this lesson.

The pace for adding stylistic techniques can be adjusted if a student needs time to practice previous dress-ups. Adjust the checklist if necessary.

Style Practice

Strong Verb Dress-Up and -ly Adverb Dress-Up

Look for other places to add strong verbs. Although *watched* is not a banned word, it is used in the source text. It is good to use your own words. On the lines below, write strong verbs to replace *watched* and -ly adverbs that you could use with the strong verbs. Use a thesaurus.

Private White *watched* the streets.

strong verbs   *scanned, studied, eyed*

-ly adverbs   *suspiciously, **warily**, anxiously, attentively, nervously*

Who/Which Clause Dress-Up

Add a *who/which* clause to each sentence. End each non-essential clause with a comma and underline the word *who* or *which*.

1. The Patriots, <u>who</u> *despised the king's treatment of them,*

   _____ often harassed the redcoats.

2. The tragic event, <u>which</u> *left five dead,*

   _____ was sure to lead to more trouble.

Vocabulary Practice

Look at the vocabulary words for Lesson 6. Fill in the blanks with a word that makes sense.

1. The Patriots liked to *provoke or confront* the soldiers.

2. The Patriots shouted *indignantly or obstinately.*

Now look at the vocabulary chart on page 322. Try to use words from Lessons 1–6 in sentences or phrases that could be in your story. Write at least two ideas below.

*The captain **endeavored** to restore peace.*

*The violence did not **subside**.*

Unit 3 Composition Checklist
Lesson 6: The Boston Massacre

Retelling
Narrative
Stories

IEW Institute for Excellence in Writing

Name: _____

STRUCTURE

☐ MLA format (see Appendix I) _____ 5 pts

☐ title centered and repeats 1–3 key words from final sentence _____ 5 pts

☐ story follows Story Sequence Chart _____ 6 pts

☐ each paragraph contains at least four sentences _____ 6 pts

☐ checklist on top, final draft, rough draft, key word outline _____ 5 pts

STYLE

¶1 ¶2 ¶3 Dress-Ups (underline one of each)   (3 pts each)

☐ ☐ ☐ -ly adverb _____ 9 pts

☐ ☐ ☐ *who/which* clause _____ 9 pts

☐ ☐ ☐ strong verb _____ 9 pts

CHECK FOR BANNED WORDS (-1 pt for each use): go/went, say/said _____ pts

MECHANICS

☐ capitalization _____ 1 pt

☐ end marks and punctuation _____ 1 pt

☐ complete sentences (Does it make sense?) _____ 2 pts

☐ correct spelling _____ 2 pts

VOCABULARY

☐ vocabulary words - label *(voc)* in left margin or after sentence

Total: _____ 60 pts

Custom Total: _____ pts

If you are using the ticket system as described on page 337, give a ticket for each vocabulary word used when you return graded papers.

Teachers are free to adjust a checklist by requiring only the stylistic techniques that have become easy, plus one new one. EZ+1

Intentionally blank so the checklist can be removed.

Lesson 7: The Boston Tea Party

Structure:	Unit 3: Retelling Narrative Stories
Style:	*because* clause
Writing Topic:	The Boston Tea Party
Literature Suggestion:	Elementary: *Ben and Me* by Robert Lawson
	Junior and Senior High: *Give Me Liberty* by L.M. Elliot

UNIT 3: RETELLING NARRATIVE STORIES

Lesson 7: The Boston Tea Party

Goals

- to practice the Unit 3 structural model
- to create a 3-paragraph KWO using the Unit 3 Story Sequence Chart
- to write a 3-paragraph story about the Boston Tea Party
- to correctly add a new dress-up: *because* clause
- to take Vocabulary Quiz 2
- to correctly use new vocabulary words: *squander, waver, cunningly, venture*

Assignment Schedule

Day 1

1. Take Vocabulary Quiz 2.
2. Complete the Review.
3. Read "The Boston Tea Party." Circle the two banned words. Do not use them in your version of the story.
4. Write a KWO by answering the Story Sequence Chart questions.
5. Cover the source text and tell the meaning of each line of notes in your own words. If a note is unclear, add what you need to in order to make it clear.

Day 2

1. Review your KWO from Day 1.
2. Complete Developing the Setting and Characters.
3. Learn a new dress-up, the *because* clause. Read New Style and complete Style Practice.
4. Look at the vocabulary cards for Lesson 7. Discuss the words and their definitions and complete Vocabulary Practice.
5. Using your KWO as a guide, begin writing a rough draft in your own words.
6. Go over the checklist. Put a check in the box for each requirement you have completed.

Day 3

1. Review all vocabulary words learned thus far.
2. Finish writing your 3-paragraph story.
3. Turn in your rough draft to your editor with the completed checklist attached.

Day 4

1. Write or type a final draft making any corrections your editor asked you to make.

2. Paperclip the checklist, final draft, rough draft, and KWO together. Hand them in.

3. If you are making a Magnum Opus Notebook, revise your Ambush in the Wilderness story from Lesson 5.

Literature Suggestion

Continue reading *Ben and Me* by Robert Lawson or *Give Me Liberty* by L.M. Elliot.

Review

Play No-Noose Hangman.

Read a sentence from your Boston Massacre story that contains either a vocabulary word or a strong verb. These should be easy to find because you labeled them.

Place quotation marks and a comma where they are needed in this sentence.

    Keep an eye on those ships   Peter told his brother.

Sidebar

No-Noose Hangman

For this lesson use the following phrases and bonus questions:

COMMAS AND PERIODS ALWAYS INSIDE

Bonus: What are commas and periods always inside of? *closing quotation marks*

Once solved review quotation rules on page 53.

Review

"Keep an eye on those ships," Peter told his brother.

Instruct students to watch for banned words. There are two: *said, went.*

UNIT 3: RETELLING NARRATIVE STORIES

Source Text

The Boston Tea Party

On a cold December evening in 1773, ships were bobbing quietly in the harbor of Boston. The streets were crowded with people. Ten-year-old Paul was among them. He was there because his older brother Peter had told him that he would see something exciting. "Keep your eyes on those three British ships filled with tea," he had advised. Peter was a member of the Sons of Liberty. What were they planning to do? Paul couldn't wait to see.

Paul knew the colonists refused to buy the tea on the ships because England was charging a tax on it. The colonists did not believe England had the right to tax them. They had told the king to take the tea back. But the Royal Governor of Boston would not let the ships sail back to England. "The king's orders must be obeyed, and the tea must be unloaded by December 17," he had said. Now it was December 16.

Suddenly the crowd began to stir. Almost one hundred "Indians" carrying axes cut through the crowd. As they passed, Paul saw that they were not Indians at all. They were the Sons of Liberty dressed like Indians. Their faces were rubbed with soot and painted with red and blue stripes. Peter winked at him as they passed. Paul watched as they boarded the ships.

Then came whack! Whack! Whack! The "Indians" were chopping open the wooden chests. In the moonlight, the crowd watched for three hours as over 340 smashed boxes of tea went into the ocean. The scent of tea filled the night air. Cheers broke out, and the crowd began to chant, "Rally Indians! Bring your axes, and tell King George we'll pay no taxes!" Paul knew King George would understand this message.

Mechanics

Use hyphens when an age comes in front of a noun: Ten-year-old Paul. Do not use hyphens when the age is after the noun: Paul was ten years old.

Sample

Key Word Outline—Story Sequence Chart

Characters and Setting

> When does the story happen?
>
> Who is in the story?
>
> What are they like?
>
> Where do they live or go?

I.   Boston, 1773, cold, Dec. eve

1.   streets, crowded, [ship] harbor

2.   Paul, 10 yrs, curious

3.   Peter, older, bro, " [eyes] exciting"

4.   Peter, Sons of Liberty

(5.)   Paul, eager, [eyes]

Conflict or Problem

> What does the main character want or need?
>
> What do the main characters do, say, think, and feel?
>
> What happens before the climax?

II.   colonists, X want, tea, [ship]

1.   [crown] tax, colonists, X right

2.   Royal Gov., X return

3.   "king, must, obeyed"

4.   unload, Dec 17

(5.)   now, Dec 16

Climax and Resolution

> What leads to the conflict being solved (the climax)?
>
> What happens as a result?
>
> What is learned? (message, moral)

III.   100, Indians → crowd

1.   Sons of Lib, disguised

2.   → ships, chopped, crates

3.   3 hrs, smashed, 340 crates, ↓ ocean

4.   crowd, cheered

(5.)   [crown] George, understand, message

Title repeats 1–3 key words from final sentence.

I. Characters and Setting

In this paragraph describe the cold weather on the streets of Boson. Tell about the main characters, Paul and Peter.

II. Conflict or Problem

In this paragraph answer questions about the big problem: the colonists do not want to pay taxes for the tea sitting in the harbor.

III. Climax and Resolution

In the final paragraph begin with the climax, which is when the "Indians" appear. Mention the tea thrown into the ocean and the colonists' message for the king.

Developing the Setting and Characters

The source text is historical fiction, which means it is based on a real event in history. You may add descriptive details to the setting as long as you do not change the basic historical facts. You may also describe the characters in more detail. As you begin your story, look for places to provide details that create strong images and feeling.

1. What is the evening like? Consider the temperature (*cool, cold, frigid, ...*), the sky (*gray, cloudy, clear, starry, ...*), the moon (*bright, hidden, covered, reflecting, ...*), the air (*still, heavy, moist, dank, icy, ...*), the wind (*howling, frigid, still, ...*). What do you picture in your mind?

    Example: *The moonlight reflected off the towering white sails as the ships rocked.*

    Describe the evening in a way that helps the readers see, hear, and feel things. You could also describe the crowd, the streets, the shops, or the ships. They are all part of the setting.

    The shops that lined the streets were empty. Seagulls squawked overhead.

    The icy wind reeked of fish and tea. The distant ships bobbed like shadows.

2. What is Paul like? Consider his looks (*hair color, eyes, height ...*), his age, his clothing. How is he feeling? What is he thinking? What is he doing? How do you picture Paul in your mind?

    Example: *Paul paced back and forth, anxious to see what would happen.*

    Describe Paul.

    Ten-year-old Paul was always full of curiosity. He admired his brother Peter

    for his ideas about liberty. Now his blue eyes scanned the docks for a clue to

    what might happen.

The *because* clause gives writers the chance to reason about cause and effect. Lead students through the information about the *because* clause.

Four dress-ups now appear on the checklist, and four dress-ups should be underlined in each paragraph written for this lesson.

The pace for adding stylistic techniques can be adjusted if a student needs time to practice previous dress-ups. Adjust the checklist if necessary.

Lesson 7: The Boston Tea Party

New Style

Because Clause Dress-Up

In this lesson you will learn another new dress-up: *because* clause.

A *because* clause helps your readers better understand what you write because a *because* clause explains why.

> Franklin offered to pay for the tea <u>because</u> he wanted to keep peace.
>
> The king closed Boston <u>because</u> the Patriots' actions angered him.

Notice:

1. A *because* clause begins with the word *because*.

   To indicate a *because* clause, underline only the first word of the clause: *because*.

2. A *because* clause contains a subject and a verb.

   > Franklin offered to pay for the tea <u>because</u> *he wanted* to keep peace.
   >
   > The king closed Boston <u>because</u> the Patriots' *actions angered* him.

3. A *because* clause is added to a sentence that is already complete.

   > *Franklin offered to pay for the tea* <u>because</u> he wanted to keep peace.
   >
   > *The king closed Boston* <u>because</u> the Patriots' actions angered him.

❜ If a *because* clause follows a complete sentence, no comma is needed. If the *because* clause is at the beginning of the sentence, a comma is required.

   > The king closed Boston <u>because</u> the Patriots' actions angered him. (no comma)
   >
   > Unfortunately <u>because</u> the king taxed tea, colonists reacted indignantly. (comma)

Practice

Add a *because* clause to these sentences. Notice that the word *because* is underlined.

1. The colonists did not want the British tea <u>because</u> *the king put an unfair tax on it.*
   _____

2. Peter told Paul to stay at the harbor <u>because</u> *there was sure to be some excitement.*
   _____

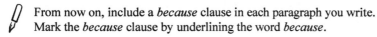 From now on, include a *because* clause in each paragraph you write.
Mark the *because* clause by underlining the word *because*.

For younger students simply encourage them to place the *because* clause after a sentence that is already complete.

Read the sentences and orally fill in the blanks several times. When students understand the pattern of the *because* clause, then direct them to write.

Style Practice

Strong Verb Dress-Up and -ly Adverb Dress-Up

On the first line below each sentence, write strong verbs that could replace the italicized banned verb. On the second line under each sentence, write ideas for -ly adverbs that you could use with the strong verbs. Use a thesaurus or your vocabulary words.

The crates of tea *went* into the ocean.

strong verbs   *plunged, splashed, plummeted*

-ly adverbs   *continually, steadily, defiantly*

Who/Which Clause Dress-Up

Add a *who/which* clause to each sentence. End each non-essential clause with a comma and underline the word *who*.

1. The colonists, <u>who</u> *indignantly complained about the taxes,*

    _____ refused to accept the British tea.

2. The Sons of Liberty, <u>who</u> *made their way through the crowd brandishing axes,*

    _____ headed toward the ships.

Vocabulary Practice

Look at the vocabulary words for Lesson 7. Fill in the blanks with a word that makes sense.

1. The Sons of Liberty ____*cunningly*____ dressed as Indians so they could not be recognized.

2. The colonists would _____*squander*_____ the tea to make their point clear.

Now look at the vocabulary chart on page 322. Try to use words from Lessons 1–7 in sentences or phrases that could be in your story. Write at least two ideas below.

*The crowd stood **transfixed** as the **zealous** Indians **audaciously ventured** onto the ships.*

*The "tea party" would certainly **provoke** the **obstinate** king.*

Unit 3 Composition Checklist
Lesson 7: The Boston Tea Party

Retelling
Narrative
Stories

Name: _____

IEW Institute for Excellence in Writing

STRUCTURE

☐ MLA format (see Appendix I) _____ 5 pts

☐ title centered and repeats 1–3 key words from final sentence _____ 5 pts

☐ story follows Story Sequence Chart _____ 6 pts

☐ each paragraph contains at least four sentences _____ 6 pts

☐ checklist on top, final draft, rough draft, key word outline _____ 5 pts

STYLE

¶1 ¶2 ¶3 **Dress-Ups** (underline one of each)   (3 pts each)

☐ ☐ ☐ -ly adverb _____ 9 pts

☐ ☐ ☐ who/which clause _____ 9 pts

☐ ☐ ☐ strong verb _____ 9 pts

☐ ☐ ☐ because clause _____ 9 pts

CHECK FOR BANNED WORDS (-1 pt for each use): go/went, say/said _____ pts

MECHANICS

☐ capitalization _____ 1 pt

☐ end marks and punctuation _____ 1 pt

☐ complete sentences (Does it make sense?) _____ 2 pts

☐ correct spelling _____ 3 pts

VOCABULARY

☐ vocabulary words - label *(voc)* in left margin or after sentence

Total: _____ 70 pts

Custom Total: _____ pts

If you are using the ticket system as described on page 337, consider giving double tickets for each vocabulary word a student uses in this story. Just a little extra motivation can yield amazing results.

Teachers are free to adjust a checklist by requiring only the stylistic techniques that have become easy, plus one new one. EZ+1

Intentionally blank so the checklist can be removed.

Lesson 8: The Shot Heard Round the World

Structure:	Unit 3: Retelling Narrative Stories
Style:	no new style
Writing Topic:	The Revolutionary War
Literature Suggestion:	Elementary: *Ben and Me* by Robert Lawson
	Junior and Senior High: *Give Me Liberty* by L.M. Elliot

UNIT 3: RETELLING NARRATIVE STORIES

Lesson 8: The Shot Heard Round the World

Goals

- to practice the Unit 3 structural model
- to create a 3-paragraph KWO using the Unit 3 Story Sequence Chart
- to write a 3-paragraph story about the beginning of the Revolutionary War
- to correctly use new vocabulary words: *persevere, compel, destined, appalled*

Assignment Schedule

Day 1

1. Complete the Review.

2. Read Historical Information.

3. Read "The Shot Heard Round the World."

4. Read Story Variation. If you desire to write a variation of the story, answer the questions at the bottom of the page.

5. Complete the KWO by answering the Story Sequence Chart questions. If you decided to change your characters, use the ideas you wrote at the bottom of Story Variation.

6. Cover the source text and tell the meaning of each line of notes in your own words. If a note is unclear, add what you need to in order to make it clear.

Day 2

1. Review your KWO from Day 1.

2. Complete Style Practice.

3. Look at the vocabulary cards for Lesson 8. Discuss the words and their definitions and complete Vocabulary Practice.

4. Using your KWO as a guide, begin writing a rough draft in your own words.

5. Go over the checklist. Put a check in the box for each requirement you have completed.

Day 3

1. Review all vocabulary words learned thus far.

2. Finish writing your 3-paragraph story.

3. Turn in your rough draft to your editor with the completed checklist attached.

Day 4

1. Write or type a final draft making any corrections your editor asked you to make.

2. Paperclip the checklist, final draft, rough draft, and KWO together. Hand them in.

3. If you are making a Magnum Opus Notebook, revise your Boston Massacre story from Lesson 6.

Literature Suggestion

Continue reading *Ben and Me* by Robert Lawson or *Give Me Liberty* by L.M. Elliot.

Review

Play the Question Game.

Add punctuation where it is needed in this sentence.

Will all this trouble lead to war   Sarah asked John.

Historical Information

The story for this lesson is based on the events that led to the beginning of the Revolutionary War. The poet Ralph Waldo Emerson used the phrase "the shot heard round the world" in 1837 to describe the first known offensive shot Americans fired at the king's soldiers. It happened on the North Bridge of Concord. The poem is called "Concord Hymn," and it begins like this:

By the rude bridge that arched the flood,
   Their flag to April's breeze unfurled,
Here once the embattled farmers stood
   And fired the shot heard round the world.

Question Game

See Appendix VII for game directions.

Choose from the questions on pages 347–349. For this lesson the following would work well: 3, 4, 5, 7, 8, 9, 33, 34, 35. Before beginning the game, renumber the chosen questions 1–9 in the margin.

Review

"Will all this trouble lead to war?" Sarah asked John.

Lesson 8: The Shot Heard Round the World

Source Text

The Shot Heard Round the World

John was a farmer who lived in Massachusetts in 1775. He lived with his wife, Sarah, and their two small sons near Lexington. King George had sent soldiers into the American towns. The colonists resented this, so conflicts often erupted. One day, John returned home quite upset. "Those blasted redcoats are everywhere! Adams and Hancock are right. We need to store up arms to protect ourselves," he told Sarah.

John soon joined the minutemen who were gathering and storing arms in case war broke out. They were hiding the arms in Concord.

Then late one April night there was a loud voice outside John's door. He leaned out the window and saw Paul Revere. "Hurry, John," he said, "the regulars are coming out!"

John knew that meant that the redcoats were headed for Concord. He woke Sarah and told her, "I must go to Lexington. We must stop the redcoats from reaching our arms."

When John reached Lexington Green, there were about seventy other minutemen ready to face the redcoats. They waited anxiously. Then early in the morning about seven hundred British troops arrived.

"Do not fire unless fired upon," Captain John Parker ordered the minutemen, "but if they mean to have a war, let it begin here!"

"Disperse, ye rebels," the British officer ordered.

The minutemen did not budge. John's heart was pounding. He prayed that the soldiers would turn back, but all of a sudden a shot rang out—then another, and another. When the shooting stopped, eight minutemen were dead, and the redcoats were marching to Concord. There, on the North Bridge, more minutemen were ready to fight. They opened fire and eventually drove the British back to Boston. The Revolutionary War had begun.

Story Variation

The source text is historical fiction, which means it is based on a real event in history. You may add descriptive details to your story as long as you do not change the basic historical facts. When you write this story, you may change the characters and some of the details. The main character does not have to be John.

As you complete the first portion of the Story Sequence Chart, one of the questions you will answer is *who is in the story*? Instead of answering *John*, change the character. You may change some of the details as well. Here are some ideas:

> You could make your main character the daughter of a minuteman. What is she like? What is she doing as her father is storing arms? She might follow her father to Lexington. What would she see when the shot was fired? Would she see who fired the first shot? Would she know any of those who were killed? What would she do after the shooting ends?

> You could make your main character the son of a minuteman who wants to go to Lexington with his father. How old is he? Does he go? Will he or his father be shot?

> You could make your main character an animal who witnesses the events. It could be a minuteman's horse, the family pet, or a forest animal.

Use the questions on the Story Sequence Chart to further develop your variation.

1. Who is the main character in your version of The Shot Heard Round the World?

    Answers will vary as each student will make up his or her characters.

2. What is this character like? Describe him or her.

    _____

    _____

3. Where is he or she when the shot is fired? How did he or she get there?

    _____

    _____

As you complete your KWO, have fun developing your variation of this historical event. The only required details are the historical facts: the storing of the arms at Concord, the minutemen going to Lexington and Concord to protect those stores, and the battles that occurred in both places. The characters and their thoughts, feelings, and actions may be determined by you.

The second paragraph contains two famous quotes. The first is Captain Parker's instructions, "Do not fire unless fired upon, but if they mean to have a war, let it begin here!" and the other is the British officer's command, "Disperse, ye rebels." Since these are famous quotes, they should be copied exactly. On the KWO students may write key words in quotation marks; then, they may refer to the source text to copy the full quotes.

I. Characters and Setting

As students write about the setting and characters, remember that they may use the characters from the source text or create their own.

II. Conflict or Problem

In this paragraph answer the questions about the big problem, the redcoats wanting to capture the ammunition at Concord. Explain how the main character discovers the problem and his/her response.

III. Climax and Resolution

In the final paragraph begin with the climax, the first shot fired at Lexington. Tell what happens as a result. The resolution starts with minutemen on the North Bridge of Concord firing on the redcoats, causing them to retreat to Boston.

Sample

Key Word Outline—Story Sequence Chart

Characters and Setting

| When does the story happen? |
| Who is in the story? |
| What are they like? |
| Where do they live or go? |

I. _Massachusetts, 1775_

1. _John, farmer, w/ wife, 2_ 👫

2. _upset,_ 👑 _soldiers, everywhere_

3. _joined, minutemen_

4. _store, ammo, Concord, protect_

(5.) _____

Conflict or Problem

| What does the main character want or need? |
| What do the main characters do, say, think, and feel? |
| What happens before the climax? |

II. _Paul Revere, "Regulars coming!"_

1. _⟳, Sarah ➔ Lexington, stop, rc_

2. _Lexington, 70 mm, waiting_

3. _AM, 700 British, rc_

4. _Capt Parker, mm, "X fire"_

(5.) _Brit officer, "Disperse, ye ... "_

Climax and Resolution

| What leads to the conflict being solved (the climax)? |
| What happens as a result? |
| What is learned? (message, moral) |

III. _standstill, suddenly, shot_

1. _more, shots_

2. _mm, XX, rc ➔ Concord_

3. _North Bridge, more mm_

4. _fire, drove, rc, Boston_

(5.) _began, Revolutionary War_

Title repeats 1–3 key words from final sentence.

Institute for Excellence in Writing

mm = minutemen   rc = redcoats

Style Practice

Because Clause Dress-up

Add a *because* clause to these sentences. Underline the word *because*.

1. The colonists were storing arms <u>because</u> *they wanted to be able to defend themselves in the case of war.*

2. Paul Revere was gathering the minutemen <u>because</u> *the redcoats were marching toward Concord.*

3. On Concord's North Bridge more minutemen prepared to fight <u>because</u> *the ammunition had to be saved.*

Strong Verb Dress-Up and -ly Adverb Dress-Up

On the first line below each sentence, write strong verbs that could replace the italicized banned verb. On the second line under each sentence, write ideas for -ly adverbs that you could use with the strong verbs. Use a thesaurus or your vocabulary words.

1. "Redcoats are everywhere!" John *said*.

   strong verbs *exclaimed, complained, lamented, grumbled*

   -ly adverbs *angrily, **indignantly**, furiously*

2. John *went* to Lexington to meet the minutemen.

   strong verbs *dashed, hurried, fled, raced*

   -ly adverbs *determinedly, immediately, **audaciously***

3. A shot *went* off.

   strong verbs *ricocheted, blasted, boomed, zoomed*

   -ly adverbs *suddenly, unexpectedly, accidentally*

UNIT 3: RETELLING NARRATIVE STORIES

Who/Which Clause Dress-Up

Add a *who/which* clause to each sentence. End each non-essential clause with a comma and underline the word *who*.

1. Sarah, who *watched her husband ride away,*

   _____ hoped there would not be trouble.

2. The minutemen, who *clutched their muskets in defiance,*

   _____ stood their ground.

Vocabulary Practice

Look at the vocabulary words for Lesson 8. Fill in the blanks with a word that makes sense.

1. The British officer was _____*appalled*_____ that the minutemen would not budge.

2. America was _____*destined*_____ for war.

Look at the vocabulary chart on page 322. Try to use words from Lessons 1–8 in sentences or phrases that could be in your story. Write at least two ideas below.

   *The minutemen **audaciously** and **zealously endeavored** to hide the ammunition.*

   ***Inevitably** the soldiers discovered the store of arms.*

Institute for Excellence in Writing

Lesson 8: The Shot Heard Round the World

Unit 3 Composition Checklist
Lesson 8: The Shot Heard Round the World

Retelling
Narrative
Stories

Name: _____

IEW Institute for Excellence in Writing

STRUCTURE

☐ MLA format (see Appendix I) _____ 5 pts

☐ title centered and repeats 1–3 key words from final sentence _____ 5 pts

☐ story follows Story Sequence Chart _____ 6 pts

☐ each paragraph contains at least four sentences _____ 6 pts

☐ checklist on top, final draft, rough draft, key word outline _____ 5 pts

STYLE

¶1 ¶2 ¶3 **Dress-Ups** (underline one of each)　　　(3 pts each)

☐ ☐ ☐ -ly adverb _____ 9 pts

☐ ☐ ☐ *who/which* clause _____ 9 pts

☐ ☐ ☐ strong verb _____ 9 pts

☐ ☐ ☐ *because* clause _____ 9 pts

CHECK FOR BANNED WORDS (-1 pt for each use): go/went, say/said _____ pts

MECHANICS

☐ capitalization _____ 1 pt

☐ end marks and punctuation _____ 1 pt

☐ complete sentences (Does it make sense?) _____ 2 pts

☐ correct spelling _____ 3 pts

VOCABULARY

☐ vocabulary words - label *(voc)* in left margin or after sentence _____

Total: _____ 70 pts

Custom Total: _____ pts

For the last assignment written in this unit, consider giving double tickets for each vocabulary word a student uses in this story. Just a little extra motivation can yield amazing results.

Teachers are free to adjust a checklist by requiring only the stylistic techniques that have become easy, plus one new one. EZ+1

UNIT 3: RETELLING NARRATIVE STORIES

Intentionally blank so the checklist can be removed.

Institute for Excellence in Writing

Lesson 9: Benjamin Franklin

Teaching Writing: Structure and Style

Structure: Unit 4: Summarizing a Reference
topic-clincher sentences

Style: no new style

Writing Topic: Benjamin Franklin

Literature Suggestion: Elementary: *Ben and Me* by Robert Lawson
Junior and Senior High: *Give Me Liberty* by L.M. Elliot

Watch the sections for Unit 4:
Summarizing a Reference.
At IEW.com/twss-help reference
the TWSS Viewing Guides.

Lesson 9: Benjamin Franklin

UNIT 4: SUMMARIZING A REFERENCE

Lesson 9: Benjamin Franklin

Goals

*   to learn the Unit 4 Summarizing a Reference structural model
*   to learn and correctly use the topic-clincher rule
*   to create a KWO
*   to write a 1-paragraph report about Benjamin Franklin
*   to correctly use new vocabulary words: *draft*, *diligently*, *acknowledge*, *resolve*

Assignment Schedule

Day 1

1. Play Vocabulary Lightning.
2. Read New Structure—Summarizing a Reference.
3. Memorize the topic-clincher rule.
4. Read "Benjamin Franklin and Our Freedom Documents" and write a KWO.

Day 2

1. Review your KWO from Day 1 and complete Structure Practice.
2. Complete Style Practice.
3. Look at the vocabulary cards for Lesson 9. Discuss the words and their definitions and complete Vocabulary Practice.
4. Using your KWO as a guide, begin writing a rough draft in your own words.
5. Go over the checklist. Put a check in the box for each requirement you have completed.

Day 3

1. Review all vocabulary words learned thus far.
2. Finish writing your report. Follow the topic-clincher rule. Highlight or bold two or three key words that repeat or reflect in the topic and clincher sentences.
3. Turn in your rough draft to your editor with the completed checklist attached.

Day 4

1. Write or type a final draft making any corrections your editor asked you to make.
2. Paperclip the checklist, final draft, rough draft, and KWO together. Hand them in.
3. If you are making a Magnum Opus Notebook, revise your Boston Tea Party story from Lesson 7.

In this new unit the KWO is formed by taking key words from interesting and important facts found in a source text. Initially, teachers will likely need to assist students as they limit their notes. Model the process. Let students choose words they think are important or interesting, limiting them to 5–7 total facts.

In this unit students learn to organize writing by beginning each paragraph with a topic sentence and ending each with a clincher sentence.

Read this page
to introduce
Unit 4:
Summarizing
a Reference.
Talk about the
difference between
the compositions
students wrote for
Unit 3 (3-paragraph
narrative stories
using the Story
Sequence
Chart) and the
compositions they
will write for Unit 4
 (1-paragraph
reports about a
single topic).

Read about the
topic and clincher
sentences and their
purpose.

UNIT 4: SUMMARIZING A REFERENCE

Literature Suggestion

Finish reading *Ben and Me* by Robert Lawson or *Give Me Liberty* by L.M. Elliot.

Acquire *Tolliver's Secret* by Esther Wood Brady (girls) or *Guns for General Washington* by Seymour Reit (boys) to read for lessons 10–11.

New Structure

Summarizing a Reference

In Unit 4 you will write reports by summarizing a reference. When you write a short report, most often you turn to an encyclopedia, textbook, or Internet article for information. These sources typically have much more information than you need. It is important to understand that you will not try to note every fact from the source text. Instead, you will choose five to seven interesting or important facts and "*SOME*-a-rize."

1 topic = 1 paragraph

When you write a report, your facts must be organized into paragraphs. Each paragraph will begin with a topic sentence, contain facts, and end with a clincher sentence.

Topic Sentence

> The topic sentence tells what the paragraph is about. For this reason, it is the first sentence of the paragraph. Every paragraph should have one clear topic. When you write the KWO, ask yourself: "What will the paragraph be about?" As you answer, write two or three key words on the Roman numeral line.

Facts

> On the other lines of the KWO, write facts that support the topic. To find facts, read the source text and look for five to seven things that you find important or interesting. To help you remember each fact that you choose, write two or three key words about the fact on the KWO. If needed, you may use two lines to write one fact, or you may combine facts so that you have two facts on one line. Remember to include symbols, numbers, and abbreviations.

Clincher Sentence

> The clincher sentence reminds the reader what the paragraph was about. For this reason, it is the last sentence of the paragraph. The KWO ends with the word *clincher*. Do not place key words on the clincher line. Instead when you form your rough draft, repeat (same word) or reflect (synonym of the word) two or three key words on the topic line.

Sample Paragraph

The following paragraph is a short report about Benjamin Franklin. Of course, there is too much information about this man to be placed in a single paragraph. Therefore, the author has chosen a specific topic about Benjamin Franklin to write about.

Benjamin **Franklin** is known as America's first **great inventor**. He labored diligently to improve life in the colonies. For example, he designed a stove to help colonists stay warm in the winter. It produced twice as much heat with less wood than other stoves of his day. This stove remains in use today because it is so efficient. It is called a Franklin stove, of course. Franklin is also famous for his experiments with lightning. After discovering that lightning was electricity, he invented the lightning rod to keep buildings safe during thunderstorms. He also invented bifocal glasses, which help people see better both far and near. **Franklin** indeed is remembered as an **exemplary inventor**.

Notice:

1. The topic sentence tells what the paragraph is about. The key words in bold are the main idea words of the topic sentence.

2. The eight sentences that follow the topic sentence each provide a fact that supports, proves, or illustrates how Franklin was a great inventor.

3. The clincher sentence states the same main idea as the topic sentence. The key words in bold repeat or reflect the same key words found in the topic sentence.

4. One can easily see that the topic-clincher rule was followed because the following words are bold: *Franklin, great, inventor* and *Franklin, exemplary, inventor*.

Help students learn the topic-clincher rule. If teaching to a classroom of students, advise students to be ready to recite the rule in order to enter class next time.

 The topic sentence and the clincher sentence MUST repeat or reflect two or three key words.

Source Text

Benjamin Franklin and Our Freedom Documents

Every American probably knows something about Benjamin Franklin. However, few probably know one of the most interesting things about him. It is the fact that he is the only man who signed all four documents that helped America become a free nation. First, in 1776 he signed the Declaration of Independence. In this document Americans proclaimed themselves free from British rule. It was considered treason by the king, so Franklin risked his life by signing it. Of course, Britain did not recognize the declaration, so America fought the Revolutionary War. During this war America needed help from France. Whom do you think they sent to obtain it? Yes, Benjamin Franklin sailed to France to ask for their help. The French people loved Franklin. In Paris he was able to obtain and sign the Treaty of Alliance with France. In this treaty France promised to send soldiers and supplies to help America. America would not have won the war without it. At the end of the war, Franklin was chosen as America's representative again, this time to return to France to sign the Treaty of Paris of 1783. This is the treaty that made peace with Britain. Finally, in 1787 at the age of eighty-one, Franklin was the oldest member of the Continental Congress to sign the Constitution of the United States of America. This document established a new government for the new, independent country. Benjamin Franklin's name remains on all four of America's freedom documents.

Mechanics

Titles of official documents are capitalized. They do not require quotation marks or italics.

Locate Key Words

Guide students to find 5–7 facts. Reread the first sentence. Ask your students, "Is that important or interesting?" If they answer yes, place a check mark by the fact or sentence.

Allow students to choose facts that they find important or interesting. Very likely their facts will differ from the ones chosen in this Teacher's Manual.

Before completing the KWO, remind students that this is a new unit and that key words are found differently. What goes on the Roman numeral line? (*key words for the topic*) Lines 1–5 (6/7) are for key words from facts, not from each sentence. Ask which facts interest them. Help them limit the number of facts they choose. If students are young, stop at five sentences. Do not put key words for a clincher on the KWO. Direct students to write the clincher sentence when they write the paragraph.

The KWOs in the Teacher's Manual are only samples. Every class and each student will have unique outlines.

Sample

Key Word Outline

Decide the topic of your paragraph. For this lesson the topic has been given to you and noted in key words on the Roman numeral line (the topic line) of the KWO.

Re-read the source text and write five to seven facts to support the topic. You will have to leave some facts out. You are *SOME-a-rizing*.

I. Topic: *BF, signed, 4, America's, documents*

1. *1st, 1776, Declaration Ind.*

2. *proclaimed, America, free* ♔

3. *Revolutionary War → France, Treaty of Alliance*

4. *help, soldiers + supplies*

5. *end → France, Treaty of Paris*

(6.) *= peace, treaty, w/ Britain*

(7.) *1787, US Constitution, @ 81 yrs, oldest*

Clincher

Use the KWO to tell each line of notes in your own words. For the clincher, repeat or reflect the words on the topic line.

Discuss ideas for a clincher using two to three key words that repeat or reflect words written on the topic sentence line.

Here is a sample clincher sentence:

*Benjamin Franklin's **signature** is prominent on all four **documents** that helped establish **America** as a free country.*

Structure Practice

Topic Sentence

The topic sentence must tell what your paragraph is about. Use the key words on the topic line (or synonyms of those words) to write a topic sentence. There are several different possibilities for communicating the topic of the paragraph, even from the same key words.

*Only one man's **name** appears on all four official **manuscripts** that led to*

***America's** independence: Benjamin Franklin.*

Style Practice

Because Clause Dress-up

Add a *because* clause to the sentence below. Underline the word *because*.

Benjamin Franklin sailed to France <u>because</u>   *America needed help to win the war.*

_____

Students may rewrite the sentence in any way that uses a strong verb rather than *went*. For example, *Benjamin Franklin sought help in France* communicates the same idea without using *went*.

Strong Verb Dress-Up

Write strong verbs that could replace the italicized banned word. Use a thesaurus or your vocabulary words. Do not use *sailed* because that is the word the source text used.

Franklin *went* to France.

strong verbs   *traveled, journeyed, **ventured**, sought help in*

Who/Which Clause Dress-Up

Add a *who/which* clause to the sentence below. Punctuate and mark correctly.

The Declaration of Independence, <u>which</u> *asserted America's freedom from Britain,*

_____ was treasonous to the king.

Vocabulary Practice

Look at the vocabulary words for Lesson 9. Fill in the blanks with a word that makes sense.

1. Britain did not _____*acknowledge*_____ the Declaration of Independence.

2. Franklin was able to _____*draft*_____ the Treaty of Alliance with France.

Look at the vocabulary chart on page 322. Try to use words from Lessons 1–9 in sentences or phrases that could be in your report. Write at least two ideas below.

  *Franklin knew that America was **destined** to be free.*

  *Franklin realized the declaration would **provoke** the king to anger.*

Unit 4 Composition Checklist
Lesson 9: Benjamin Franklin

Summarizing
a Reference

Institute for
Excellence in
Writing

Name: _____

STRUCTURE

☐ MLA format (see Appendix I)   _____   2   pts

☐ title centered and repeats 1–3 key words from final sentence   _____   3   pts

☐ topic-clincher sentences repeat or reflect 2–3 key words (highlight or bold)   _____   3   pts

☐ checklist on top, final draft, rough draft, key word outline   _____   1   pt

STYLE

¶1 Dress-Ups (underline one of each)   (3 pts each)

☐ -ly adverb   _____   3   pts

☐ *who/which* clause   _____   3   pts

☐ strong verb   _____   3   pts

☐ *because* clause   _____   3   pts

CHECK FOR BANNED WORDS (-1 pt for each use): go/went, say/said   _____   pts

MECHANICS

☐ capitalization   _____   1   pt

☐ end marks and punctuation   _____   1   pt

☐ complete sentences (Does it make sense?)   _____   1   pt

☐ correct spelling   _____   1   pt

VOCABULARY

☐ vocabulary words - label *(voc)* in left margin or after sentence

Total: _____   25   pts

Custom Total: _____   pts

Notice that the checklist requires students to highlight or bold topic-clincher key words.

Dress-ups should continue to be underlined.

Teachers are free to adjust a checklist by requiring only the stylistic techniques that have become easy, plus one new one. EZ+1

UNIT 4: SUMMARIZING A REFERENCE

Intentionally blank so the checklist can be removed.

Lesson 10: George Washington

Structure:	Unit 4: Summarizing a Reference
Style:	quality adjective, banned words: *good, bad*
Writing Topic:	George Washington
	Bonus: Quality Adjective Poem
Literature Suggestion:	Girls: *Tolliver's Secret* by Esther Wood Brady
	Boys: *Guns for General Washington* by Seymour Reit

UNIT 4: SUMMARIZING A REFERENCE

Lesson 10: George Washington

Goals

- to practice the Unit 4 structural model
- to create a KWO
- to write a 1-paragraph report about George Washington
- to correctly add a new dress-up: quality adjective
- to ban weak adjectives: *good, bad*
- to correctly use new vocabulary words: *exemplary, esteemed, prominent, conceive*

Assignment Schedule

Day 1

1. Complete the Review.
2. Read "George Washington" and write a KWO.

Day 2

1. Review your KWO from Day 1 and complete Structure Practice.
2. Learn a new dress-up, the quality adjective. Read New Style and complete Style Practice.
3. Look at the vocabulary cards for Lesson 10. Discuss the words and their definitions and complete Vocabulary Practice.
4. Using your KWO as a guide, begin writing a rough draft in your own words.
5. Go over the checklist. Put a check in the box for each requirement you have completed.

Day 3

1. Review all vocabulary words learned thus far.
2. Finish writing your report. Follow the topic-clincher rule. Highlight or bold two or three key words that repeat or reflect in the topic and clincher sentences.
3. Turn in your rough draft to your editor with the completed checklist attached.

Day 4

1. Write or type a final draft making any corrections your editor asked you to make.
2. Paperclip the checklist, final draft, rough draft, and KWO together. Hand them in.
3. If you are making a Magnum Opus Notebook, revise your Shot Heard Round the World story from Lesson 8.

Note: There is a bonus activity, an adjective poem, on pages 97–98. Your teacher will decide when you will complete this activity.

Students will likely need continued help. Model the process by writing a sample KWO on the whiteboard for them to see. Help students limit which interesting or important facts they choose.

Study for Vocabulary Quiz 3. It will cover words from Lessons 1–10.

Literature Suggestion

Begin reading *Tolliver's Secret* by Esther Wood Brady or *Guns for General Washington* by Seymour Reit.

Review

Play Around the World.

What is the topic-clincher rule?

When summarizing a reference, do you take words from every sentence in your source text?

Review

The topic sentence and the clincher sentence MUST repeat or reflect two or three key words.

When summa-rizing a reference, you do not take words from every sentence in the source text. Instead, notes are based on facts. Choose 5–7 interesting or important facts.

Directions at the end of this lesson explain how to write a descriptive poem of America following this model. Your teacher will decide when you will complete this activity.

AMERICA, Land of ...

Sunlit, dazzling seashores
with radiant and soft sunsets

Dense, lush forests
with fragrance and grace

Misty, majestic mountains
that tower bravely

Rolling, golden plains
with placid and immeasurable space

Icy, raging rivers
with sparkling and rhythmic waters

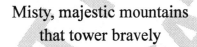

AMERICA, Land of ...

Proud, diverse people
who strive for liberty

Heroic, patriotic people
who love their country

The free and the brave

GOD BLESS AMERICA, MY HOME SWEET HOME

Julianna Gilson, grade 8

2009–2010

Source Text

George Washington

George Washington was a skillful leader who helped America become a great nation. During the Revolutionary War he was the general who led the Continental Army to victory. After the war he was chosen to lead the Constitutional Convention. This is the convention that created the new government for the new country. They wrote the Constitution of the United States. The Constitution established the highest office of government to be the president. Although Washington preferred to return home to a quiet life after the completion of the Constitution, friends convinced him to run for president. He won readily. Washington served as the nation's president in New York City for two terms from 1789–1797. The people wanted him to run for a third term, but he refused. He did not believe one man should hold the highest office for so long. He did not want one man to have too much power because that would be too much like a king. Washington retired and returned home. He died a few years later. He was revered by the people and called "the Father of His Country."

His face is now on the dollar bill and on the quarter. The nation's current capital city is named after him. George Washington was "first in war, first in peace, and first in the hearts of his countrymen."

Mechanics _____

Contractions are not used in academic writing.

He didn't want one man to have too much power. (incorrect)

Institute for Excellence in Writing

Sample

Key Word Outline

Decide the topic of your paragraph. Note it in key words on the topic line of the KWO.
Re-read the source text and write five to seven facts to support the topic.

I.   Topic: *G.W. + leader, various, roles*

   1.   *Rev War, led, US, victory*

   2.   *led, Constitutional Convention*

   3.   *→ establish, new, gov't*

   4.   *led, US, president, 2 terms (1789–1797)*

   5.   *X run, 3rd, ppl, wanted*

  (6.)   *⬭, 1 ⚲, X much, power*

  (7.)   *XX, revered, "Father ... Country"*

   Clincher

Use the KWO to tell each line of notes in your own words. For the clincher, repeat or reflect the
words on the topic line.

Structure Practice

Topic Sentence

Use the key words that you wrote on the KWO topic line (or synonyms of those words) to write
a topic sentence for your paragraph.

*George Washington assumed **various roles** that distinguished him as one of*

*America's greatest **leaders**.*

New Style

Quality Adjective Dress-Up

In this lesson you will learn another dress-up: quality adjective.

An adjective is a describing word. An adjective describes a noun—a person, place, thing, or idea. Here is the adjective test. If the word fits in the blank, it is an adjective.

the _____ pen or person

Use the adjective test. Underline six adjectives below.

dog	chew	<u>ravishing</u>	<u>elegant</u>	<u>hideous</u>
<u>brave</u>	<u>zealous</u>	<u>prominent</u>	pair	table

Banned Words

Boring adjectives like boring verbs should be avoided in writing. For this reason you will not be allowed to use certain adjectives in the writing you do for this class.

Good and *bad* are not very descriptive; they are ordinary. Quality adjectives like *glorious* and *sinister* add more detail and provide a strong image and feeling.

What quality adjectives might be more descriptive than *good* and *bad*? On the lines below, add to the list of synonyms.

Synonyms for *good* *talented, revered, valiant , excellent, favorable*

Synonyms for *bad* *abominable, appalling, foul , dreadful, disagreeable*

From now on in these lessons, the words *good* and *bad* are banned. To help yourself avoid these banned words, use a thesaurus or your vocabulary words or look at the -ly adverb list on the *Portable Walls for Structure and Style Students* or the IEW Writing Tools App. Dropping the -ly from the words on the -ly adverb list will transform them into quality adjectives.

 From now on, include a quality adjective in each paragraph you write.
Mark the quality adjective by underlining it.

⊘ BANNED WORDS   VERBS: SAY/SAID, GO/WENT   ADJECTIVES: GOOD, BAD

Institute for Excellence in Writing

Encourage students to rapidly give many adjectives to describe the pen or person.

red, fat, fancy, old, new, broken, delightful, silly, terrible, etc.

For the rest of this course, one quality adjective should be underlined in every paragraph of the students' compositions.

Style Practice

Quality Adjective Dress-Up

On the line below each sentence, write quality adjectives that could replace the italicized banned adjective. Use a thesaurus or your vocabulary words. Be sure to consider the context of the sentence.

1. George Washington had been a *good* general in the Revolutionary War.

    __cunning, adroit, skillful, successful__

2. George Washington was a *good* president.

    *wise, humble, **esteemed**, revered*

3. Washington believed that one man possessing too much power for too long would be *bad*.

    *detrimental, **imprudent**, ruinous, unwise*

Because Clause Dress-up

Add a *because* clause to this sentence. Underline the word *because*.

George Washington did not run for a third term as president <u>because</u> _____

he believed it important to limit the power of one man.

Strong Verb Dress-Up

When you write from a source text, do not use the exact words found in the text. On the blank below each sentence, write strong verbs that are synonyms of the italicized words. Use a thesaurus.

1. The Constitutional Convention *created* a new government for the new country.

    strong verbs *adopted, **drafted, conceived**, formulated*

2. Washington *retired* from the office of president.

    strong verbs *stepped down, resigned, departed*

Who/Which Clause Dress-Up

Add a *who/which* clause to the sentence below. Punctuate and mark correctly.

George Washington, <u>who</u> ___*led America during its infancy,*_____

_____ is still greatly esteemed.

-ly Adverb Dress-Up

Write an idea for adding an -ly adverb to any of the sentences you will write in your paragraph.

___*Washington <u>humbly</u> refused to run for a third term.*_____

_____

Vocabulary Practice

Look at the vocabulary words for Lesson 10. Fill in the blanks with a word that makes sense.

1. George Washington was greatly _____*esteemed*_____ by his countrymen.

2. Washington is certainly one of America's most __*prominent, esteemed, or exemplary*__ men.
   (Three words work here.)

Look at the vocabulary chart on page 322. Try to use words from Lessons 1–10 in sentences or phrases that could be in your report. Write at least two ideas below.

___*Washington helped American troops **persevere** through the hardships of the war.*___

___***Inevitably** the people elected Washington as America's first president.*___

Bonus Activity

Adjective Poem

The following assignment will help you practice using quality adjectives. If you are making a Magnum Opus Notebook, it can also serve as the cover for it.

Read the poem on page 91 about America by Julianna Gilson. This poem is filled with quality adjectives. You will use this same model to write your own poem. Begin by listing possible adjectives that you may use in your poem. Then use the template on the next page to write your poem.

Quality Adjectives

Use a thesaurus or your vocabulary words to find adjectives to describe each of the nouns below.

1. seashores _____ *sandy, serene, welcoming, shimmering* _____

_____

2. forests _____ *frosty, piney, misty, tranquil* _____

_____

3. mountains _____ *majestic, snowcapped, massive, breathtaking* _____

_____

4. rivers _____ *roaring, refreshing, clear, sapphire* _____

_____

5. plains _____ *golden, vast, fruited, waving* _____

_____

6. people of America _____ *patriotic, diverse, hardworking, hopeful* _____

_____

Commas should be used to separate two or more coordinate adjectives before a noun, such as *sunny, salty seashores*. Commas should not be used to separate cumulative adjectives in which the first adjective modifies both the second adjective and the noun as in *towering snowcapped mountains* or *many diverse people*.

There are two tricks to help distinguish coordinate from cumulative. Adjectives are coordinate and need a comma

1) if you can reverse their order (Both *sunny, salty seashores* and *salty, sunny seashores* sounds good.)

2) if you can insert *and* between them. (*Sunny and salty seashores* sounds good, but *many and diverse people* sounds awkward.)

UNIT 4: SUMMARIZING A REFERENCE

Bonus Activity

Adjective Poem

Adjectives come in three sizes: words, phrases, and clauses. Use the model below to help you write a poem about America that is filled with all sizes of adjectives. You may make some changes to the model; it is a general guide. Rhyming is optional.

1. Place 1–2 quality adjectives on each line before the noun.

2. Place a phrase or clause that begins with *that*, *of*, *which*, or *who* on each line after the noun.

    Sunlit, salty seashores covered in sand

3. If you desire, add other nouns, such as cities, farms, churches, historical landmarks, etc.

4. To end the poem, write one or two unique lines or copy these:

    The free and the brave

    God Bless America, My Home Sweet Home.

America, Land of ...

Sunny, salty	seashores	*covered in sand*
Tranquil, fragrant	forests	*that fill the land*
Towering snowcapped	mountains	*that reach to the sky*
Rushing, roaring	rivers	*flowing nearby*
Vast, golden	plains	*that wave in the wind*

America, Land of ...

Many diverse	people	*who share a common home*
Proud, patriotic	people	*who stand for freedom*

The free and the brave,

God bless America, my home sweet home.

Name and Grade

School Year

Challenge advanced students to make the poem sound more poetic by incorporating rhyme and alliteration.

Both of these techniques are used in the sample.

    Institute for Excellence in Writing

Unit 4 Composition Checklist

Lesson 10: George Washington

Summarizing
a Reference

Name: _____

Institute for **Excellence** in **Writing**

STRUCTURE

☐ MLA format (see Appendix I) _____ 2 pts

☐ title centered and repeats 1–3 key words from final sentence _____ 3 pts

☐ topic-clincher sentences repeat or reflect 2–3 key words (highlight or bold) _____ 5 pts

☐ checklist on top, final draft, rough draft, key word outline _____ 1 pt

STYLE

¶1 Dress-Ups (underline one of each) (3 pts each)

☐ -ly adverb _____ 3 pts

☐ *who/which* clause _____ 3 pts

☐ strong verb _____ 3 pts

☐ *because* clause _____ 3 pts

☐ quality adjective _____ 3 pts

CHECK FOR BANNED WORDS (-1 pt for each use): go/went, say/said, good, bad _____ pts

MECHANICS

☐ capitalization _____ 1 pt

☐ end marks and punctuation _____ 1 pt

☐ complete sentences (Does it make sense?) _____ 1 pt

☐ correct spelling _____ 1 pt

VOCABULARY

☐ vocabulary words - label *(voc)* in left margin or after sentence

Total: _____ 30 pts

Custom Total: _____ pts

Point out all the banned words on the checklist. Each of these words must be avoided when writing.

Teachers are free to adjust a checklist by requiring only the stylistic techniques that have become easy, plus one new one. EZ+1

Intentionally blank so the checklist can be removed.

Lesson 11: Thomas Jefferson

Structure:	Unit 4: Summarizing a Reference
Style:	*www.asia* clause
Writing Topic:	Thomas Jefferson
Literature Suggestion:	Girls: *Tolliver's Secret* by Esther Wood Brady
	Boys: *Guns for General Washington* by Seymour Reit

Lesson 11: Thomas Jefferson

UNIT 4: SUMMARIZING A REFERENCE

Lesson 11: Thomas Jefferson

Goals

- to practice the Unit 4 structural model
- to create a KWO
- to write a 1-paragraph report about Thomas Jefferson
- to correctly add a new dress-up: *www.asia* clause
- to take Vocabulary Quiz 3
- to correctly use new vocabulary words: *stirring, affirm, tyrant, adept*

Assignment Schedule

Day 1

1. Play Two Strikes and You're Out.
2. Take Vocabulary Quiz 3.
3. Read "Thomas Jefferson" and write a KWO.

Day 2

1. Review your KWO from Day 1 and complete Structure Practice.
2. Learn a new dress-up, the *www.asia* clause. Read New Style and complete Style Practice.
3. Look at the vocabulary cards for Lesson 11. Discuss the words and their definitions and complete Vocabulary Practice.
4. Using your KWO as a guide, begin writing a rough draft in your own words.
5. Go over the checklist. Put a check in the box for each requirement you have completed.

Day 3

1. Review all vocabulary words learned thus far.
2. Finish writing your report. Follow the topic-clincher rule. Highlight or bold two or three key words that repeat or reflect in the topic and clincher sentences.
3. Turn in your rough draft to your editor with the completed checklist attached.

Day 4

1. Write or type a final draft making any corrections your editor asked you to make.
2. Paperclip the checklist, final draft, rough draft, and KWO together. Hand them in.
3. If you are making a Magnum Opus Notebook, revise your Benjamin Franklin report from Lesson 9.

Two Strikes and You're Out

As you prepare to play the game, include the following words: proficient, profound, compose, conceive, draft, revere.

Feel free to add other quality adjectives and strong verbs.

Literature Suggestion

Finish reading *Tolliver's Secret* by Esther Wood Brady or *Guns for General Washington* by Seymour Reit.

Acquire *By the Great Horn Spoon!* by Sid Fleischman to read for Lessons 12–14.

Source Text

Thomas Jefferson

Thomas Jefferson was an amazing man with many talents and bold ideas. He was one of America's greatest architects. He designed his own magnificent home, called Monticello, which is a National Historical Landmark today. It is the building pictured on the back of today's nickel. Jefferson's profile is on the front of the coin. Jefferson was an excellent lawyer, an accomplished musician, a scientist, and a politician. He spoke six languages fluently, and he was an eloquent writer and great thinker. His writings inspired many people in America's fight for independence. In fact, Jefferson is probably most famous for writing the Declaration of Independence. It took him only seventeen days. In it he included the idea that all men have rights such as "Life, Liberty, and the pursuit of Happiness." He called King George a tyrant who was denying Americans their rights. He believed that men should govern themselves, not be ruled by a king. After the Revolutionary War he became America's first secretary of state. He was America's second vice president (under John Adams) and America's third president. While in office, he upheld the ideals of limited government and rule by the will of the people. He died July 4, 1826, exactly fifty years after the Declaration of Independence was adopted. He will always be remembered as one of America's greatest founding fathers.

> If students wish to include "Life, Liberty, and the pursuit of Happiness," they must copy it exactly as it appears in the source text and place the phrase in quotation marks.

Thomas Jefferson is the subject of the assignment. The topics are the divisions, the things within the subject. After reading the source text, ask students who the text indicates Jefferson was. He was a talented individual, an inspirational writer, and an American statesman. Students should choose one of these three topics and place the words on the topic line. Guide students to look for 5–7 important or interesting facts that support the chosen topic and to ignore the other facts.

Sample

Lesson 11: Thomas Jefferson

Key Word Outline

Decide the topic of your paragraph. Note it in key words on the topic line of the KWO. Re-read the source text and write five to seven facts to support the topic.

I. Topic: ___TJ, writer, inspired 🯄 🯄___

1. ___++ famous, Declaration Ind, 17 days___

2. ___w/ ideas, all, 🯄 🯄, rights___

3. ___Ex: "Life, Liberty, + pursuit"___

4. ___+ rule, by, will, ppl___

5. ___🯄 🯄, govern, selves, X 👑___

(6.) ___3rd, US pres, upheld, writings___

(7.) _____

Clincher

Use the KWO to tell each line of notes in your own words. For the clincher, repeat or reflect the words on the topic line.

Structure Practice

Topic Sentence

Use the key words that you wrote on the KWO topic line (or synonyms of those words) to write a topic sentence for your paragraph.

Thomas Jefferson was an influential **writer** who **inspired people** to fight for freedom.

A *www.asia* clause contains both a subject and a verb.

As a president is not a clause because *As a president* does not contain a subject and verb.
As a president is a prepositional phrase.

As the president declared is a clause because *As the president declared* contains a subject (*president*) and verb (*declared*).

Recite the *www.asia* words over and over with students.

UNIT 4: SUMMARIZING A REFERENCE

New Style

www.asia **Clause Dress-Up**

In this lesson you will learn the sixth and final dress-up: *www.asia* clause.

This clause is just like a *because* clause except it begins with one of these words: *when, while, where, as, since, if, although.* Memorize these words. An acronym can help: *www.asia.*

> Jefferson developed the idea for Monticello <u>when</u> he was twenty-one.
> America doubled in size <u>while</u> Jefferson served as president.

www.asia

when

while

where

as

since

if

although

Notice:

1. A *www.asia* clause begins with *when, while, where, as, since, if, although.*

    To indicate a *www.asia* clause, underline only the first word of the clause: *when, while, where, as, since, if, although.*

2. A *www.asia* clause contains a subject and a verb.

    > Jefferson developed the idea for Monticello <u>when</u> *he was* twenty-one.

    > America doubled in size <u>while</u> *Jefferson served* as president.

3. A *www.asia* clause is added to a sentence that is already complete.

    > *Jefferson developed the idea for Monticello* <u>when</u> he was twenty-one.

    > *America doubled in size* <u>while</u> Jefferson served as president.

, If a *www.asia* clause follows a complete sentence, no comma is needed.
If the *www.asia* clause is at the beginning of the sentence, a comma is required.

> Jefferson developed the idea for Monticello <u>when</u> he was twenty-one. (no comma)

> Today <u>if</u> you look at a nickel, you may see Jefferson. (comma)

Practice

Add a *www.asia* clause to this sentence.

Thomas Jefferson called King George a tyrant *when he penned the Declaration of Independence.*

 From now on, include a *www.asia* clause in each paragraph you write.
Mark the *www.asia* clause by underlining the first word of the clause.

For younger students simply encourage them to place the *www.asia* clause after a sentence that is already complete.

Read the sentences and orally fill in the blanks several times. When students understand the pattern of the *www.asia* clause, then direct them to write.

Style Practice

Quality Adjective

The source text called Thomas Jefferson *amazing* and Monticello *magnificent*. Do not copy these exact words. What other quality adjectives could describe Jefferson and Monticello? Use a thesaurus or your vocabulary words to find synonyms.

Synonyms for *amazing*   *incredible, inspiring, influential, impressive*

Synonyms for *magnificent*   *grandiose, palatial, splendid, radiant, striking*

Because Clause Dress-up

Add a *because* clause to this sentence. Underline the word *because*.

Thomas Jefferson was an incredible man <u>because</u> *his words inspired people to*

fight for the rights of all men.

Strong Verb Dress-Up

Avoid repeating the same key word or forms of the same key word. The source text uses the words *writer*, *writings*, and *writing* in three consecutive sentences. Avoid doing this in your paragraph. What synonyms could replace *wrote* in the following sentence. Use a thesaurus or your vocabulary words.

Thomas Jefferson *wrote* the Declaration of Independence in seventeen days.

strong verbs ***drafted**, penned, composed, authored, **conceived***

Who/Which Clause Dress-Up

Add a *who/which* clause to the sentence below. Punctuate and mark correctly.

Thomas Jefferson, <u>who</u> *detested the idea of a king,*

_____ believed men should govern themselves.

-ly Adverb Dress-Up

Write an idea for adding an -ly adverb to any of the sentences you will write in your paragraph.

*Jefferson **audaciously** wrote about the rights of all men.*

Vocabulary Practice

Look at the vocabulary words for Lesson 11. Fill in the blanks with a word that makes sense.

1. Jefferson was a (an) _____*stirring or adept*_____ writer. (Two words work here.)

2. In the Declaration of Independence, Jefferson _____*affirmed*_____ (ed)

   that all men have rights that a government should not take away.

Look at the vocabulary chart on pages 322–323. Try to use words from Lessons 1–11 in sentences or phrases that could be in your report. Write at least two ideas below.

*Jefferson's ideas **compelled** many to action.*

*Jefferson **indignantly** accused King George of being a **tyrant**.*

Unit 4 Composition Checklist
Lesson 11: Thomas Jefferson

Summarizing a Reference

Name: _____

STRUCTURE

- ☐ MLA format (see Appendix I) _____ 2 pts
- ☐ title centered and repeats 1–3 key words from final sentence _____ 3 pts
- ☐ topic-clincher sentences repeat or reflect 2–3 key words (highlight or bold) _____ 2 pts
- ☐ checklist on top, final draft, rough draft, key word outline _____ 1 pt

STYLE

¶1 Dress-Ups (underline one of each)   (3 pts each)

- ☐ -ly adverb _____ 3 pts
- ☐ *who/which* clause _____ 3 pts
- ☐ strong verb _____ 3 pts
- ☐ *because* clause _____ 3 pts
- ☐ quality adjective _____ 3 pts
- ☐ *www.asia* clause _____ 3 pts

CHECK FOR BANNED WORDS (-1 pt for each use): go/went, say/said, good, bad _____ pts

MECHANICS

- ☐ capitalization _____ 1 pt
- ☐ end marks and punctuation _____ 1 pt
- ☐ complete sentences (Does it make sense?) _____ 1 pt
- ☐ correct spelling _____ 1 pt

VOCABULARY

- ☐ vocabulary words - label *(voc)* in left margin or after sentence

Total: _____ 30 pts
Custom Total: _____ pts

Teachers are free to adjust a checklist by requiring only the stylistic techniques that have become easy, plus one new one. EZ+1

Intentionally blank so the checklist can be removed.

Lesson 12: The Louisiana Purchase

Structure:	Unit 4: Summarizing a Reference
Style:	#2 prepositional opener, banned words: *pretty, big, small*
Writing Topic:	the Louisiana Purchase
Literature Suggestion:	*By the Great Horn Spoon!* by Sid Fleischman

UNIT 4: SUMMARIZING A REFERENCE

Lesson 12: The Louisiana Purchase

Goals

- to practice the Unit 4 structural model
- to create a KWO
- to write a 2-paragraph report about the Louisiana Purchase
- to learn about variety in sentence openers
- to ban weak adjectives: *pretty, big, small*
- to correctly add a new sentence opener: #2 prepositional opener
- to correctly use new vocabulary words: *grueling, stupendous, extensive, formidable*

Assignment Schedule

Day 1

1. Play Find the *www.asia* Clause Starters.

2. Read "The Louisiana Purchase."

3. In this lesson you will write two paragraphs about the Louisiana Purchase. The Louisiana Purchase is the subject of the paper. Each paragraph must be about a specific topic within the subject. As you read the source text, you likely saw many facts that described the territory and other facts that explained the significance of the purchase. These two topics, the description of the Louisiana Territory and the significance of the Louisiana Purchase, are the topics you will write about when you write your paper. Using key words, write each topic on the topic lines of the KWO.

4. Re-read the source text and note five to seven facts that support the first topic, the description of the Louisiana Territory. Facts will come from both paragraphs. Be a detective and note only the facts that describe the territory. You will leave much information out.

5. Re-read the source text and note five to seven facts that support the second topic, the significance of the Louisiana Purchase. Because facts can be found in both paragraphs, you must again be a detective and search only for facts that indicate the significance of the purchase.

6. Cover the source text and tell the meaning of each line of notes in your own words. If a note is unclear, check the source text and add what you need to in order to make it clear. For each clincher, repeat or reflect two or three key words on the topic line for the paragraph.

Day 2

1. Review your KWO from Day 1.

2. Learn about sentence openers. Read New Style and complete Style Practice.

3. Look at the vocabulary cards for Lesson 12. Discuss the words and their definitions and complete Vocabulary Practice.

4. Using your KWO as a guide, begin writing a rough draft in your own words.

5. Go over the checklist. Put a check in the box for each requirement you have completed.

Day 3

1. Review all vocabulary words learned thus far.

2. Finish writing your 2-paragraph report. Follow the topic-clincher rule in each paragraph.

3. Turn in your rough draft to your editor with the completed checklist attached.

Day 4

1. Write or type a final draft making any corrections your editor asked you to make.

2. Paperclip the checklist, final draft, rough draft, and KWO together. Hand them in.

3. If you are making a Magnum Opus Notebook, revise your George Washington report from Lesson 10.

Literature Suggestion

Begin reading *By the Great Horn Spoon!* by Sid Fleischman.

Source Text

The Louisiana Purchase

Everyone enjoys getting a good deal. Thomas Jefferson, our third president, got a great deal for America! He bought the entire Louisiana Territory from France for just $.04 per acre. It was a vast territory. This territory stretched from west to east from the Mississippi River to the Rocky Mountains and south to north from the Gulf of Mexico to the Canadian border. The purchase almost doubled the size of the United States, making the young country seem more formidable to enemies. It also made the country wealthy in resources. Interestingly, the land was acquired almost by accident. It was owned and controlled by France, and it included the port city of New Orleans. President Jefferson knew how important this city was for trade, so he sent men to France to try to buy it. When they arrived, Emperor Napoleon Bonaparte was in desperate need of money for wars, so he wanted to sell not just New Orleans, but the entire Louisiana Territory. He sold all 828,000 square miles for just $15 million. It was one of the greatest accomplishments of Jefferson's presidency.

President Jefferson sent Meriwether Lewis and William Clark to explore and map America's new, vast land. In May of 1804 they headed west with a team of about forty men. As they traveled, they met many Native Americans from over fifty different tribes. Most were friendly. They were fortunate that one of the Native Americans, a young woman named Sacagawea, joined them as an interpreter and guide. With her help, they traveled the vast territory. The expedition discovered that the land was very pretty with unfamiliar plants and animals like grizzly bears and prairie dogs. Some areas seemed to have endless forests while other areas were perfect as farming and grazing land. In addition, the territory was abundant in natural resources, including precious metals like gold and silver. Lewis and Clark were in awe of the land. After their expedition, many Americans were inspired to settle the western frontier. As they did, over time the land gave the United States part or all of fifteen new states, the first of which was Louisiana. America would be a very different country without the Louisiana Purchase.

Sample

Key Word Outline

For this lesson the topic of each paragraph has been given to you. Next to the first Roman numeral write: *LA Territory*, *vast*, *rich*. Re-read the source text and write five to seven facts to support the first topic.

Next to the second Roman numeral write *LA Purchase*, *significant*. Re-read the source text and write five to seven facts to support the second topic.

I.   Topic: _____*LA Territory, vast, rich*_____

  1. _____*E-W, Mississippi River ➜ Rocky Mts*_____

  2. _____*S-N, Gulf of Mexico ➜ Canada*_____

  3. _____*++ resources, gold, silver*_____

  4. _____*828,000 sq. miles*_____

  5. _____*met, Native Americans, 50 tribes*_____

  (6.) _____*new, plants, animals*_____

  (7.) _____*beautiful, w/ forests, farmland*_____

  Clincher

II. Topic: _____*LA Purchase, significant*_____

  1. _____*2x, size, America*_____

  2. _____*formidable, enemies*_____

  3. _____*increased, wealth, resources*_____

  4. _____*w/ port, easier, trade*_____

  5. _____*inspired, settlers, W, frontiers*_____

  (6.) _____*gave, 15, new states, 1st ➜ LA*_____

  (7.) _____

  Clincher

Use the KWO to tell each line of notes in your own words. For the clincher, repeat or reflect the words on the topic line.

The students now know all of the dress-ups. Remember, dress-ups are placed within a sentence to dress-up the writing. Students indicate a dress-up has been placed in a sentence by underlining it. Now it's time to teach your students sentence openers. Sentence openers teach sentence variety. Students indicate a sentence opener has been used by inserting a number in front of it.

UNIT 4: SUMMARIZING A REFERENCE

New Style

Sentence Openers

You are already familiar with dress-ups. In this lesson you will learn a second element of style: sentence openers.

Sentence openers are descriptive words, phrases, or clauses that you add to the beginning of a sentence. You will learn six openers—six ways to open or begin a sentence. Using various sentence openers will help your writing sound more sophisticated. To indicate that you have begun a sentence with an opener, you should number it. You can number it by putting a number in the margin on the same line as the sentence or by putting a number in brackets directly before the sentence. Although you may use more than one specific type of sentence opener in a paragraph, only number one of each type in each paragraph.

To help you appreciate this stylistic device, read the following two versions of part of a paragraph about the westward expansion.

Version 1

Many settlers and pioneers headed into the Louisiana Territory. America formed more states there. The first was named Louisiana. It was admitted in 1812. It was the eighteenth state to join the union. Next was Indiana in 1816. Mississippi followed in 1817. America included forty-four states by 1890.

Version 2

After President Jefferson's Louisiana Purchase, many settlers and pioneers headed into the Louisiana Territory. As towns were built, America formed more states there. Not surprisingly the first was named Louisiana. It was admitted in 1812 as the eighteenth state to join the union. Next was Indiana in 1816. Mississippi followed in 1817. By 1890 America included forty-four states.

In the paragraphs above you should have noticed that in Version 1 all the sentences begin with the subject and are about the same length. This makes the paragraph boring to read. When you begin your sentences with different types of openers, your writing sounds more sophisticated because your sentences begin with something other than the subject and the sentences vary in length. Can you see how Version 2 accomplished both of these things?

We call a sentence that opens with a subject the #1 subject opener. Most young writers' sentences begin with a subject. We explain the #1 subject opener to the students after they know all of the other openers.

New Style

#2 Prepositional Opener

In this lesson you will learn the first sentence opener: the #2 prepositional opener. (You will learn more sentence openers later that will be given other numbers.) The prepositional opener is a prepositional phrase placed at the beginning of a sentence.

> [2] After President Jefferson's Louisiana Purchase, many settlers and pioneers headed into the Louisiana Territory.

> [2] By 1890 America included forty-four states.

Notice:

1. A prepositional phrase contains at least two words and begins with a preposition.

2. A prepositional phrase ends with a noun. A prepositional phrase never contains a verb.

    There might be other words between the preposition and the noun, but there is never a verb in a prepositional phrase. Here are some examples of prepositional phrases:

    > in wagons   after several years   during the Westward Movement

3. To indicate that a sentence begins with a prepositional opener, label it with a 2 in the left margin or place a [2] right before the sentence.

🛇 If the prepositional phrase has five words or more, follow it with a comma. A comma is optional but usually not recommended with shorter phrases.

Practice

Write a sentence with a #2 prepositional opener. Follow the pattern: preposition + noun (no verb). Label it with a [2]. Do not underline the phrase.

[2] After the purchase America was destined for greatness.

_____

✎ From now on, include a #2 prepositional opener in each paragraph you write. Label it with a 2 in the margin or place a [2] before the sentence.

Prepositions

above

across

around

after

by

during

for

from

in

inside

into

near

of

off

on

outside

over

past

through

to

under

up

with

without

Encourage students to memorize the pattern: preposition + noun (no verb).

When short prepositional openers work transitionally, they will need a comma.

For example, In addition, On the other hand,

If a student writes a prepositional opener that is also a transitional opener, explain the comma is needed because the phrase is working as a transition.

Students benefit from looking at word lists like those listed on this page. A longer list of prepositions can be found on the *Portable Walls for Structure and Style Students* as well as the IEW Writing Tools App.

As students write prepositional openers, remind them to follow the pattern: preposition + noun (no verb).

If a verb is included, the student likely wrote an adverb clause. For example, *As they explored* includes a subject (*they*) and verb (*explored*). *As they explored* is a *www.asia* clause. *As explorers*, however, is not a clause because *As explorers* does not contain a subject and verb. *As explorers* is a prepositional phrase.

UNIT 4: SUMMARIZING A REFERENCE

Style Practice

#2 Prepositional Opener

Prepositional openers begin with a preposition. Look at the list of prepositions on page 115. Try to memorize as many as you can before next week.

Begin each sentence with a #2 prepositional opener. Follow the comma rule on page 115.

1. _____*[2] As explorers*_____ Lewis and Clark

   discovered many forests and natural resources.

2. _____*[2] Over time*_____ settlers moved west.

Quality Adjective Dress-Up

We have not only banned verbs, but we have also banned the adjectives *good* and *bad*. In this lesson three more adjectives are banned: *big*, *small*, *pretty*.

Banned Words

Look at the italicized adjective in each sentence below. Underline the word that creates a strong image or feeling in your mind.

1. The *big* trees filled the forest.   The *towering* trees filled the forest.

2. The *pretty* house stands as a monument.   The *majestic* house stands as a monument.

Write several ideas for quality adjectives that could replace the banned adjectives in these sentences. Use a thesaurus or your vocabulary words.

1. The Louisiana Territory was *big*.

   quality adjectives _____*immense, **extensive**, expansive, enormous*_____

2. The land was *pretty*.

   quality adjectives _____*stunning, lush, breathtaking, **unfathomable***_____

⊘ **BANNED WORDS**   VERBS: SAY/SAID, GO/WENT   ADJECTIVES: GOOD, BAD, BIG, SMALL, PRETTY

Institute for Excellence in Writing

Dress-Ups

Although this lesson does not contain specific practice exercises for each of the six dress-ups you have learned, you must include one of each in both paragraphs you write. Look at your KWO and consider where you can include various clauses as well as strong verbs, quality adjectives, and -ly adverbs. When you write your paper, follow your checklist!

Vocabulary Practice

Look at the vocabulary words for Lesson 12. Fill in the blanks with a word that makes sense.

1. The Louisiana Territory was ___*extensive or stupendous.*___

2. What a ___*stupendous*___ deal President Jefferson got!

Look at the vocabulary chart on pages 322–323. Try to use words from Lessons 1–12 in sentences or phrases that could be in your report. Write at least two ideas below.

   __Extensive, formidable__ mountains __loomed__ across the land.

   The Louisiana Purchase furthered the __prosperity__ of America.

Unit 4 Composition Checklist
Lesson 12: The Louisiana Purchase

Summarizing
a Reference

Name: _____

Institute for Excellence in Writing
Listen Speak Read Write Think!

STRUCTURE

☐ MLA format (see Appendix I) _____ 1 pt

☐ title centered and repeats 1–3 key words from final sentence _____ 2 pts

☐ topic-clincher sentences repeat or reflect 2–3 key words (highlight or bold) _____ 6 pts

☐ checklist on top, final draft, rough draft, key word outline _____ 5 pts

STYLE

¶1 ¶2 **Dress-Ups** (underline one of each)   (3 pts each)

☐ ☐ -ly adverb _____ 6 pts

☐ ☐ *who/which* clause _____ 6 pts

☐ ☐ strong verb _____ 6 pts

☐ ☐ *because* clause _____ 6 pts

☐ ☐ quality adjective _____ 6 pts

☐ ☐ *www.asia* clause _____ 6 pts

Sentence Openers (number; one of each as possible)   (3 pts each)

☐ ☐ [2] prepositional _____ 6 pts

CHECK FOR BANNED WORDS (-1 pt for each use): go/went, say/said, good, bad, pretty, big, small _____ pts

MECHANICS

☐ capitalization _____ 1 pt

☐ end marks and punctuation _____ 1 pt

☐ complete sentences (Does it make sense?) _____ 1 pt

☐ correct spelling _____ 1 pt

VOCABULARY

☐ vocabulary words - label *(voc)* in left margin or after sentence

Total: _____ 60 pts

Custom Total: _____ pts

Because students are writing a 2-paragraph report, they should underline twelve words, six dress-ups in each paragraph.

In addition, students should include and mark one prepositional phrase opener in each paragraph.

Teachers are free to adjust a checklist by requiring only the stylistic techniques that have become easy, plus one new one. EZ+1

Intentionally blank so the checklist can be removed.

Lesson 13: The Westward Movement

Structure:	Unit 5: Writing from Pictures
Style:	no new style
Writing Topic:	The Westward Movement
Literature Suggestion:	*By the Great Horn Spoon!* by Sid Fleischman

Teaching Writing: Structure and Style

Watch the sections for Unit 5: Writing from Pictures. At IEW.com/twss-help reference the TWSS Viewing Guides.

Lesson 13: The Westward Movement

UNIT 5: WRITING FROM PICTURES

Lesson 13: The Westward Movement

Goals

- to learn the Unit 5 Writing from Pictures structural model
- to create a KWO from a series of three pictures: the Westward Movement
- to write a 3-paragraph composition from the KWO
- to learn to ask questions to get ideas for writing
- to correctly use new vocabulary words: *laden, fathom, incessant, trepidation*

Assignment Schedule

Day 1

1. Complete the Review.
2. Read Historical Information.
3. Read New Structure—Writing from Pictures.
4. Write your KWO.

Day 2

1. Review your KWO from Day 1 and complete Structure Practice.
2. Complete Style Practice.
3. Look at the vocabulary cards for Lesson 13. Discuss the words and their definitions and complete Vocabulary Practice.
4. Using your KWO as a guide, begin writing your 3-paragraph rough draft.
5. Go over the checklist. Put a check in the box for each requirement you have completed.

Day 3

1. Review all vocabulary words learned thus far.
2. Finish writing your 3-paragraph composition. Ensure that the clincher sentence of each paragraph repeats or reflects two or three key words of the central fact of the picture.
3. Turn in your rough draft to your editor with the completed checklist attached.

Day 4

1. Write or type a final draft making any corrections your editor asked you to make.
2. Paperclip the checklist, final draft, rough draft, and KWO together. Hand them in.
3. If you are making a Magnum Opus Notebook, revise your Thomas Jefferson report from Lesson 11.

In this new unit the KWO is formed by looking at three pictures and asking good questions related to the pictures. The key words are formed from the answers to the questions.

This unit is not story telling but rather event description. Help students form the topic sentence by focusing on the central fact of each picture. Develop the outline by asking questions to describe the event.

Literature Suggestion

Continue reading *By the Great Horn Spoon!* by Sid Fleischman.

Review

A #2 prepositional opener begins with a _____, ends with a _____, and never includes a _____.

How do you indicate a #2 prepositional opener?

Read a sentence that begins with a #2 prepositional opener from your Louisiana Purchase report.

Play Preposition Round Robin.

Historical Information

After the Louisiana Purchase, settlers began heading into the American West. Some wanted to escape crowded cities, others sought adventure, and still others just wanted a new life and free land. The Oregon Trail and gold in California also lured people west. Many Americans believed in what they called *Manifest Destiny*. This was the idea that the United States was destined to control and spread its ways across the entire continent of North America.

Those who migrated had to first sell their homes and everything they could not take with them. The journeys were long and difficult. For example, the journey to Oregon could take up to a year, and one in ten people who attempted the journey died along the way. Rough terrain, wild animals, hostile Native Americans, and disease constantly threatened the travelers. For those traveling on the Oregon Trail, Independence Rock marked the halfway point. The goal was to reach this landmark by July 4 in order to avoid severe winter weather toward the end of the journey. Over five thousand travelers wrote their names on Independence Rock.

Review

A #2 prepositional opener begins with a preposition, ends with a noun, and never includes a verb.

Indicate a #2 prepositional opener by placing a *2* in the margin or a [2] directly before the sentence.

Lesson 13: The Westward Movement

New Structure

Writing from Pictures

In Unit 5 instead of using source texts, you will write three paragraphs from a series of three pictures. Although it may seem as if you are telling a story, your task it to describe each event.

Each paragraph will begin with a central fact, contain details, and end with a clincher sentence.

if 1 topic = 1 paragraph

then 3 topics = 3 paragraphs

Central Fact

> The central fact tells what you see in the picture. It is the topic sentence of the paragraph. Think of this sentence as the caption that describes the picture. When you write the KWO, ask yourself: "What do I see in the picture?" As you answer, write three key words on the Roman numeral line.

Details

> On the other lines of the KWO, explain in more detail what is happening and how it came to be that way. Where do you find out what is happening? Just like Unit 3, ask yourself questions. Brain-helping questions are listed on the KWO. These helpful questions include:
>
> > **Who** is in the picture? **What** is the history of this picture? **Where** exactly is this? **How** is this being done or said? **Why** is this situation happening? **When** did this begin? What are they **doing**? **thinking**? **feeling**? **saying**? What happened just **before** the picture? What might happen **after** this picture? What might be just **outside** the picture?

The answers to your questions become the details for the outline. As you answer a question, place two or three key words on the KWO. Use symbols, numbers, and abbreviations when possible. You do not have to answer every question or ask in the order they are written. Keep your answers brief. You can add more details when you write your paragraphs.

Clincher Sentence

> The clincher sentence reminds the reader what you see in the picture. Because it is the clincher sentence, it must repeat or reflect two or three key words placed on the central fact line. What rule does that remind you of?

The topic sentence and the clincher sentence MUST repeat or reflect two or three key words.

Look at the series of pictures. The first picture is of a family loading their wagon. The second picture is of the wagon crossing a high river. The third picture is of the family sitting around a campfire. After you discuss the pictures, emphasize that students should write what they see in the picture on the central fact line. Stick with the facts, the things you see. Then, teach students to ask questions to determine what to place for notes on the rest of the KWO. Every class and each student will have unique outlines.

Sample

Key Word Outline

This is a 3-paragraph assignment. Each paragraph will begin with the central fact, a topic sentence which describes the picture. The clincher also describes the picture. If students add conversation, do not make them indent if the speakers change.

I.   Central fact: _loading, wagon, possessions_

1.   _Pa, X busy, city_
2.   _find, land, W frontier_
3.   _kids, excited, new 🏠_
4.   _Ma, worried, dangerous_
5.   _miss, friends, 💬 goodbyes_

Clincher repeats or reflects 2–3 key words of central fact.

II. Central fact: _wagon, cross, river_

1.   _Pa ➡ H₂O, led, horse_
2.   _"Billy, reins, steady"_
3.   _wagon, rocking, Spot, ⬇_
4.   _Ma, clutched, baby_
5.   _Sarah, scared, "Spot!"_

Clincher repeats or reflects 2–3 key words of central fact.

III. Central fact: _family, around, campfire_

1.   _Pa, "See, Independence Rock?"_
2.   _rock = mean ½ way_
3.   _plan, Oregon, < snow_
4.   _Ma, relieved_
5.   _children, dance, joy_

Clincher repeats or reflects 2–3 key words of central fact.
Title repeats 1–3 key words from final sentence.

?

who?
what?
when?
where?
why?
how?
doing?
thinking?
feeling?
saying?
before?
after?
outside?

A topic sentence tells the reader what the rest of the paragraph is about. In Unit 5 the topic is the picture. To write the topic sentence of the paragraph, students write a sentence that contains the three words they placed on the topic line of the KWO. Following the topic-clincher rule, the clincher sentence also uses those same three words or synonyms of them. The topic sentence and the clincher sentence become captions for the picture.

Structure Practice

Topic Sentence

Use your KWO to guide you as you write your composition. Begin by looking at the words on the central fact line, the words that indicate what you see in the picture.

If you wrote *loading*, *wagon*, *possessions* on the central fact line next to the first picture, your topic sentence could be:

The Smiths were **loading** their **wagon** with their most precious **possessions**.

Use the key words that you wrote on the KWO next to the first central fact (the topic line) to write a sentence that tells what you see in the picture. Remember to highlight or bold the key words.

Answers will vary.
_____

Continue your composition by forming sentences from the key words placed on the KWO. When you reach the clincher line, write a sentence that repeats or reflects two or three key words of the central fact. The clincher for the sample above might be:

The **wagon** pulled away **loaded** with all they now **owned**.

Style Practice

#2 Prepositional Opener

Begin each sentence with a #2 prepositional opener. Follow the comma rule on page 115.

1. _[2] For days_ _____ they had been loading the wagon.

2. _[2] In the rapid current_ _____ the wagon rocked violently.

3. _[2] With happy hearts_ _____ they sang along as Dad played his fiddle.

Quality Adjective Dress-Up

There are many things that you could describe, and you might describe the same thing differently in different paragraphs. For example, the children might be *excited* in paragraph I, *terrified* in paragraph II, and *relieved* in paragraph III.

Next to each noun write ideas for adjectives. Choose adjectives that create strong images and tell what each thing looks like, sounds like, or feels like. Avoid banned adjectives.

1. the wagon ____*rickety, overstuffed, sturdy, floundering*____

2. the river ____*violent, rushing, raging, turbulent*____

3. the campfire ____*warm, crackling, dancing, bright*____

4. the rock ____*massive, **prominent**, famous, lone*____

Strong Verb Dress-Up and -ly Adverb Dress-Up

On the first line under each sentence, write strong verbs that could replace the italicized banned verb. On the second line under each sentence, write ideas for -ly adverbs that you could use with the strong verbs. Use a thesaurus or your vocabulary words.

1. "Do you really think it is safe?" Ma *said*.

    strong verbs ____*questioned, wondered, whispered, cautioned*____

    -ly adverbs ____*nervously, anxiously, apprehensively*____

2. "Hold those reins tightly," Pa *said*.

    strong verbs ____*insisted, commanded, demanded, urged*____

    -ly adverbs ____*sternly, suddenly, sharply, intently*____

3. The wagon *went* across the river.

    strong verbs ____*struggled, floated, lumbered, labored*____

    -ly adverbs ____***perilously**, unsteadily, slowly, precariously*____

Because Clause Dress-up

Add a *because* clause to this sentence. Underline the word *because*.

Pa decided to move west <u>because</u>   *he disliked the busy city.* _____

_____

www.asia Clause Dress-Up

Add a *www.asia* clause to this sentence. Underline the first word of the clause.

Spot jumped from the wagon   <u>*when*</u> *he spied Pa in the water.* _____

Who/Which Clause Dress-Up

Add a *who/which* clause to each sentence below. Punctuate and mark correctly.

1. Ma, <u>who</u>   *felt the wagon teeter,* _____

    _____ clutched baby Jane tightly.

2. The rock, <u>which</u> *towered over the land in the distance,* _____

    _____ told them they were halfway there.

Vocabulary Practice

Look at the vocabulary words for Lesson 13. Fill in the blanks with a word that makes sense.

1. They looked at the river with *trepidation.* _____

2. The *incessant* _____ slapping of the water on the wagon frightened Mary.

Look at the vocabulary chart on pages 322–323. Try to use words from Lessons 1–13 in sentences or phrases that could be in your composition. Write at least two ideas below.

   *The wagon was **laden** with everything they now owned.* _____

   *The journey west seemed a **formidable** one to Ma, but Pa was **resolved** to begin a new life.*

UNIT 5: WRITING FROM PICTURES

Institute for Excellence in Writing

Lesson 13: The Westward Movement

Unit 5 Composition Checklist
Lesson 13: The Westward Movement

Writing
from
Pictures

Name: _____

IEW Institute for Excellence in Writing

STRUCTURE

☐ MLA format (see Appendix I) _____ 1 pt

☐ title centered and repeats 1–3 key words from final sentence _____ 2 pts

☐ clincher sentences repeat or reflect 2–3 key words of central fact (highlight or bold) _____ 6 pts

☐ checklist on top, final draft, rough draft, key word outline _____ 5 pts

STYLE

¶1 ¶2 ¶3 Dress-Ups (underline one of each)   (2 pts each)

☐ ☐ ☐ -ly adverb _____ 6 pts

☐ ☐ ☐ *who/which* clause _____ 6 pts

☐ ☐ ☐ strong verb _____ 6 pts

☐ ☐ ☐ *because* clause _____ 6 pts

☐ ☐ ☐ quality adjective _____ 6 pts

☐ ☐ ☐ *www.asia* clause _____ 6 pts

Sentence Openers (number; one of each as possible)   (2 pts each)

☐ ☐ ☐ [2] prepositional _____ 6 pts

CHECK FOR BANNED WORDS (-1 pt for each use): go/went, say/said, good, bad, pretty, big, small _____ pts

MECHANICS

☐ capitalization _____ 1 pt

☐ end marks and punctuation _____ 1 pt

☐ complete sentences (Does it make sense?) _____ 1 pt

☐ correct spelling _____ 1 pt

VOCABULARY

☐ vocabulary words - label *(voc)* in left margin or after sentence

Total: _____ 60 pts
Custom Total: _____ pts

Teachers are free to adjust a checklist by requiring only the stylistic techniques that have become easy, plus one new one. EZ+1

UNIT 5: WRITING FROM PICTURES

Intentionally blank so the checklist can be removed.

Lesson 14: The Underground Railroad

Structure:	Unit 5: Writing from Pictures
Style:	#3 -ly adverb opener
Writing Topic:	The Underground Railroad
Literature Suggestion:	*By the Great Horn Spoon!* by Sid Fleischman

UNIT 5: WRITING FROM PICTURES

Lesson 14: The Underground Railroad

Goals

- to practice the Unit 5 structural model
- to create a KWO from a series of three pictures: the Underground Railroad
- to write a 3-paragraph composition from the KWO
- to correctly add a new sentence opener: #3 -ly adverb opener
- to correctly use new vocabulary words: *deplorable, loom, imperative, distraught*

Assignment Schedule

Day 1

1. Complete the Review.
2. Read Historical Information.
3. Review New Structure on page 123 and write your KWO.

Day 2

1. Review your KWO from Day 1 and complete Structure Practice.
2. Learn a new sentence opener, the #3 -ly adverb opener. Read New Style and complete Style Practice.
3. Look at the vocabulary cards for Lesson 14. Discuss the words and their definitions and complete Vocabulary Practice.
4. Using your KWO as a guide, begin writing your 3-paragraph rough draft.
5. Go over the checklist. Put a check in the box for each requirement you have completed.

Day 3

1. Review all vocabulary words learned thus far.
2. Finish writing your 3-paragraph composition. Ensure that the clincher sentence of each paragraph repeats or reflects two or three key words of the central fact of the picture.
3. Turn in your rough draft to your editor with the completed checklist attached.

Day 4

1. Write or type a final draft making any corrections your editor asked you to make.
2. Paperclip the checklist, final draft, rough draft, and KWO together. Hand them in.
3. If you are making a Magnum Opus Notebook, revise your Louisiana Purchase report from Lesson 12.

Study for Vocabulary Quiz 4. It will cover words from Lessons 1–14.

Literature Suggestion

Finish reading *By the Great Horn Spoon!* by Sid Fleischman.

Acquire *Mr. Lincoln's Drummer* by G. Clifton Wisler (elementary) or *Behind Rebel Lines: The Incredible Story of Emma Edmonds, Civil War Spy* by Seymour Reit (junior/senior high) to read for Lessons 15–17.

Review

Play Two Strikes and You're Out.

Read a topic (central fact) sentence and clincher sentence from one of the paragraphs you wrote for Lesson 13.

Historical Information

Prior to the Civil War a network of people formed to help slaves escape to freedom in the North and Canada. They called their network the *Underground Railroad*. The Underground Railroad consisted of former slaves who had escaped as well as white men and women who opposed slavery. The former slaves were often the ones who led runaways in their flight. They were called *conductors*. The most famous conductor was Harriet Tubman. People who housed and hid runaways were called *station masters*, and their homes were called *stations*. Often their homes had secret hiding places such as spaces between walls or under the floor.

The people of the Underground Railroad used many secret codes and signals to let runaways know where, how, and when to flee. For example, code words in songs might have indicated it was time to flee. Owl hoots or quail calls might have directed slaves to a conductor. The people of the Underground Railroad also used clever disguises and tricks to help slaves. For example, wagons sometimes had false bottoms so that slaves could be hidden between the false bottom and the real bottom. Most journeys took many weeks or even months. Runaways were often on their own, guided only by the Big Dipper for much of the time. The trips were filled with hardships and danger. Despite all of this, between 1830 and 1862 thousands of slaves escaped to freedom on the Underground Railroad.

Two Strikes and You're Out

As you prepare to play the game, include the following words: distraught, imperative, deplorable, incessant, laden, formidable, grueling, loom, affirm, fathom, conceive.

Feel free to add other quality adjectives and strong verbs.

Look at the series of pictures. The first picture is of slaves running through the forest in search of freedom. The second picture is of two men and dogs stopping a wagon. The third picture is of a family near a man on a raft on a river. After you discuss the pictures, remind the students to use key words to write what they see in the picture on the central fact line. Students come up with ideas that describe the event in order to write the rest of the paragraph. Asking questions is key.

Sample

Lesson 14: The Underground Railroad

Key Word Outline

I.   Central fact: *slaves, running, freedom*

1.   *overheard, owners, $, baby*
2.   *packed, food, blanket*
3.   ☾*, followed, Big Dipper, N*
4.   ♥*, pounding, wary*
5.   *meet, conductor, URR*

Clincher repeats or reflects 2–3 key words of central fact.

II.   Central fact: *wagon, ◯, 2 men + dogs*

1.   *hid, false, bottom*
2.   *Mary, baby, quiet*
3.   *hunters, "see runaways?"*
4.   👀*, wagon, held, breath*
5.   *X find, relieved*

Clincher repeats or reflects 2–3 key words of central fact.

III.   Central fact: *reached, river,* 🧍 *+ raft*

1.   *boarded, drifted*
2.   *distance, dogs, barking*
3.   *thanked, God, safe*
4.   *fell, asleep*
5.   *shore, awoke,* ☺

Clincher repeats or reflects 2–3 key words of central fact.
Title repeats 1–3 key words from final sentence.

who?
what?
when?
where?
why?
how?
doing?
thinking?
feeling?
saying?
before?
after?
outside?

UNIT 5: WRITING FROM PICTURES

Structure Practice

Topic Sentence

Use your KWO to guide you as you write your composition. Begin by looking at the words on the central fact line, the words that indicate what you see in the picture.

If you wrote *slaves*, *running*, *freedom* on the central fact line next to the first picture, your topic sentence could be:

> **James**, **Mary**, and little **Eli** were **running** away to **freedom**.

Use the key words that you wrote on the KWO next to the first central fact (the topic line) to write a sentence that tells what you see in the picture. Remember to highlight or bold the key words.

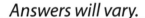

Answers will vary.

Continue your composition by forming sentences from the key words placed on the KWO. When you reach the clincher line, write a sentence that repeats or reflects two or three key words of the central fact. The clincher for the sample above might be:

> Nothing was going to stop the **family** in their **quest** for **freedom**.

Institute for Excellence in Writing

New Style

#3 -ly Adverb Opener

In this lesson you will learn another sentence opener: the #3 -ly adverb opener.

The -ly adverb opener is an -ly adverb placed at the beginning of a sentence. You have been using -ly adverbs as dress-ups. Here are examples of the -ly adverb opener:

[3] Frantically they grabbed some food and fled.

[3] Clearly, their little Elijah would be sold.

Notice:

1. An -ly adverb that begins a sentence is called an -ly adverb opener. Label it with a 3 in the left margin or place a [3] right before the sentence.

2. An -ly adverb that does not begin a sentence is called an -ly adverb dress-up. It is marked with an underline.

> If the -ly adverb opener modifies the main verb, the comma is optional but discouraged. If the -ly adverb opener modifies the entire sentence, the comma is required.
>
> Frantically they *grabbed* some food and *fled*. The -ly adverb modifies the verbs, not the entire sentence. You cannot say it was frantic that they grabbed some food. The comma is not needed.
>
> Clearly, *their little Elijah would be sold.* The -ly adverb does not modify the verb. *Clearly* modifies the entire sentence because you can say *It is clear that their little Elijah would be sold.* The comma is required.

Practice

Which -ly adverbs might open these sentences? Use a thesaurus or your vocabulary words or look at the -ly adverb word list on the *Portable Walls for Structure and Style Students* or the IEW Writing Tools App. Label with a [3]. Do not underline the -ly adverb opener.

1. ___*[3] Silently*_____ the family tiptoed through the woods.

2. ___*[3] Futilely*_____ the men searched for the missing slaves.

> From now on, include two -ly adverbs—an opener and a dress-up in each paragraph you write. Label the opener with a 3 in the margin or place a [3] before the sentence. Underline the dress-up.

Six dress-ups and two openers now appear on the checklist.

Style Practice

#2 Prepositional Opener

Begin each sentence with a #2 prepositional opener. Follow the comma rule on page 115.

1. _____ *[2] Through the dark, dense woods,* _____ they moved as quietly as possible.

2. _____ *[2] In his arms* _____ James held Eli still.

3. _____ *[2] From the river* _____ they would reach the North.

www.asia Clause Dress-Up

Add a *www.asia* clause to each sentence below. Underline the first word of the clause.

1. They knew they had to run away *when they learned of their owners' plan to sell baby Eli.*

2. They squeezed in the false bottom of the wagon *where they would be hidden for the journey.*

Quality Adjective Dress-Up

Next to each noun write ideas for adjectives. Choose adjectives that create strong images and tell what each thing looks like, sounds like, or feels like. Avoid banned adjectives.

1. the forest _____ *dark, menacing, **eerie**, still*

2. the dogs _____ *snarling, yapping, moaning, terrifying*

3. the river _____ *gentle, gurgling, tranquil, winding*

4. the slave hunters _____ *determined, **indignant**, baffled, gruff*

Describe two additional things the runaways might see, hear, or feel on their journey.

_____ *The dim light of the moon was just enough to help them through the misty forest.*

_____ *Twigs snapped and mud oozed under their feet.*

Because Clause Dress-up

Write a sentence with a *because* clause that you could use in your composition. Remember to add the clause to a sentence that is already complete. Punctuate and mark correctly.

They kept their eyes on the Big Dipper <u>because</u> it would guide them north.

Strong Verb Dress-Up and -ly Adverb Dress-Up

On the first line below each sentence, write strong verbs that could replace the italicized banned verb. On the second line under each sentence, write ideas for -ly adverbs that you could use with the strong verbs. Use a thesaurus or your vocabulary words.

1. The family *went* through the forest.

   strong verbs *fled, trudged, tiptoed, wandered*

   -ly adverbs *cautiously, **warily**, silently, watchfully*

2. The wagon *went* down the road.

   strong verbs *bounced, rocked, crept, continued*

   -ly adverbs *gently, steadily, safely, carefully*

3. The dogs *went* around the wagon.

   strong verbs *darted, sniffed, circled, advanced*

   -ly adverbs *ferociously, eagerly, meticulously*

4. "Seen any runaways?" the man *said*.

   strong verbs *inquired, snapped, bellowed, panted*

   -ly adverbs *suspiciously, angrily, gruffly, frantically*

Who/Which **Clause Dress-Up**

Write a sentence you could use in your composition that contains a *who/which* clause. Remember the comma rule. Underline the word *who* or *which*.

The Quaker, who detested slavery, hid them in his wagon.

Vocabulary Practice

Look at the vocabulary words for Lesson 14. Fill in the blanks with a word that makes sense.

1. Mary became _____*distraught*_____ when she heard that Master would sell her little Eli.

2. It was _____*imperative*_____ that they reach the river before daybreak.

Look at the vocabulary chart on pages 322–323. Try to use words from Lessons 1–14 in sentences or phrases that could be in your composition. Write at least two ideas below.

*Silhouettes of dogs **loomed** down the road.*

*Despite much **trepidation**, John and Mary decided to **venture** to freedom.*

Lesson 14: The Underground Railroad

Unit 5 Composition Checklist
Lesson 14: The Underground Railroad

Writing
from
Pictures

Name: _____

Institute for **Excellence** in **Writing**

STRUCTURE

☐ MLA format (see Appendix I) _____ 1 pt

☐ title centered and repeats 1–3 key words from final sentence _____ 2 pts

☐ clincher sentences repeat or reflect 2–3 key words of central fact (highlight or bold) _____ 5 pts

☐ checklist on top, final draft, rough draft, key word outline _____ 5 pts

STYLE

¶1 ¶2 ¶3 **Dress-Ups** (underline one of each) (2 pts each)

☐ ☐ ☐ -ly adverb _____ 6 pts

☐ ☐ ☐ *who/which* clause _____ 6 pts

☐ ☐ ☐ strong verb _____ 6 pts

☐ ☐ ☐ *because* clause _____ 6 pts

☐ ☐ ☐ quality adjective _____ 6 pts

☐ ☐ ☐ *www.asia* clause _____ 6 pts

Sentence Openers (number; one of each as possible) (2 pts each)

☐ ☐ ☐ [2] prepositional _____ 6 pts

☐ ☐ ☐ [3] -ly adverb _____ 6 pts

CHECK FOR BANNED WORDS (-1 pt for each use): go/went, say/said, good, bad, pretty, big, small

MECHANICS

☐ capitalization _____ 1 pt

☐ end marks and punctuation _____ 1 pt

☐ complete sentences (Does it make sense?) _____ 1 pt

☐ correct spelling _____ 1 pt

VOCABULARY

☐ vocabulary words - label *(voc)* in left margin or after sentence

Total: _____ 65 pts

Custom Total: _____ pts

Teachers are free to adjust a checklist by requiring only the stylistic techniques that have become easy, plus one new one. EZ+1

UNIT 5: WRITING FROM PICTURES

Intentionally blank so the checklist can be removed.

Lesson 15: The Civil War

Structure:	Unit 5: Writing from Pictures
Style:	no new style
Writing Topic:	The Civil War
Literature Suggestion:	Elementary: *Mr. Lincoln's Drummer* by G. Clifton Wisler
	Junior and Senior High: *Behind Rebel Lines* by Seymour Reit

Lesson 15: The Civil War

UNIT 5: WRITING FROM PICTURES

Lesson 15: The Civil War

Goals

- to practice the Unit 5 structural model
- to create a KWO from a series of three pictures: the Civil War
- to write a 3-paragraph composition from the KWO
- to take Vocabulary Quiz 4
- to correctly use new vocabulary words: *diminish, awestruck, solemn, encounter*

Assignment Schedule

Day 1

1. Play Around the World or Vocabulary Lightning.
2. Take Vocabulary Quiz 4.
3. Read Historical Information.
4. Write your KWO.

Day 2

1. Review your KWO from Day 1 and complete Structure Practice.
2. Complete Style Practice.
3. Look at the vocabulary cards for Lesson 15. Discuss the words and their definitions and complete Vocabulary Practice.
4. Using your KWO as a guide, begin writing your 3-paragraph rough draft.
5. Go over the checklist. Put a check in the box for each requirement you have completed.

Day 3

1. Review all vocabulary words learned thus far.
2. Finish writing your 3-paragraph composition. Ensure that the clincher sentence of each paragraph repeats or reflects two or three key words of the central fact of the picture.
3. Turn in your rough draft to your editor with the completed checklist attached.

Day 4

1. Write or type a final draft making any corrections your editor asked you to make.
2. Paperclip the checklist, final draft, rough draft, and KWO together. Hand them in.
3. If you are making a Magnum Opus Notebook, revise your Westward Movement composition from Lesson 13.

UNIT 5: WRITING FROM PICTURES

Literature Suggestion

Begin reading *Mr. Lincoln's Drummer* by G. Clifton Wisler or *Behind Rebel Lines* by Seymour Reit.

Historical Information

During the Civil War (1861–1865) Americans fought Americans. When Abraham Lincoln was elected president, the Southern states feared that slavery would eventually be outlawed. The South had many huge cotton and tobacco plantations that depended upon slave labor, so the Southern states tried to leave the Union to form their own separate nation called the *Confederate States of America.* They even elected their own president, Jefferson Davis.

President Lincoln did not believe the South had the right to leave the country, so he did not remove U.S. soldiers from the South. On April 12, 1861, Southern Confederate soldiers attacked Union soldiers at Ft. Sumter in South Carolina. The Civil War began. Both sides fought for what they believed was a just cause. The war was America's bloodiest and deadliest war ever, killing about 620,000 men and boys.

The Civil War is sometimes called the *Boys' War* because so many teens fought in it. Some of the youngest boys were drummer boys. They had the important role of relaying orders across a camp or battlefield with their drum beats. Drummer boys were also stretcher bearers. It was their job to search the battlefields for wounded soldiers and bring them to the medics.

Some drummer boys became fighting soldiers. Johnny Clem joined the Union army as a drummer boy at nine years old. He became a sergeant at twelve years old and was most likely the youngest Union soldier.

Look at the series of pictures. The first picture is of a drummer boy marching beside soldiers. The second picture is of a drummer boy standing beside two wounded soldiers. The third picture is of a drummer boy receiving a medal. After you discuss the pictures, remind the students to use key words to write what they see in the picture on the central fact line. Students come up with ideas that describe the event in order to write the rest of the paragraph. Asking questions is key.

Sample

Key Word Outline

I. Central fact: *Johnny, marching, drum*

1.   *wanted, fight*

2.   *12, young, infantry*

3.   *heard, battle, ahead*

4.   *yelling, cannons, bullets*

5.   *X long, reached*

Clincher repeats or reflects 2–3 key words of central fact.

II. Central fact: *J. @ cannon, soldiers, wounded*

1.   *Johnny, 👀, alone*

2.   *drum, down, fired*

3.   *> battle, chaos*

4.   *finally, enemy, retreated*

5.   *Johnny, relieved*

Clincher repeats or reflects 2–3 key words of central fact.

III. Central fact: *Johnny, medal, valor*

1.   *promoted, private*

2.   *traded, drum, rifle*

3.   *fought, bravely, rest*

4.   *soon, war, ended*

5.   *Johnny, 🏠*

Clincher repeats or reflects 2–3 key words of central fact.
Title repeats 1–3 key words from final sentence.

?

who?

what?

when?

where?

why?

how?

doing?

thinking?

feeling?

saying?

before?

after?

outside?

Structure Practice

Topic Sentence

Use your KWO to guide you as you write your composition. Begin by looking at the words on the central fact line, the words that indicate what you see in the picture.

If you wrote *Johnny*, *marching*, *drum* on the central fact line next to the first picture, your topic sentence could be:

With his **drum Johnny** proudly **marched** alongside the Union troops.

Use the key words that you wrote on the KWO next to the first central fact (the topic line) to write a sentence that tells what you see in the picture. Remember to highlight or bold the key words.

_____ *Answers will vary.* _____

_____

Continue your composition by forming sentences from the key words placed on the KWO. When you reach the clincher line, write a sentence that repeats or reflects two or three key words of the central fact. The clincher for the sample above might be:

Keeping in step with the Union soldiers, **Johnny marched** and **drummed**.

Style Practice

#2 Prepositional Opener

Begin each sentence with a #2 prepositional opener. Follow the comma rule on page 115.

1. ___*[2] On this day*_____ they were headed to battle.

2. ___*[2] To his shock*_____ the gunners lay severely wounded.

3. ___*[2] With much humility*_____ Johnny accepted the medal.

#3 -ly Adverb Opener

Begin each sentence with a #3 -ly adverb opener. Follow the comma rule on page 135.

1. ___*[3] Proudly*_____ Johnny beat his drum.

2. ___*[3] Resolutely*_____ Johnny fired the cannon.

www.asia Clause Dress-Up

Write a sentence with a *www.aisa* clause that you could use in your composition. Remember to add the clause to a sentence that is already complete. Punctuate and mark correctly.

Johnny continued to fire <u>while</u> bullets whizzed all around him.

_____

Because Clause Dress-up

Write a sentence with a *because* clause that you could use in your composition. Remember to add the clause to a sentence that is already complete. Punctuate and mark correctly.

Johnny had signed up <u>because</u> he wanted to support President Lincoln.

_____

Who/Which Clause Dress-Up

Add a *who/which* clause to the sentence below. Punctuate and mark correctly.

Johnny, <u>who</u> _____ *realized he was alone at the site,* _____ manned the cannon.

Quality Adjective Dress-Up

Next to each noun write ideas for adjectives. Choose adjectives that create strong images and tell what each thing looks like, sounds like, or feels like. Avoid banned adjectives.

1. the soldiers _____ **zealous**, *eager,* **wary** _____

2. the drummer boy _____ *determined,* **resolute**, *frantic* _____

3. the road _____ *dusty, perilous, rocky, muddy* _____

4. the battle _____ *chaotic, fierce, bloody* _____

Describe two additional things the soldiers might see, hear, or feel.

He kept a steady, rhythmic beat as the tired soldiers marched in step along the dusty path.

Their blue tattered uniforms now looked gray.

Strong Verb Dress-Up and -ly Adverb Dress-Up

On the first line below each sentence, write strong verbs that could replace the italicized banned verb. On the second line under each sentence, write ideas for -ly adverbs that you could use with the strong verbs. Use a thesaurus or your vocabulary words.

1. The soldier *went* along the muddy road.

    strong verbs ___ *marched, trudged, advanced, progressed* ___

    -ly adverbs ___ *eagerly, laboriously, **warily**, watchfully* ___

2. Bullets *went* by Johnny's head.

    strong verbs ___ *whizzed, rocketed, zoomed, buzzed* ___

    -ly adverbs ___ ***incessantly**, mercilessly, haphazardly* ___

3. "The Union is proud of your service," the general *said*.

    strong verbs ___ *proclaimed, announced, **affirmed**, expressed* ___

    -ly adverbs ___ *proudly, joyfully, meaningfully, positively* ___

Vocabulary Practice

Look at the vocabulary words for Lesson 15. Fill in the blanks with a word that makes sense.

1. He hoped the Rebel firing would ___ *diminish.* ___

2. The Rebel army was a ___ *solemn* ___ force.

Look at the vocabulary chart on pages 322–323. Try to use words from Lessons 1–15 in sentences or phrases that could be in your composition. Write at least two ideas below.

*The Rebels were a **formidable** foe **looming** on the open field.*

*Johnny fought **adeptly** during the **grueling** and **extensive battle**.*

Unit 5 Composition Checklist
Lesson 15: The Civil War

Writing
from
Pictures

Name: _____

Institute for Excellence in Writing
Listen. Speak. Read. Write. Think.

STRUCTURE

☐ MLA format (see Appendix I)	_____	1 pt
☐ title centered and repeats 1–3 key words from final sentence	_____	2 pts
☐ clincher sentences repeat or reflect 2–3 key words of central fact (highlight or bold)	_____	5 pts
☐ checklist on top, final draft, rough draft, key word outline	_____	5 pts

STYLE

¶1 ¶2 ¶3 Dress-Ups (underline one of each)   (2 pts each)

☐ ☐ ☐ -ly adverb	_____	6 pts
☐ ☐ ☐ *who/which* clause	_____	6 pts
☐ ☐ ☐ strong verb	_____	6 pts
☐ ☐ ☐ *because* clause	_____	6 pts
☐ ☐ ☐ quality adjective	_____	6 pts
☐ ☐ ☐ *www.asia* clause	_____	6 pts

Sentence Openers (number; one of each as possible)   (2 pts each)

☐ ☐ ☐ [2] prepositional	_____	6 pts
☐ ☐ ☐ [3] -ly adverb	_____	6 pts

CHECK FOR BANNED WORDS (-1 pt for each use): go/went, say/said, good, bad, pretty, big, small   _____   pts

MECHANICS

☐ capitalization	_____	1 pt
☐ end marks and punctuation	_____	1 pt
☐ complete sentences (Does it make sense?)	_____	1 pt
☐ correct spelling	_____	1 pt

VOCABULARY

☐ vocabulary words - label *(voc)* in left margin or after sentence	

Total: _____ 65 pts

Custom Total: _____ pts

Teachers are free to adjust a checklist by requiring only the stylistic techniques that have become easy, plus one new one. EZ+1

UNIT 5: WRITING FROM PICTURES

Intentionally blank so the checklist can be removed.

Institute for Excellence in Writing

Lesson 16: Oklahoma Land Rush of 1889

Structure:	Unit 6: Summarizing Multiple References
	source and fused outlines
Style:	no new style
Writing Topic:	The Oklahoma Land Rush
Literature Suggestion:	Elementary: *Mr. Lincoln's Drummer* by G. Clifton Wisler
	Junior and Senior High: *Behind Rebel Lines* by Seymour Reit

Watch the sections for Unit 6: Summarizing Multiple References. At IEW.com/twss-help reference the TWSS Viewing Guides.

UNIT 6: SUMMARIZING MULTIPLE REFERENCES

Lesson 16: Oklahoma Land Rush of 1889

Goals

- to learn the Unit 6 Summarizing Multiple References structural model
- to create source outlines from multiple references
- to create a fused outline
- to write a 1-paragraph report about the Oklahoma Land Rush
- to review vocabulary words

Assignment Schedule

Day 1

1. Read New Structure—Summarizing Multiple References.

3. Read "The Mad Dash" and take notes about the Oklahoma Land Rush of 1889 by writing a source outline as directed on page 154.

3. Read "Free Land" and take additional notes about the Oklahoma Land Rush of 1889 by writing another source outline. Note that the words on the topic line for this source outline are the same as the previous source outline because you are taking notes about the same topic. As you take notes, do not note facts that you already noted from the first source.

4. Using notes from both source outlines, write a fused outline.

Day 2

1. Review your fused outline.

2. Complete Style Practice.

3. Complete Vocabulary Practice. There are no new words for this lesson.

4. Using your fused outline as a guide, begin writing your rough draft.

5. Go over the checklist. Put a check in the box for each requirement you have completed.

Day 3

1. Review all vocabulary words learned thus far.

2. Finish writing your 1-paragraph report. Follow the topic-clincher rule.

3. Turn in your rough draft to your editor with the completed checklist attached.

In this new unit the KWO is formed by taking key words from interesting and important facts, similar to Unit 4. In this unit students receive multiple sources related to each topic. For each topic students take 3–5 notes from each source to form a source outline. Using the source outlines, students combine the notes to form a fused outline. Help students limit which facts they choose.

Each paragraph is about a specific topic and should follow the topic-clincher rule.

Day 4

1. Write or type a final draft making any corrections your editor asked you to make.

2. Paperclip the checklist, final draft, rough draft, and KWO together. Hand them in.

3. If you are making a Magnum Opus Notebook, revise your Escape on the Underground Railroad composition from Lesson 14.

Literature Suggestion

Continue reading *Mr. Lincoln's Drummer* by G. Clifton Wisler or *Behind Rebel Lines* by Seymour Reit.

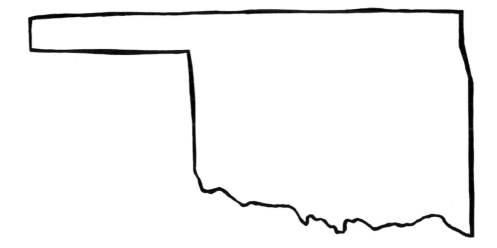

Read this page to introduce the new structural unit, Unit 6: Summarizing Multiple References. Like Unit 4, students take notes from the source text to write a report. Because there are two source texts, students will take notes from both texts and then fuse them into one KWO. Students will write from the fused outline.

Lesson 16: Oklahoma Land Rush of 1889

New Structure

Summarizing Multiple References

In Unit 6 you will again write reports. Remember when you write a report, your facts must be organized into paragraphs. Just like Unit 4 you will find the facts to support your topic in source texts, except this time you will use several sources from which to gather facts.

Each paragraph will begin with a topic sentence, contain facts, and end with a clincher sentence.

1 topic = 1 paragraph

Topic Sentence

> The topic sentence tells what the paragraph is about. When you write the KWO, ask yourself: "What will the paragraph be about?" As you answer, write two or three key words on the Roman numeral line of the source outlines and the fused outline. In this book the topics of the paragraphs for the first few Unit 6 lessons will be given to you.

Facts

> Gather facts by writing source outlines. Create one source outline for each source text. Once you have chosen your topic, read each of your sources and look for important or interesting facts that support the topic. Select three to five facts from each source and place them on the appropriate source outline using key words, symbols, numbers, and abbreviations.

> Organize facts by writing a fused outline. Select five to seven facts from the source outlines and transfer them to the fused outline.

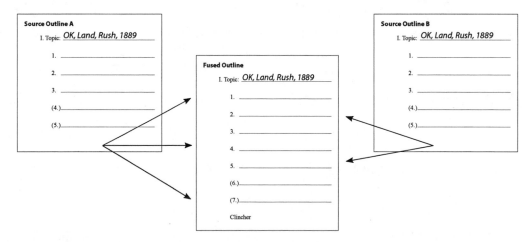

Clincher Sentence

> The clincher sentence reminds the reader what the paragraph was about. Like Unit 4 the KWO ends with the word *clincher*. Do not place key words on the clincher line. Instead when you write your rough draft, repeat or reflect two or three key words on the topic line.

Source A

The Mad Dash

On April 22, 1889, right at noon, over 50,000 people rushed into Oklahoma Territory to claim free land. What enabled them to do this? Who provided free land? The land was provided by the United States government. In an attempt to encourage people to move from the crowded eastern cities to the undeveloped western territories, Congress passed the Homestead Act in 1862. This act allowed the government to give away up to 160 acres of land to anyone. The stipulations were few. People who wanted the land had to be older than twenty-one, arrange to live on the land for five years, and agree to make improvements to the land. The only fee that potential landowners had to pay to the government was an $18 filing fee, which made the claim official. This Homestead Act offered new hope to struggling farmers, freed slaves, and immigrants. Different territories opened at different times. On April 22, 1889, almost two million acres in Oklahoma were scheduled to become available. In anticipation, thousands of people prepared to claim land. Many camped all around the land waiting for the signal to enter; however, some people snuck in ahead of time to find the best land. They were called the "Sooners." Once the cannons boomed at noon, people quickly dashed in and claimed the land. Within a short period of time, cities, farms, and ranches were established. By1907 Oklahoma officially became the forty-sixth state of the United States.

Mechanics _____

When a date includes the month, day, and year, place a comma between the day and year. If the date is placed in the middle of a sentence, place a comma on both sides of the year.

Source B

Free Land

The Oklahoma Land Rush occurred on April 22, 1889. Seven weeks prior to this, President Harrison announced that the government would put almost two million acres of land up for grabs. This was part of the government's plan to encourage white people to settle the western United States. This particular government give-away took place in the Oklahoma Indian Territory. Initially the president chose land that had not yet been assigned to any particular Indian tribe. Although anyone could claim a stake of this land, they had to wait until noon on April 22 to do so. More than fifty thousand settlers desiring free land camped around the territory waiting for the race to begin. They were nicknamed "Boomers." Some dared to enter early. They were nicknamed the "Sooners." At noon on that particular April day, cannons boomed, and a frantic rush ensued. Fifty to sixty thousand hopefuls entered in wagons, on horseback, and by foot. Hours of chaos followed. By the end of the day, tens of thousands of claims had been staked. Around 10,000 claims were in one area. The very next day that area was established as Oklahoma City. Almost overnight other towns were developed. In the following years additional more controlled land rushes occurred in the Oklahoma Territory. Eventually white Americans took over what was supposed to be Indian Territory, and Oklahoma became an official state in 1907.

Mechanics _____

Separate a city and state with a comma. When a city and state are placed in the middle of a sentence, place a comma on both sides of the state.

Sample

Source Outlines

The assigned topic for this paragraph is the Oklahoma Land Rush of 1889. The titles of the source texts are on the Source line. The assigned topic is written in key words on the Roman numeral topic lines. Complete each source outline by looking at the appropriate source and noting three to five interesting or important facts about the topic.

1 paragraph = 1 topic

Topic: *Oklahoma land rush of 1889*

Source A: *"The Mad Dash"*

I. Topic: *OK, land, rush, 1889*

1. *Apr 22, 50,000 ppl, free, land*

2. *Homestead Act, gov't, 160 acres* ➔ *anyone*

3. *2 million acres, available*

(4.) *early,* 🏠 *snuck, "Sooners"*

(5.) 🕐 *cannon, ppl, rushed, claim*

Source B: *"Free Land"*

I. Topic: *OK, land, rush, 1889*

1. *gov't, encouraged, settlers, western US*

2. *must, wait, noon, Apr 22*

3. *50,000, ppl,* 🏠 *"Boomers," cannon, rushed*

(4.) *10,000 + claims, towns, overnight*

(5.) *OK, state, 1907*

The topic on the source and fused outlines is identical. This is because students choose a topic to write about and then gather facts from both sources about the chosen topic. Only the fused outline has a clincher line because students write the paragraph using the fused outline.

Sample

Fused Outline

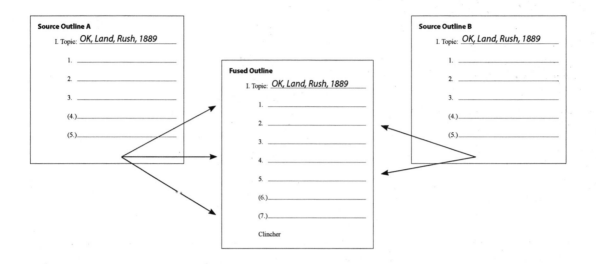

Select five to seven facts from the source outlines to transfer to the fused outline.

I. Topic: *OK, land, rush, 1889*

1. _____ *Apr 22, 50,000 ppl, free, land* _____

2. _____ *Homestead Act, gov't, 160 acres ➜ anyone* _____

3. _____ *encouraged, settlers, western US* _____

4. _____ *must, wait, noon* _____

5. _____ *early,* 🏠 *snuck, "Sooners"* _____

(6.) _____ *ppl, rushed, "Boomers," 10,000 + claims* _____

(7.) _____ *towns, overnight, OK, state, 1907* _____

Clincher

Tell back the facts on the fused outline in complete sentences. Fix any notes you do not understand. For the clincher, repeat or reflect two or three key words from the topic line.

Style Practice

#2 Prepositional Opener and #3 -ly Adverb Opener

The checklist will require that you include both of the sentence openers you have learned. Write sentences that can be used in your paragraph.

1. #2 prepositional opener ___*[2] At noon the cannons boomed.*___

2. #3 -ly adverb opener ___*[3] Immediately an onrush of hopefuls poured in.*___

Dress-Ups

Although this lesson does not contain specific practice exercises for the six dress-ups you have learned, you must include one of each in the paragraph you write. Look at your KWO and consider where you can include various clauses as well as strong verbs, quality adjectives, and -ly adverbs. When you write your paper, follow your checklist!

Vocabulary Practice

Look at the vocabulary chart on pages 322–323. Try to use words from Lessons 1–15 in sentences or phrases that could be in your report. Write at least two ideas below.

*It is difficult to **fathom** the **extensive** amount of land that was given away.*

*The government **conceived** the Homestead Act to **compel settlers** west.*

Unit 6 Composition Checklist
Lesson 16: Oklahoma Land Rush of 1889

Summarizing
Multiple
References

Name: _____

Institute for Excellence in Writing

STRUCTURE

☐ MLA format (see Appendix I) _____ 2 pts

☐ title centered and repeats 1–3 key words from final sentence _____ 2 pts

☐ topic-clincher sentences repeat or reflect 2–3 key words (highlight or bold) _____ 6 pts

☐ checklist on top, final draft, rough draft, key word outline _____ 5 pts

STYLE

¶1 Dress-Ups (underline one of each)   (2 pts each)

☐ -ly adverb _____ 2 pts

☐ *who/which* clause _____ 2 pts

☐ strong verb _____ 2 pts

☐ *because* clause _____ 2 pts

☐ quality adjective _____ 2 pts

☐ *www.asia* clause _____ 2 pts

Sentence Openers (number; one of each as possible)   (2 pts each)

☐ [2] prepositional _____ 2 pts

☐ [3] -ly adverb _____ 2 pts

CHECK FOR BANNED WORDS (-1 pt for each use): go/went, say/said, good, bad, pretty, big, small _____ pts

MECHANICS

☐ capitalization _____ 1 pt

☐ end marks and punctuation _____ 1 pt

☐ complete sentences (Does it make sense?) _____ 1 pt

☐ correct spelling _____ 1 pt

VOCABULARY

☐ vocabulary words - label *(voc)* in left margin or after sentence

Total: _____ 35 pts

Custom Total: _____ pts

Teachers are free to adjust a checklist by requiring only the stylistic techniques that have become easy, plus one new one. EZ+1

UNIT 6: SUMMARIZING MULTIPLE REFERENCES

Intentionally blank so the checklist can be removed.

Lesson 17: Transportation Milestones, Part 1

Structure:	Unit 6: Summarizing Multiple References
Style:	#6 vss opener
Writing Topic:	transportation
Literature Suggestion:	Elementary: *Mr. Lincoln's Drummer* by G. Clifton Wisler
	Junior and Senior High: *Behind Rebel Lines* by Seymour Reit

Lesson 17: Transportation Milestones, Part 1

UNIT 6: SUMMARIZING MULTIPLE REFERENCES

Lesson 17: Transportation Milestones, Part 1

Goals

- to practice the Unit 6 structural model
- to practice scanning multiple sources to determine topics for research
- to create source outlines from multiple references
- to create a fused outline
- to write the first paragraph of a 3-paragraph report about transportation
- to correctly add a new sentence opener: #6 vss
- to review vocabulary words

Assignment Schedule

Day 1

1. Play No-Noose Hangman with phrases provided in the Teacher's Manual.

2. In Lessons 17–18 you will use more than one source of information to write a 3-paragraph report. This lesson contains three different articles about transportation milestones in America. You are going to use some of the information in these articles to write your report—one paragraph at a time.

3. Before you begin taking notes, you must determine what topics are available to write about. Scan the paragraphs in each source text, reading just enough of each paragraph to discern its topic. The first and last sentence of each paragraph should help. Write the topic of each paragraph in the boxes in the margin. (The first paragraph of each source is labeled background because each of these paragraphs provides background information for the remaining topic paragraphs.)

4. For your first paragraph, choose a topic that is covered in two sources. Do not choose background. Write the topic on the topic line on page 168. Complete the source outlines from the two sources that contain information about your topic.

5. Using notes from both source outlines, write a fused outline.

Day 2

1. Review your fused outline.

2. Learn a new sentence opener, the #6 vss opener. Read New Style and complete Style Practice.

3. Complete Vocabulary Practice. There are no new words for this lesson.

4. Using your fused outline as a guide, begin writing your rough draft.

5. Go over the checklist. Put a check in the box for each requirement you have completed.

In Lessons 17–18 students will follow the same process introduced in Lesson 16. However, in Lessons 17–18, students will write a three-paragraph report. The subject (transportation milestones) is assigned, but students will need to choose their own three topics about transportation milestones. Before students can choose topics to write about, they must scan the source texts and determine which topics are covered in the source material.

No-Noose Hangman

For this lesson use the following phrases and bonus questions:

ABSOLUTELY NECESSARY

Bonus: What is the vocabulary word? *imperative*

FUSED OUTLINE

Bonus: What is the a fused outline? *An outline made by selecting facts from multiple source outlines. It is the outline used to write the paragraph.*

Day 3

1. Review all vocabulary words learned thus far.

2. Finish writing your paragraph. Follow the topic-clincher rule.

3. Turn in your rough draft to your editor with the completed checklist attached.

Day 4

1. Write or type a final draft making any corrections your editor asked you to make.

2. Paperclip the checklist, final draft, rough draft, and KWO together. Hand them in.

3. If you are making a Magnum Opus Notebook, revise your Civil War composition from Lesson 15.

Literature Suggestion

Finish reading *Mr. Lincoln's Drummer* by G. Clifton Wisler or *Behind Rebel Lines* by Seymour Reit.

Acquire *Hattie Big Sky* by Kirby Larson to read for Lessons 18–21.

Scan the source text with the students to determine what each paragraph is about.

Source A

Milestones in American Transportation

background

In the early nineteenth century, transportation across America's western frontiers was crude and uncomfortable. Roads, especially, were horrendous and dangerous for traveling long distances. But as the country grew, the need for ways to connect the East and West became apparent. The Industrial Revolution brought innovations to transportation that transformed America forever.

Erie Canal

The first major milestone in providing long distance travel for both people and goods was the building of the Erie Canal in 1825. This canal is a manmade waterway across the state of New York that connects Lake Erie to the Hudson River. It was 363 miles long when first built. The Hudson River continues south to New York City. This means that the waterway connects the Great Lakes region with New York City and the Atlantic Ocean. The building of the canal enabled goods to be moved for one-tenth of what it used to cost in less than half the time. This encouraged people to move West and helped cities grow around the Great Lakes. The canal also resulted in the huge economic growth of New York City. It became the center of commerce in America. Because of the success of the Erie Canal, many more canals were built.

Transcontinental RR

Probably the most significant transportation achievement of the 1800s was the Transcontinental Railroad. Early railroads did not travel far. During the Gold Rush trips from the East Coast to California by land were extremely difficult and dangerous. For this reason many people took ships, but they had to sail all the way around South America! People soon realized the need for a railroad that would connect the entire country. In 1862 two of the largest railway companies began construction on a transcontinental railroad. The Central Pacific Company began their track in Sacramento, California, and built toward the East while the Union Pacific Company began in Omaha, Nebraska, and built toward the West. In 1869 the lines met. The country celebrated as a railroad official pounded a ceremonial gold spike into the ground. The railway brought not only people across the country but transported goods and raw materials. Railroads replaced canals as the major means of transportation of goods. The Transcontinental Railroad helped transform America.

The motor car, or automobile, also remarkably changed America, but not until it became affordable for the average American. Henry Ford made this possible. Ford did not invent motor cars, but he created a way to build them quickly and cheaply. He hired many factory workers. He had each man work on only one part of the car, so each worker became fast and skilled at his job. These men were part of an assembly line. With this system Ford was able to mass produce cars that were exactly alike. He called his car a Model T Ford, but people nicknamed it the "Tin Lizzie."* By 1927 the Ford Motor Company had manufactured 15 million Model T Fords. Eventually almost every family in America could own a car. This meant people could travel longer distances quickly and conveniently. The Model T is another transportation innovation that changed American life.

car (margin note)

Bibliography (fictitious)

Doe, John. "Milestones in American Transportation." *Transportation in America*, US Transport, 15 May 2018, mrsv.org/transportation.

*For Fun _____

Find out how the Model T got its nickname of "Tin Lizzie."

Source B

Transportation Innovations of the 1800s

background

America was a young nation in the 1800s, and it was expanding. People were settling the western frontiers, but the frontier was cut off from many of the goods of the East. Factories or stores where people could buy even basic things like food, furniture, and household items did not exist. Furthermore, people were discovering that the West had valuable resources that could be used by factories in the East. The problem was finding ways to easily transport goods and people between the East and the West.

Erie Canal

The Erie Canal was the first answer to the transportation problem. It provided a way to move goods and resources between New York City and the Great Lakes region. The Appalachian Mountains made this difficult by land. Building the canal was a huge engineering feat. In fact, many people did not think it could be done and made fun of the idea. The project took seven years. Men with shovels digging through mountainous terrain built the canal. When they finally finished in October of 1825, the canal was 363 miles long and 40 feet wide. The canal brought shipping costs way down, so more goods and resources flowed between East and West. New York City became the chief city of commerce in the United States. Many people moved to New York. Many people also moved to the Great Lakes region, and cities grew there. The Erie Canal remained the chief mode of transportation of goods until the mid-1800s when railroads grew and took over.

In the mid-1800s America needed a railroad that could cross the entire county—a transcontinental railroad. In 1862 President Abraham Lincoln signed

Transcontinental RR

the Pacific Railroad Act. This act gave railroad companies land on which to build tracks that would connect the East to the West. The two companies chosen were the Central Pacific Company, which began its tracks in California and headed east, and the Union Pacific Company, which began in Nebraska and headed west. Building the railroad was very difficult work. In the West, the Sierra Nevada Mountains proved a challenging obstacle. Many tunnels had to be blasted through mountainsides. Blasting was slow, only getting through about one foot per day. The Union Pacific Line had to deal with angry Native Americans. The natives knew that the "Iron Horse" would lead to more white men taking more of their land, so they sometimes raided and attacked railroad stations and workers. However, on May 10, 1869, the track was complete. The two halves met in Utah. An official from each railroad company drove in the last spike, which was called both the "Final Spike" and the "Golden Spike." The Transcontinental Railroad moved people and goods from coast to coast. The Transcontinental Railroad has been called by some the most monumental feat of the nineteenth century.

Bibliography (fictitious)

Verstegen, Lori. "Transportation Innovations of the 1800s." *U.S. History-Based Writing Lessons*. Institute for Excellence in Writing, 2020, pp. 163–164.

Mechanics _____

Capitalize *north*, *south*, *east*, and *west* when they refer to a region or proper name. Do not capitalize these words when they indicate direction. Do not capitalize the words *northern*, *southern*, *eastern*, or *western*.

Source C

Transporting Americans

background

In the 1800s most people did not travel more than one hundred miles from their homes. People usually were born, grew up, and died in the same town. However, access to the automobile and then to air travel changed that. Today many people often travel across the country and even across the world.

In the early 1900s Henry Ford made automobiles available to middle-class Americans. He had said he wanted to make "a motor car for the great multitude," instead of only for the rich. He succeeded because of his assembly line factory. In his factory each worker added one part to a car as it moved down a belt. This process cut the production time of a car from fourteen hours to one and a half hours. The only drawback was that every car was exactly alike. But that did not

car

stop Americans all over from buying his Model T Ford. Other companies soon followed. By the end of 1929, a staggering twenty-six million automobiles had been sold since Ford's first Model T in 1908. The mass production of automobiles transformed America in many ways. Steel, petroleum, and rubber industries grew. Suburbs developed where workers could live outside of the big cities and drive to work. People could travel farther than they ever had before, easily and comfortably. America was evolving, and the Model T Ford became the symbol of its modernization.

The other invention that truly opened not just the entire country to Americans but the world as well is the airplane. In 1903 two brothers, Orville and Wilbur Wright, developed the first successful motorized airplane that could carry

airplane

a person. They tested it on December 17 at Kitty Hawk, North Carolina. Orville

made the first flight. He flew 120 feet in 12 seconds. Wilbur made the longest

flight that day. He flew 852 feet in 59 seconds. That might not seem like much,

but the brothers continued to work on improving their craft. By 1905 their flights

were up to 39 minutes. In 1908 they made their first flight for the public to see. It

was in France. Later they began the Wright Company to build and sell aircraft. In

1909 the U.S. government bought its first plane from the Wright brothers. It could

travel more than 40 miles per hour. In 1911 the Wrights built a plane that crossed

the entire United States. Although it stopped 70 times and took 84 days, it made it.

Other inventors began to improve the airplane, and eventually jets were invented.

Today air travel is common. People can travel all the way across the country in a

matter of hours. They can also travel the world.

Bibliography (fictitious)

"Transporting Americans." *Verstegen's Encyclopedia*, ABC Publishers,

2017, p. 165.

Lesson 17: Transportation Milestones, Part 1

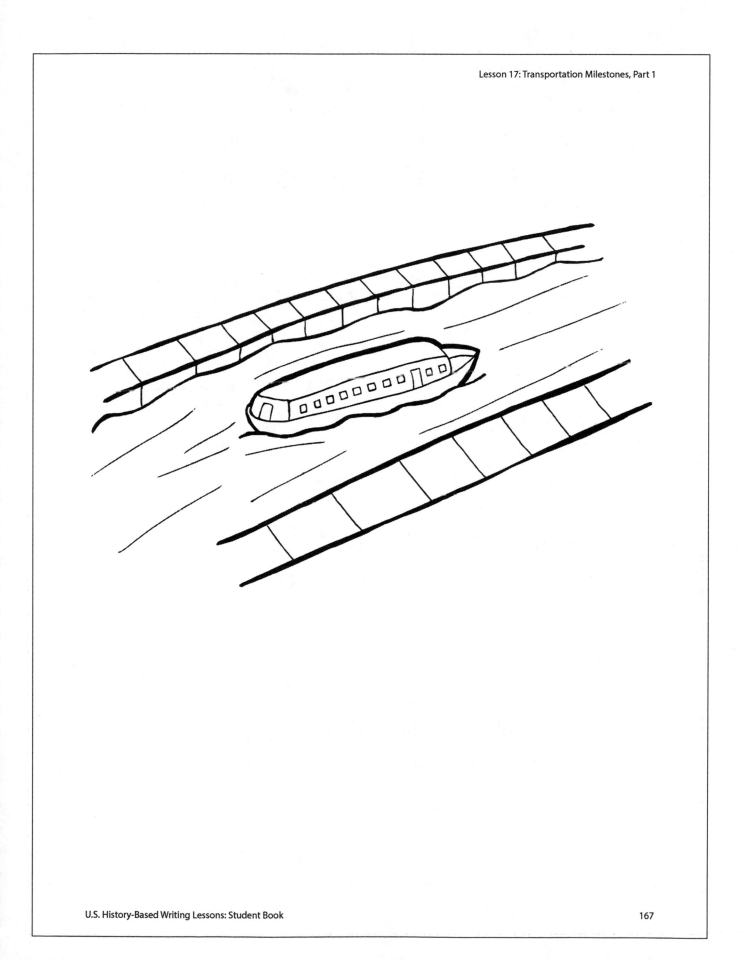

Students often confuse subjects and topics. The subject of the report is the entire thing being written about. In this case, the subject is transportation milestones. The topics are the divisions—the things within the subject. Students will choose a specific topic about transportation milestones (car, canal, railroad) to write for this paragraph. All the facts gathered should support, prove, or illustrate the chosen topic.

Sample

Source Outlines

The topic sentence tells what a paragraph is about.
Write the topic of your first paragraph on the line below.

1 paragraph = 1 topic

First Topic: *Erie Canal, the first transportation milestone in America*

Using key words, write the topic on the Roman numeral line of each source outline. Each topic line will have the same words. Look at the appropriate paragraphs of the source texts and note three to five interesting facts about the topic. Since each topic is only found in two of the sources, you will only complete two source outlines.

Source A: *"Milestones in American Transportation"*

I. Topic: *Erie Canal, 1st, transportation, milestone, Amer.*

   1.   *built, 1825, waterway ➜ ← NY*

   2.   *363 mi, connect, Gr Lakes, NYC*

   3.   *cost, transport, 1/10 previous*

   (4.)   *cities, ⬆ around, Gr Lakes*

   (5.)   *$ ➜ NYC, center, commerce*

Source B: *"Transportation Innovations of the 1800s"*

I. Topic: *Erie Canal, 1st transportation, milestone, Amer.*

   1.   *moved, goods, resources*

   2.   *engineering, feat, ppl, 💬 impossible*

   3.   *7 yrs, men, w/, shovels, ➜ 🏔, terrain*

   (4.)   *363 mi. long, 40 ft wide*

   (5.)   *chief, transport, until, RR*

Sample

Source C: *"Transporting Americans"*

I. Topic: *This source does not contain information about the Erie Canal.*

1. _____

2. _____

3. _____

(4.) _____

(5.) _____

Fused Outline

Place the topic you are writing about on the topic line. Select five to seven facts from the source outlines to transfer to the fused outline.

I. Topic: *Erie Canal, 1st transportation, milestone, Amer.*

1. *built, 1825, men, w/, shovels, 7 yrs*

2. *engineering, feat, ppl, ⟲ impossible*

3. *363 mi, 40 ft wide, connect, Gr Lakes, NYC*

4. *moved, goods, resources*

5. *cities, ⬆, around, Gr Lakes*

(6.) *$ ➜ NYC, center, commerce*

(7.) *chief, transport, until, RR*

Clincher

Tell back the facts on the fused outline in complete sentences. Fix any notes you do not understand. For the clincher, repeat or reflect two or three key words from the topic line.

New Style

#6 Vss Opener

In this lesson you will learn another sentence opener: the #6 very short sentence (vss).

This opener is simply a short sentence that contains two to five words. Remember that variety in sentence structure is important in good writing. In each paragraph you should have some sentences that are long, some that are of medium length, and some that are short.

Purposefully adding a very short sentence will help break up the pattern of sentences in a stylish way. It catches the reader's attention. As a result, it is best placed in a spot where you would like to emphasize something. Here is a portion of Source A, which contains a very short sentence.

> The Central Pacific Company began their track in Sacramento, California, and built toward the East while the Union Pacific Line began in Omaha, Nebraska, and built toward the West. [6] In 1869 the lines met. The country celebrated as railroad officials pounded a ceremonial gold spike into the ground.

Notice:

1. A very short sentence contains at least two but no more than five words. Each word counts as one.

    The Transcontinental Railroad revolutionized the nation. (not a vss)

    Although *The Transcontinental Railroad* is one name, it counts as three words.

2. A very short sentence is a complete sentence. It is not a fragment.

    It revolutionized the nation! (sentence)

    Revolutionized at last! (fragment)

3. To indicate a very short sentence, label it with a 6 in the left margin or place a [6] right before the sentence.

Practice

Write a sentence with a #6 vss opener. Label it with a [6].

_____ *[6] Men labored for seven years.* _____

_____

 From now on, each paragraph you write should include a #6 vss opener. Label it with a 6 in the margin or place a [6] before the sentence.

The #6 vss must contain a written subject and verb.

Challenge advanced students to include a strong verb so that their very short sentences pack a punch.

Style Practice

Sentence Openers

The checklist will require that you include all of the sentence openers you have been introduced to thus far. Write sentences that can be used in your paragraph.

1. #2 prepositional opener *[2] With shovels in hand men labored for seven years.*

2. #3 -ly adverb opener *[3] Eventually the canal joined the Great Lakes and New York City.*

3. #6 vss opener, 2–5 words *[6] Adept workers succeeded.*

Dress-Ups

Look at your KWO and consider where you can include various clauses as well as strong verbs, quality adjectives, and -ly adverbs. When you write your paper, follow your checklist!

Vocabulary Practice

Look at the vocabulary chart on pages 322–323. Try to use words from Lessons 1–15 in sentences or phrases that could be in your report. Write at least two ideas below.

*The workers likely **encountered** many difficulties and much ridicule, but they worked **diligently**.*

***Inevitably** cities sprang up around the Great Lakes.*

Unit 6 Composition Checklist
Lesson 17: Transportation Milestones, Part 1

Summarizing
Multiple
References

IEW Institute for Excellence in Writing

Name: _____

STRUCTURE

☐ MLA format (see Appendix I)	_____	2 pts
☐ topic-clincher sentences repeat or reflect 2–3 key words (highlight or bold)	_____	2 pts
☐ checklist on top, final draft, rough draft, key word outline	_____	2 pts

STYLE

¶1 Dress-Ups (underline one of each)   (2 pts each)

☐ -ly adverb	_____	2 pts
☐ *who/which* clause	_____	2 pts
☐ strong verb	_____	2 pts
☐ *because* clause	_____	2 pts
☐ quality adjective	_____	2 pts
☐ *www.asia* clause	_____	2 pts

Sentence Openers (number; one of each as possible)   (2 pts each)

☐ [2] prepositional	_____	2 pts
☐ [3] -ly adverb	_____	2 pts
☐ [6] vss	_____	2 pts

CHECK FOR BANNED WORDS (-1 pt for each use): go/went, say/said, good, bad, pretty, big, small   _____ pts

MECHANICS

☐ capitalization	_____	1 pt
☐ end marks and punctuation	_____	2 pts
☐ complete sentences (Does it make sense?)	_____	1 pt
☐ correct spelling	_____	2 pts

VOCABULARY

☐ vocabulary words - label *(voc)* in left margin or after sentence		

Total:	_____	30	pts
Custom Total:	_____		pts

Teachers are free to adjust a checklist by requiring only the stylistic techniques that have become easy, plus one new one. EZ+1

UNIT 6: SUMMARIZING MULTIPLE REFERENCES

Intentionally blank so the checklist can be removed.

Lesson 18: Transportation Milestones, Part 2

Structure:	Unit 6: Summarizing Multiple References bibliography
Style:	no new style
Writing Topic:	transportation
Literature Suggestion:	*Hattie Big Sky* by Kirby Larson

UNIT 6: SUMMARIZING MULTIPLE REFERENCES

Lesson 18: Transportation Milestones, Part 2

Goals

- to practice the Unit 6 structural model
- to create source outlines from multiple references
- to create a fused outline
- to write the second and third paragraphs of a 3-paragraph report about transportation
- to correctly add a bibliography
- to correctly use new vocabulary words: *milestone, thrive, innovative, profound*

Assignment Schedule

Day 1

1. Play Around the World.

2. In this lesson you will complete the 3-paragraph report using the source texts provided in Lesson 17. Then you will add a bibliography page.

3. For the second paragraph of your report, choose a second topic about transportation milestones that is covered in two of the sources found on pages 161–166. Write the topic on the topic line on page 178 and complete the source outlines.

4. Using notes from your source outlines, write a fused outline.

Day 2

1. For the third paragraph of your report, choose a third topic about transportation milestones that is covered in two of the sources. Write the topic on the topic line on page 180 and complete the source outlines.

2. Using notes from your source outlines, write a fused outline.

3. Complete Style Practice.

4. Look at the vocabulary cards for Lesson 18. Discuss the words and their definitions and complete Vocabulary Practice.

5. Using your fused outlines as a guide, begin writing your rough draft.

6. Go over the checklist. Put a check in the box for each requirement you have completed.

Day 3

1. Review all vocabulary words learned thus far.

2. Finish writing the second and third paragraphs of your 3-paragraph report. Follow the topic-clincher rule.

3. Read New Structure—Bibliography. Create a bibliography for your report. Begin by arranging the bibliography information at the bottom of each source text (pages 162, 164, and 166) in alphabetical order. The first source you list on your bibliography page will be Doe, John. Copy the bibliography information from page 162. Finish your bibliography page by copying the bibliography information for the remaining entries.

4. Turn in your rough draft and bibliography to your editor with the completed checklist attached.

Day 4

1. Write or type a final draft making any corrections your editor asked you to make. Place the two paragraphs written in this lesson after the paragraph you wrote for Lesson 17 so that you have one 3-paragraph report. Include the bibliography.

2. Paperclip the checklist, final draft, rough draft, and KWO together. Hand them in.

3. If you are making a Magnum Opus Notebook, revise your Oklahoma Land Rush report from Lesson 16.

Note: The paragraphs you wrote in Lessons 17–18 will be used to compose a 5-paragraph report with an introduction and a conclusion in Lesson 25.

In Lesson 19 you will write a report about the sinking of the *Lusitania*. One source of information will be provided for you. You must find two additional sources either from the library or the Internet. Choose fairly short, simple sources. History text books, encyclopedia articles, short children's books, and Internet articles labeled "for kids" usually work well.

Literature Suggestion

Begin reading *Hattie Big Sky* by Kirby Larson.

New Structure

Bibliography

A bibliography is a list of the sources that were used to write a research report. It is placed as the last page of the report. To write a bibliography follow these general guidelines:

Center the title (Bibliography) at the top of the page.

Double-space the entire page.

List sources in alphabetical order. (Use the first word of each entry, but ignore *A*, *An*, *The*.)

Do not indent the first line, but indent the following lines of the same entry ½ inch from left.

Books

Begin with the author's name. If a book has two authors, order the authors in the order they are presented in the book. If there are three or more authors, list only the first author followed by the phrase *et al*. Book titles are italicized. (If handwriting, underline.)

Last Name, First Name. "Chapter of Book." [in quotes] *Title of Book,*

[in italics] Publisher, Publication Date, p. #. [page number(s)]

Encyclopedia Articles

Cite encyclopedias like books. If the article has an author, begin with the name. Otherwise, begin with the title of the article.

Last Name, First Name. [if given] "Article Title." [in quotes] *Title of*

Encyclopedia, [in italics] Publisher, Publication Date, p. #. [page number(s)]

Websites

Often websites have a Cite icon, which can prove helpful. If the article has an author, begin with the name. Otherwise, begin with the title of the article, which is the logo at the top of the page (not the URL).

Last Name, First Name. [if given] "Title of Article." [in quotes] *Title of Website,*

[in italics] Publisher or sponsor, Day Month Year the article was posted,

[if available (If there is no publication date, use latest copyright date at the

bottom of the webpage.)] URL.

Sample

Source Outlines

The topic sentence tells what a paragraph is about.
Write the topic of your second paragraph on the line below.   **1 paragraph = 1 topic**

Second Topic: _Transcontinental Railroad, the most significant accomplishment of the 1800s_

Using key words, write the topic on the Roman numeral line of each source outline. Each topic line will have the same words. Look at the appropriate paragraphs of the source texts and note three to five interesting facts about the topic. Since each topic is only found in two of the sources, you will only complete two source outlines.

Source A: _"Milestones in American Transportation"_

II. Topic: ___TRR, ++ significant, accomplishment, 1800s___

   1. ___U.S., needed, RR, connect, E ➔ W___

   2. ___1862, 2, RR, companies, began, TRR___

   3. ___1st, Sacramento ➔ E, 2nd, Omaha ➔ W___

  (4.) ___1869, ✳, met, golden spike___

  (5.) ___TRR, replaced, canals, goods + ppl___

Students may use "the most monumental feat of the 19th century" in their paragraph if they place the phrase in quotation marks. They may not use the exact words as their own.

Source B: _"Transportation Innovations of the 1800s"_

II. Topic: ___TRR, ++ significant, accomplishment, 1800s___

   1. ___Pacific Railroad Act, land, build, ✳___

   2. ___difficult, blast, ➔ mts.___

   3. ___fight, angry, Native Amer.___

  (4.) ___✳ met, Utah___

  (5.) ___"most monumental feat 19th cent"___

Sample

Source C: *"Transporting Americans"*

II. Topic: *This source does not contain information about the*

1.   *Transcontinental Railroad.*

2.   _____

3.   _____

(4.)   _____

(5.)   _____

Fused Outline

Place the topic you are writing about on the topic line. Select five to seven facts from the source outlines to transfer to the fused outline.

II. Topic: *TRR, ++ significant, accomplishment, 1800s*

1.   *U.S., needed, RR, connect, E ➜ W*

2.   *1862, 2, RR, companies, began, TRR*

3.   *1st, Sacramento ➜ E*

4.   *2nd, Omaha ➜ W*

5.   *difficult, blast, mts, ☺, Native Amer.*

(6.)   *1869, met, UT, golden spike*

(7.)   *TRR, replaced, canals, goods + ppl*

Clincher

Tell back the facts on the fused outline in complete sentences. Fix any notes you do not understand. For the clincher, repeat or reflect two or three key words from the topic line.

The fact that *the TRR was called "the most monumental feat of the 19th century"* is not in the fused KWO because the idea could be used in a clincher sentence. If the exact words are used, however, they should be placed in quotation marks.

Sample

Source Outlines

The topic sentence tells what a paragraph is about.
Write the topic of your third paragraph on the line below.   **1 paragraph = 1 topic**

Third Topic: _Automobile, the transportation milestone which transformed America_

Using key words, write the topic on the Roman numeral line of each source outline. Each topic line will have the same words. Look at the appropriate paragraphs of the source texts and note three to five interesting facts about the topic. Since each topic is only found in two of the sources, you will only complete two source outlines.

Source A: *"Milestones in American Transportation"*

III. Topic: _automobile, transformed, America_

   1. _Henry Ford, car, affordable, ppl_

   2. _built, quickly, cheaply_

   3. _assembly line, ++ cars =_

  (4.) _Model T, ppl, "Tin Lizzie"_

  (5.) _1927, 15 mil, sold, most, Amer._

Source B: *"Transportation Innovations of the 1800s"*

III. Topic: _This source does not contain information about the automobile._

   1. _____

   2. _____

   3. _____

  (4.) _____

  (5.) _____

Institute for Excellence in Writing

Sample

Source C: *"Transporting Americans"*

III. Topic: __automobile, transformed, America__

  1. ____1900s, HF, "motor car > multitude," X $$____

  2. ____1929, 26 mil, sold, since, 1st____

  3. ____transformed, Amer, ↑, industry____

  (4.) ____ppl, outside, cities, suburbs____

  (5.) ____Model T, symbol, modernization____

Fused Outline

Place the topic you are writing about on the topic line. Select five to seven facts from the source outlines to transfer to the fused outline.

III. Topic: __automobile, transformed, America__

  1. ____1900s, HF, car, affordable, ppl____

  2. ____built, quickly, cheaply____

  3. ____assembly line, ++ cars =____

  4. ____Model T, ppl, "Tin Lizzy"____

  5. ____1927, 15 mil, sold, most, Amer.____

  (6.) ____caused, industries, ↑____

  (7.) ____ppl, outside, cities, suburbs____

Clincher

Tell back the facts on the fused outline in complete sentences. Fix any notes you do not understand. For the clincher, repeat or reflect two or three key words from the topic line.

HF = Henry Ford. Since his full name has already been noted, the initials can now replace it.

Style Practice

Sentence Openers

The checklist will require that you include all of the sentence openers you have been introduced to thus far. Write sentences that can be used in your paragraph.

1. #2 prepositional opener ____*[2] In the 1900s Henry Ford manufactured the Model T.*____

    _____

2. #3 -ly adverb opener ____*[3] Diligently Ford worked on a way to mass produce cars that*____

    ____*would be affordable.*____

3. #6 vss opener, 2–5 words ____*[6] Cars transformed America.*____

    _____

Dress-Ups

Look at your KWO and consider where you can include various clauses as well as strong verbs, quality adjectives, and -ly adverbs. When you write your paper, follow your checklist!

Vocabulary Practice

Look at the vocabulary words for Lesson 18. Fill in the blanks with a word that makes sense.

1. _____*Innovative*_____ men transformed transportation in the 1800s.

2. New modes of transportation brought _____*profound*_____ changes to America.

Look at the vocabulary chart on pages 322–323. Try to use words from Lessons 1–18 in sentences or phrases that could be in your report. Write at least two ideas below.

___*Ford **cunningly conceived** the idea of an assembly line.*___

___*The automobile industry was **thriving**, and the Model T was **prominent**.*___

Unit 6 Composition Checklist
Lesson 18: Transportation Milestones, Part 2

Summarizing
Multiple
References

IEW Institute for Excellence in Writing

Name: _____

STRUCTURE

☐ MLA format (see Appendix I) _____ 2 pts

☐ title centered and repeats 1–3 key words from final sentence _____ 2 pts

☐ topic-clincher sentences repeat or reflect 2–3 key words (highlight or bold) _____ 2 pts

☐ bibliography entries in proper format _____ 5 pts

☐ checklist on top, final draft, rough draft, key word outline _____ 2 pts

STYLE

¶2 ¶3 Dress-Ups (underline one of each) (1 pt each)

☐ ☐ -ly adverb _____ 2 pts

☐ ☐ *who/which* clause _____ 2 pts

☐ ☐ strong verb _____ 2 pts

☐ ☐ *because* clause _____ 2 pts

☐ ☐ quality adjective _____ 2 pts

☐ ☐ *www.asia* clause _____ 2 pts

Sentence Openers (number; one of each as possible) (1 pt each)

☐ ☐ [2] prepositional _____ 2 pts

☐ ☐ [3] -ly adverb _____ 2 pts

☐ ☐ [6] vss _____ 2 pts

CHECK FOR BANNED WORDS (-1 pt for each use): go/went, say/said, good, bad, pretty, big, small _____ pts

MECHANICS

☐ capitalization _____ 1 pt

☐ end marks and punctuation _____ 1 pt

☐ complete sentences (Does it make sense?) _____ 1 pt

☐ correct spelling _____ 1 pt

VOCABULARY

☐ vocabulary words - label *(voc)* in left margin or after sentence

Total: _____ 35 pts

Custom Total: _____ pts

The checklist indicates ¶2 and ¶3 because this checklist is for the second and third paragraph of the 3-paragraph composition. ¶1 was written in the last lesson.

Teachers are free to adjust a checklist by requiring only the stylistic techniques that have become easy, plus one new one. EZ+1

UNIT 6: SUMMARIZING MULTIPLE REFERENCES

Intentionally blank so the checklist can be removed.

Institute for Excellence in Writing

Lesson 19: The Sinking of the *Lusitania*

Structure:	Unit 6: Summarizing Multiple References
Style:	no new style
Writing Topic:	the *Lusitania*
Literature Suggestion:	*Hattie Big Sky* by Kirby Larson

UNIT 6: SUMMARIZING MULTIPLE REFERENCES

Lesson 19: The Sinking of the *Lusitania*

Goals

- to practice the Unit 6 structural model
- to create source outlines from multiple references
- to create a fused outline
- to write a 2-paragraph report about the *Lusitania*
- to review vocabulary words

Assignment Schedule

Day 1

1. Complete the Review.

2. In this lesson you will write a 2-paragraph report about the *Lusitania* using a source text provided in this lesson as well as two additional sources that you found at the library or from the Internet. Then you will add a bibliography page.

3. Before you begin taking notes, you must determine what topics are available to write about. The subject is the *Lusitania*. Scan each source text to discern possible topics. You will likely find the description of the ship, events and warnings prior to the sinking, how it sunk, and reactions to the sinking from America as well as other nations. There will be many topics on this subject.

4. Read Structure—Refining the Topic.

5. For your first paragraph, choose a topic that is covered in at least two sources. It is possible that the topic you choose may not be covered in the source text provided in this lesson. Write the topic on the topic line on page 190. Follow the pattern: *subject*, *topic*, one more word *about the topic*. Complete the source outlines using the sources that contain information about your topic.

6. Using notes from your source outlines, write a fused outline.

Day 2

1. For the second paragraph, choose another topic that is covered in at least two sources. Write the topic on the topic line on page 192. Again, follow the pattern: *subject*, *topic*, one more word *about the topic*. Complete the source outlines using the sources that contain information about your topic.

2. Using notes from your source outlines, write a fused outline.

3. Complete Style Practice.

4. Complete vocabulary practice. There are no new words for this lesson.

In this lesson the report subject (*Lusitania*) is assigned. Students will need to choose their own topics.

In Lessons 17–18 simplified source texts were provided; therefore, identifying topics to write about was relatively easy.

In this lesson one source text is provided. Students must also find sources outside of this book. Encourage students to look for books in the juvenile section of the library or Internet articles labeled "for kids." It will be easier to identify topics in these types of sources than it will be in longer, more mature sources.

5. Using your fused outlines as a guide, begin writing your rough draft.

6. Go over the checklist. Put a check in the box for each requirement you have completed.

Day 3

1. Review all vocabulary words learned thus far.

2. Finish writing your 2-paragraph report. Ensure you follow the topic-clincher rule.

3. Write a bibliography that includes all three sources you used. Follow the format on page 177.

4. Turn in your rough draft and bibliography to your editor with the completed checklist attached.

Day 4

1. Write or type a final draft making any corrections your editor asked you to make.

2. Paperclip the checklist, final draft, rough draft, and KWO together. Hand them in.

Literature Suggestion

Continue reading *Hattie Big Sky* by Kirby Larson.

Review

Play Tic-Tac-Toe with questions provided in the Teacher's Manual.

What must you do when you write the name of a ship?

How do you punctuate a date when it is placed in the middle of a sentence?

Review

When you write a report, the names of ships are italicized. If a report is handwritten, the ship name is underlined. (See Appendix III.)

When a date includes the month, day, and year, place a comma between the day and year. If the date is placed in the middle of a sentence, place a comma on both sides of the year. (See Appendix III.)

Tic-Tac-Toe

1. What is a fused outline? *(An outline made by selecting facts from multiple source outlines. It is the outline from which the paragraph will be written.)*

2. Once you know your subject and have chosen your topics for a report from multiple sources, will your first set of outlines be all from the same source or all for the same topic? *(topic)*

3. When writing source outlines, what should you write on the top (Roman numeral) line of each? *(the topic of the paragraph you are working on)*

4. What is a bibliography and where is it placed? *(a list of sources used, placed after the report as a separate page)*

5. In what order should you list your sources on a bibliography? *(alphabetical)*

6. Do you indent the first line of each entry on a bibliography? *(no)*

7. If a bibliography entry (one of your sources) requires more than one line, what must you do to the second line? *(indent five spaces)*

8. What should a bibliography entry begin with, if known? *(author's last name, first name)*

9. In a bibliography what must you do to titles of websites? *(italicize)*

10. In a bibliography what must you do to titles of articles within a website? *(quotation marks)*

Use vocabulary definitions if more questions are needed. Students answer by telling the vocabulary word.

Source A

The *Lusitania*

The *Lusitania* was a British luxury liner completed in 1906. At that time it was
the largest passenger ship in the world. The British Admiralty had helped build
it in order to compete with German passenger ships. It was, therefore, made part
of the Royal Naval Fleet Reserve. This means it could be used by the military if
necessary. The newest, fastest turbine engines powered the ship. It boasted 50%
more passenger space than any other ship. It could carry 3,048 passengers and
crew, and it flaunted seven first class decks. The ship routinely traveled across the
Atlantic Ocean between Liverpool, England, and New York.

The *Lusitania* became famous not for her luxurious journeys across the
Atlantic Ocean but for her tragic sinking. During World War I, Britain and
Germany were enemies. America was neutral for a while. Germany declared the
waters around Britain a war zone. They warned that they would not hesitate to fire
at any ship in those waters. In fact, both the German Embassy and the American
government published warnings in many newspapers advising Americans not to
travel in the waters around Britain. One of these warnings was placed directly
across from an advertisement for the *Lusitania*, which would soon leave
New York.

In May of 1915, the *Lusitania* made journey number 202 across the Atlantic.
The British Admiralty had warned the captain to avoid the waters around Ireland,
but the captain did not take heed. The ship was just eleven miles from Ireland when
it was hit by a German torpedo. The captain tried to take the crippled ship to shore,

but is was no use. The ship was sinking quickly. He ordered all to abandon ship. The 787-foot-long ship sank in twenty minutes. The crew did not have enough time to put more than six of the forty-eight life boats in the water. As a result, more than a thousand passengers perished.

The sinking of this passenger ship angered the world, including America, which lost 128 people in the attack. Germany tried to justify the attack by claiming that the ship was carrying war supplies and ammunition. While it likely was carrying supplies, the ship was not armed. Even though it had been built with mounts for cannons, the weapons were never added. Many Americans believed America should enter the war. A flood of books and articles were written urging Americans to prepare for war. In response, Congress passed and President Woodrow Wilson signed the Army Reorganization Bill that increased troops to 200,000. However, President Wilson still wanted to stay out of the war. It was not until 1917 after Germany had sunk several American merchant ships that America declared war. The phrase "Remember the *Lusitania*" helped recruit and embolden soldiers.

Bibliography

Verstegen, Lori. "The *Lusitania*." *U.S. History-Based Writing Lessons*, Locust
    Grove: Institute for Excellence in Writing, 2020, pp. 187–188.

When students fail to refine their topics, they often write paragraphs that contain an odd collection of facts about a subject. It can sound like a grocery list.

Guide students to choose the third word for the topic line by asking questions. If the topic is ship, ask, "what kind of ship?" or "what about the ship?"

New Structure
Refining the Topic

The topic sentence tells what the paragraph is about. When you write your KWO, you begin by placing key words on the topic line. When writing multi-paragraph compositions, it helps to follow the pattern: *subject*, *topic*, one more word *about the topic*.

Subject

The subject of a report is the entire thing being written about. For this assignment the subject is the *Lusitania*. The first word you place on the KWO topic line is *Lusitania*.

Topic

The topics are the divisions—the things within the subject. Because the assignment is to write two paragraphs, you must scan the source texts and find two topics about the *Lusitania*.

if 1 topic = 1 paragraph
then 2 topics = 2 paragraphs

The second word you place on the KWO will indicate your chosen topic. If you choose to describe the ship, you may write *ship*. If you choose to write about events prior to the sinking, you may write *events*. If you choose to write about warnings from Germany, you may write *Ger. warnings*. If you choose to describe the sinking, you may write *sinking*. If you choose to write about various nations' reactions, you may write *reactions*. Many possibilities exist.

About the Topic

A well written paragraph will be focused. You do not want it to sound like a list of items. To further narrow the topic, choose one specific thing to focus on by asking *what about the topic?*

When you chose your topic, if you chose ship description, you will now ask *what about the ship?* Your answer becomes the third word on KWO topic line.

If you choose to describe the Lusitania as a luxury liner, your KWO topic line may look like this: Topic: I. *Lusitania, ship, luxury*

If you choose to describe the Lusitania as a resource for the British Naval Force, your KWO topic line may look like this: Topic: I. *Lusitania, ship, naval*

The three key words you place on the topic line determine the facts that you search for during the research process.

By refining a topic, students are forced to limit the type of information they choose to insert on the KWO and ultimately in the paragraph. This results in a more focused paragraph with facts that support, prove, and illustrate the topic.

Sample

Source Outlines

Write the name of the first topic you will research on the line below.

First Topic: ____*the Lusitania, a luxury liner*_____

Choose your first source. Write the title on the Source line. Using key words, write the topic on the Roman numeral line. Complete the source outline by noting three to five interesting facts about the topic. Repeat the process with the second source and, if applicable, with the third.

Source A: ___*The Lusitania*_____

I. Topic: ____*Lusitania, ship, luxury*_____

   1. _____*1906, ++ passenger, ship*_____

   2. _____*newest, fastest, turbine, eng.*_____

   3. _____*50%+, passenger, space, 3040 ppl*_____

  (4.) _____*7, 1st class decks, 787 ft. long*_____

  (5.) _____*mounts, cannons, 0 weapons*_____

Source B: _____

I. Topic: ____*Lusitania, ship, luxury*_____

   1. _____

   2. _____

   3. _____

  (4.) _____

  (5.) _____

Source C: _____

I. Topic: ____*Lusitania, ship, luxury*_____

   1. _____

   2. _____

   3. _____

  (4.) _____

  (5.) _____

Institute for Excellence in Writing

The topic indicates what the paragraph will be about. Therefore, the words on the topic lines of the source and fused outlines are identical. Only the fused outline has a clincher line because students write the paragraph using the fused outline.

Sample

Fused Outline

Source Outline A

I. Topic: _____

  1. _____

  2. _____

  3. _____

  (4.) _____

  (5.) _____

Source Outline B

I. Topic: _____

  1. _____

  2. _____

  3. _____

  (4.) _____

  (5.) _____

Source Outline C

I. Topic: _____

  1. _____

  2. _____

  3. _____

  (4.) _____

  (5.) _____

Fused Outline

I. Topic: _____

  1. _____

  2. _____

  3. _____

  4. _____

  5. _____

  (6.) _____

  (7.) _____

  Clincher

Place the topic you are writing about on the topic line. Select five to seven facts from the source outlines to transfer to the fused outline.

I. Topic: _Lusitania, ship, luxury_

  1. _The fused outline will depend upon each student's choice of topic and additional sources._

  2. _____

  3. _____

  4. _____

  5. _____

  (6.) _____

  (7.) _____

  Clincher

Tell back the facts on the fused outline in complete sentences. Fix any notes you do not understand. For the clincher, repeat or reflect two or three key words from the topic line.

Sample

Source Outlines

Write the name of the second topic you will research on the line below.

Second Topic: *the Lusitania, sunk by Germans in WWI*

Choose your first source. Write the title on the Source line. Using key words, write the topic on the Roman numeral line. Complete the source outline by noting three to five interesting facts about the topic. Repeat the process with the second source and, if applicable, with the third.

Source A: *The Lusitania*

II. Topic: *Lusitania, sunk, Germans, WWI*

   1.   *Germ, ⌒⌒⌒➤, Britain, war, zone*

   2.   *May, 1915, Lusitania, 202nd, journey*

   3.   *@ Ireland, torpedoed, sank, 20 min*

 (4.)   *> 1000, ppl, died, 128 Americans*

 (5.)   *Amer ☺, eventually, entered, WWI*

Source B:

II. Topic: *Lusitania, sunk Germans, WWI*

   1.

   2.

   3.

 (4.)

 (5.)

Source C:

II. Topic: *Lusitania, sunk Germans, WWI*

   1.

   2.

   3.

 (4.)

 (5.)

Sample

Fused Outline

Place the topic you are writing about on the topic line. Select five to seven facts from the source outlines to transfer to the fused outline.

II. Topic: *Lusitania, sunk Germans, WWI*

1.   *The fused outline will depend upon each student's choice of topic and additional sources.*

2. _____

3. _____

4. _____

5. _____

(6.) _____

(7.) _____

Clincher

Tell back the facts on the fused outline in complete sentences. Fix any notes you do not understand. For the clincher, repeat or reflect two or three key words from the topic line.

Style Practice

Sentence Openers

The checklist will require that you include all of the sentence openers you have been introduced to thus far. Write sentences that can be used in your paragraph.

1. #2 prepositional opener ___*[2] During its approach to Ireland, a German torpedo struck*___

   ___*the Lusitania.*___

2. #3 -ly adverb opener ___*[3] Immediately the ship began to sink.*___

   _____

3. #6 vss opener, 2–5 words ___*[6] The act outraged America.*___

   _____

Dress-Ups

Look at your KWO and consider where you can include various clauses as well as strong verbs, quality adjectives, and -ly adverbs. When you write your paper, follow your checklist!

Vocabulary Practice

Look at the vocabulary chart on pages 322–323. Try to use words from Lessons 1–18 in sentences or phrases that could be in your report. Write at least two ideas below.

___*Germany was **hostile** toward all ships in British waters and **audaciously** torpedoed the*___

___*Lusitania. **Inevitably**, America declared war on Germany.*___

Unit 6 Composition Checklist
Lesson 19: The Sinking of the *Lusitania*

Summarizing
Multiple
References

IEW Institute for Excellence in Writing

Name: _____

STRUCTURE

☐ MLA format (see Appendix I)	_____	1 pt
☐ title centered and repeats 1–3 key words from final sentence	_____	3 pts
☐ topic-clincher sentences repeat or reflect 2–3 **key** words (highlight or bold)	_____	5 pts
☐ bibliography entries in proper format	_____	5 pts
☐ checklist on top, final draft, rough draft, key word outline	_____	1 pt

STYLE

¶2 ¶3 Dress-Ups (underline one of each)   (2 pts each)

☐ ☐ -ly adverb	_____	4 pts
☐ ☐ *who/which* clause	_____	4 pts
☐ ☐ strong verb	_____	4 pts
☐ ☐ *because* clause	_____	4 pts
☐ ☐ quality adjective	_____	4 pts
☐ ☐ *www.asia* clause	_____	4 pts

Sentence Openers (number; one of each as possible)   (2 pts each)

☐ ☐ [2] prepositional	_____	4 pts
☐ ☐ [3] -ly adverb	_____	4 pts
☐ ☐ [6] vss	_____	4 pts

CHECK FOR BANNED WORDS (-1 pt for each use): go/went, say/said, good, bad, pretty, big, small   _____ pts

MECHANICS

☐ capitalization	_____	1 pt
☐ end marks and punctuation	_____	1 pt
☐ complete sentences (Does it make sense?)	_____	1 pt
☐ correct spelling	_____	1 pt

VOCABULARY

☐ vocabulary words - label *(voc)* in left margin or after sentence

Total:	_____	55 pts
Custom Total:	_____	pts

Teachers are free to adjust a checklist by requiring only the stylistic techniques that have become easy, plus one new one. EZ+1

Intentionally blank so the checklist can be removed.

Lesson 20: Hopes and Dreams, Part 1

Structure: Unit 7: Inventive Writing
body paragraphs

Style: no new style

Writing Topic: Statue of Liberty

Literature Suggestion: *Hattie Big Sky* by Kirby Larson

Teaching Writing: Structure and Style

Watch the sections for Unit 7: Inventive Writing. At IEW.com/twss-help reference the TWSS Viewing Guides.

Lesson 20: Hopes and Dreams, Part 1

UNIT 7: INVENTIVE WRITING

Lesson 20: Hopes and Dreams, Part 1

Goals

- to learn the Unit 7 Inventive Writing structural model
- to create a KWO from a writing prompt
- to write the body paragraphs of a 4-paragraph composition
- to correctly use new vocabulary words: *espouse, adverse, aspire, lofty*

Assignment Schedule

Day 1

1. Play a vocabulary game such as Around the World or Vocabulary Lightning.
2. Read New Structure—Inventive Writing: Body Paragraphs and the prompt.
3. Read Notes from the Brain and follow the instructions to write a 2-paragraph KWO.

Day 2

1. Complete Style Practice.
2. Look at the vocabulary cards for Lesson 20. Discuss the words and their definitions and complete Vocabulary Practice.
3. Using your KWO as a guide, begin writing your 2-paragraph rough draft.
4. Go over the checklist. Put a check in the box for each requirement you have completed.

Day 3

1. Review all vocabulary words learned thus far.
2. Finish writing your 2-paragraph composition. Follow the topic-clincher rule.
3. Turn in your rough draft to your editor with the completed checklist attached.

Day 4

1. Write or type a final draft making any corrections your editor asked you to make.
2. Paperclip the checklist, final draft, rough draft, and KWO together. Hand them in.
3. If you are making a Magnum Opus Notebook, revise your Transportation Milestones composition from Lessons 17–18.

Note: Next week you will write an introduction and a conclusion to add to the paragraphs written for this lesson.

> Study for Vocabulary Quiz 5. It will cover words from Lessons 1–20.

In this new unit students do not have a source text or even pictures to look at. The KWO is formed by asking good questions. Key words for the outline are found in the answers to the questions. Be patient with yourself and your student. This is a practicable skill that will take time to perfect.

Literature Suggestion

Continue reading *Hattie Big Sky* by Kirby Larson.

New Structure

Inventive Writing: Body Paragraphs

In Unit 7 you will write compositions that begin with an introduction and end with a conclusion. Look at the 5-paragraph model below: three body paragraphs plus an introduction and a conclusion. The model can be adapted by simply changing the number of body paragraphs.

	I.	Introduction	*attention getter, background, state topics*
Body	II.	Topic A	*topic, 5–7 details, clincher*
	III.	Topic B	*topic, 5–7 details, clincher*
Paragraphs	IV.	Topic C	*topic, 5–7 details, clincher*
	V.	Conclusion	*restate topics, most significant/why, last sentence ➜ title*

Your entire composition should be about one subject. Once you know what the subject of the composition is, you determine how many body paragraphs to write. Once you know the number of body paragraphs, you determine the topics. Each body paragraph equals one topic. When you follow this model, write from the inside out beginning with the body paragraphs.

Sometimes you are given a prompt and asked to write a response. Where do you find the information for your paper? When learning to write from the "blank page," one technique to help develop content is to ask yourself questions. In Unit 5 when you wrote from a series of pictures, you began with brain-helping questions. You will again use those same questions in Unit 7. The ability to ask questions and develop answers is the core skill required for all inventive writing.

Analyze the prompt below and then ask yourself questions.

> ### Prompt
>
> The Statue of Liberty was a gift from France to America. The statue symbolizes the freedom and opportunity for which America is known. Standing in New York Harbor, she holds a torch in one hand and the Declaration of Independence in the other. Broken chains lie at her feet. Lady Liberty represents the hopes and dreams of a bright future for the many immigrants who have come to America since 1886.
>
> What hopes and dreams do you have for your future? Write about two things you hope to do or accomplish in either the near or far future.

Notice that the first body paragraph begins with Roman numeral II. The first paragraph of the composition will be written in Lesson 21.

Notes from the Brain

When learning to write from the "blank page," one technique to help come up with content is to ask yourself questions about the prompt. Based on the prompt, what is the subject of this composition? Does the prompt provide a clue to how many body paragraphs you need to write to complete the assignment?

The prompt for this lesson assigned the subject of your paper—your hopes and dreams. Because the prompt directs you to *write about two things you hope to do or accomplish,* you will write two paragraphs. Each paragraph will be about a specific hope or dream. The topic sentence of each paragraph will state a specific hope or dream that you have. Begin by writing your topics on the Roman numeral lines of the KWO. Follow this pattern:

hopes/dreams (subject), topic, one more word *about the topic.*

When choosing a topic consider what you might like to do or places you might like to visit. Think also about goals you would like to reach in school, sports, hobbies, or other extracurricular activities. Do you know what occupation you may pursue when you grow up? How do you picture your life as an adult?

if 1 topic = 1 paragraph

then 2 topics = 2 paragraphs

On the lines under the first Roman numeral, describe the first topic by asking yourself questions. Brain-helping questions are listed on the KWO. These helpful questions include:

Who might be part of my hope or dream?

When would I like to accomplish it?

What must I do now or in the future in order to accomplish it?

Why do I want to do it?

How can I prepare?

Where will I be? **What** will I see, hear, feel?

What will I **do**? **think**? **feel**?

The answers to your questions become the details for the outline. As you answer a question, place two or three key words on the KWO. Use symbols, numbers, and abbreviations when possible. You do not have to answer every question, nor do you need to ask in the order they are written. Keep your answers brief. You can add more details when you write your composition.

Repeat this process for the second topic.

Help the students ask questions to discover possible topics. As they ask and answer questions, make a list of possible topics.

Once students have chosen two topics to write about, ask additional questions to refine the topic. If a students dreams of traveling, ask where, how, or when.

If a student hopes to become a teacher, ask what kind (*art, history, computers*) and where (*classroom, online, church*).

As students ask questions, encourage them to write their answers using key words on the KWO.

The key to the process is asking questions.

In this lesson students write two body paragraphs. Once the composition is completed, these paragraphs will be the second and third paragraphs of the paper. Thus, the first body paragraph is marked with Roman numeral II and the second with III.

The key to the process is asking questions. Here are the questions asked that resulted in the sample KWO.

Topic A

What is the subject? (*hope*)

What is your specific topic for this paragraph? Which hope or dream will you write about? (*traveling*)

Where do you dream of traveling? (*American National Parks*)

1. Who will you travel with?

2. How will you travel and for how long?

3. Which parks do you especially want to visit?

4. What will you do and how will you feel while doing it? (notes 4–5)

5. What do you want to see? Describe what you think they will look like. (notes 6–7)

Topic B

What is the subject? (*hope*)

What is your specific topic for this paragraph? Which hope or dream will you write about? (*becoming a teacher*)

What kind of a teacher? (*elementary school*)

1. Why would you like to be a teacher?

2. Why do you prefer elementary school?

3. What do you think is the most important thing to teach?

4. How can you prepare to become a teacher?

5. What do you like in your teachers?

6. What do you mean by kind and fun? Give examples of what kind, fun teachers do. (notes 6–7)

UNIT 7: INVENTIVE WRITING

Sample

II. Topic A: hope, travel, Amer. parks

   1.   w/ Dad, Mom, brother

   2.   RV, all, summer

   3.   Yosemite, Yellowstone

   4.   hike, awestruck, hills, + 🌳

   5.   swim, refreshed, carefree

  (6.) 👀, ++ bison, cute, p. dogs

  (7.) gushing, geysers, hot springs

Clincher

III. Topic B: hope, teacher, elementary

   1.   I, ♥, learn, share

   2.   children, admire, teachers

   3.   teach, subjects + character

   4.   👀, my, teachers, examples

   5.   like, ☺ kind, fun

  (6.) encouraging, words, inspire

  (7.) games, motivate

Clincher

?

who?
what?
when?
where?
why?
how?
how feel?
problems?
solutions?
best thing?
worst thing?
value?
significance?
meaning?
examples?
description?

Style Practice

Sentence Openers

The checklist will require that you include all of the sentence openers you have been introduced to thus far. Write sentences that can be used in your body paragraphs.

1. #2 prepositional opener *[2] During our hike I would stop to sketch some of the wildlife nearby.*

2. #3 -ly adverb opener *[3] Eagerly I read all kinds of books.*

3. #6 vss opener, 2–5 words *[6] Numerous adventures await.*

Dress-Ups

Write ideas for various dress-up you could use in your body paragraphs. Use a thesaurus or your vocabulary words.

1. strong verbs ***venture*, *encounter*, *desire*, *value*, *admire*, *esteem***

2. -ly adverbs ***diligently*, *earnestly*, *zealously*, *prudently***

3. quality adjectives *stunning*, ***stupendous***, *expansive*, ***exemplary***

Vocabulary Practice

Look at the vocabulary words for Lesson 20. Fill in the blanks with a word that makes sense.

1. I _____ *aspire* _____ to be a mechanical engineer.

2. I may have _____ *lofty* _____ goals, but if I persist, I will succeed despite any adversity.

Look at the vocabulary chart on pages 322–323. Try to use words from Lessons 1–20 in sentences or phrases that could be in your composition. Write at least two ideas below.

*I am **awestruck** at the land's beauty.*

*Sometimes hopes and dreams require **diligent** or even **grueling** work to attain.*

Unit 7 Composition Checklist
Lesson 20: Hopes and Dreams, Part 1 body paragraphs

Inventive Writing

Institute for Excellence in Writing

Name: _____

STRUCTURE

☐ MLA format (see Appendix I) _____ 2 pts

☐ checklist on top, final draft, rough draft, key word outline _____ 2 pts

Body

☐ topic-clincher sentences repeat or reflect 2–3 key words (highlight or bold) _____ 5 pts

☐ facts stay on topic _____ 5 pts

STYLE

¶2 ¶3 Dress-Ups (underline one of each)   (2 pts each)

☐ ☐ -ly adverb _____ 4 pts

☐ ☐ *who/which* clause _____ 4 pts

☐ ☐ strong verb _____ 4 pts

☐ ☐ *because* clause _____ 4 pts

☐ ☐ quality adjective _____ 4 pts

☐ ☐ *www.asia* clause _____ 4 pts

Sentence Openers (number; one of each as possible)   (2 pts each)

☐ ☐ [2] prepositional _____ 4 pts

☐ ☐ [3] -ly adverb _____ 4 pts

☐ ☐ [6] vss _____ 4 pts

CHECK FOR BANNED WORDS (-1 pt for each use): go/went, say/said, good, bad, pretty, big, small _____ pts

MECHANICS

☐ spelling, grammar, and punctuation (-1 pt per error) _____ pts

VOCABULARY

☐ vocabulary words - label *(voc)* in left margin or after sentence

Total: _____ 50 pts

Custom Total: _____ pts

Teachers are free to adjust a checklist by requiring only the stylistic techniques that have become easy, plus one new one. EZ+1

UNIT 7: INVENTIVE WRITING

Intentionally blank so the checklist can be removed.

Lesson 21: Hopes and Dreams, Part 2

Structure:	Unit 7: Inventive Writing introduction and conclusion
Style:	#5 clausal opener, *www.asia.b* clause
Writing Topic:	Statue of Liberty
Literature Suggestion:	*Hattie Big Sky* by Kirby Larson

UNIT 7: INVENTIVE WRITING

Lesson 21: Hopes and Dreams, Part 2

Goals

- to practice the Unit 7 structural model
- to create KWOs for an introduction and a conclusion paragraph
- to write an introduction and a conclusion paragraph
- to complete a 4-paragraph composition
- to correctly add a new sentence opener: #5 clausal opener
- to take Vocabulary Quiz 5
- to correctly use new vocabulary words: *enthrall, persistent, emblem, elated*

Assignment Schedule

Day 1

1. Take Vocabulary Quiz 5.
2. Play Find the *www.asia* Clause Starters.
3. Read New Structure—Inventive Writing: Introduction and Conclusion. Both paragraphs have their own unique structure. Take time to memorize the components.
4. Write a KWO for a conclusion and then write a KWO for an introduction.

Day 2

1. Review both KWOs from Day 1.
2. Read New Style and complete Style Practice.
3. Look at the vocabulary cards for Lesson 21. Discuss the words and their definitions and complete Vocabulary Practice.
4. Using your conclusion KWO as a guide, write your conclusion. Highlight or bold the topic key words.
5. Go over the checklist. Put a check in the box for each requirement you have completed.

Day 3

1. Review all vocabulary words learned thus far.
2. Using your introduction KWO as a guide, write your introduction. Highlight or bold the topic key words.
3. Turn in your rough draft to your editor with the completed checklist attached.

In this lesson students add an introduction paragraph and a conclusion paragraph to the body paragraphs written in Lesson 20. Help students understand that these paragraphs are not about specific topics. Therefore, neither contain topic nor clincher sentences. Both paragraphs follow their own unique structure.

Encourage students to memorize the components of the introduction and of the conclusion.

Day 4

1. Write or type a final draft making any corrections your editor asked you to make. Add the introduction and the conclusion to the final draft body paragraphs written in Lesson 20.

2. Paperclip the checklist, final draft, rough drafts, and KWOs together. Hand them in.

3. If you are making a Magnum Opus Notebook, revise your *Lusitania* composition from Lesson 19.

Literature Suggestion

Finish reading *Hattie Big Sky* by Kirby Larson.

Acquire *Journey to Topaz* by Yoshiko Uchida to read for Lessons 22–25.

New Structure

Inventive Writing: Introduction and Conclusion

Now that you have completed the body paragraphs, you are ready to add the introduction and conclusion. Look at the model below and notice the components that make up the introduction and conclusion. These two paragraphs are not about specific topics. Therefore, neither contain topic nor clincher sentences. Both paragraphs follow their own unique structure.

I.   Introduction   *attention getter, background, state topics*

          Body Paragraphs

IV.   Conclusion   *restate topics, most significant/why, last sentence ➜ title*

Read sample paragraphs on page 210. The introduction must get the readers' attention by enticing readers to keep reading. It also introduces the readers to the subject of the paper and states the topics. The conclusion reminds the readers of the topics and then indicates what is most important about the subject and why. The conclusion also brings finality to the paper.

It is important that the conclusion flows smoothly from the final body paragraph. Since you have just written the body paragraphs and the details are fresh on your mind, you will outline and write the conclusion before you write the introduction.

Key Word Outline—Conclusion

Restate the Topics

> Write a sentence or two about each topic. Try to convey the main idea of each body paragraph; in other words, reword the topic sentences. Highlight or bold the topic key words.

Most Significant and Why

> What is the most important, most interesting, or most significant thing to remember about all that you wrote and why? You may consider explaining why it is important to have hopes and dreams. You may tell what impact hopes and dreams have on you now or how they may impact your future. You may choose one of your topics and tell why it is the most significant, or you may choose something that tells the importance of the entire subject.

Final Sentence

> End with a sentence from which you can create a title. Be sure that your paper sounds complete.

Sample

Key Word Outline for Conclusion

IV.   Topic A: _____ *hope, travel, Amer. Parks* _____

      Topic B: _____ *hope, teacher, elementary* _____

      Most significant _____ *accomplish, both* _____

      Why? _____ *future, excites, motivates* _____

      _____ *work + determination, possible* _____

      _____ *new, adventures, X fear* _____

Title repeats 1–3 key words from final sentence.

Highlight or bold the topic key words in your paragraph.

Key Word Outline—Introduction

Attention Getter

Start your introduction with a sentence that encourages your reader to continue reading. Create three different attention getters. When you are done, choose the one you like the best.

1. Ask your reader a question.

    Example*: Who doesn't have hopes and dreams?*

    Write a question that you might use to begin your introduction:

    What do you look forward to?

2. Write a very short sentence (#6 vss).

    Example*: Dreams motivate.*

    Write a very short sentence that you might use to begin your introduction:

    Dreams can become reality.

3. State a famous quote or fact. (If you do not know one, search on the Internet for a quote about hopes and dreams.)

    Example*: "If you can dream it, you can do it" (Walt Disney).*

    Write a quote or fact that you might use to begin your introduction:

    "In every walk with nature one receives far more than he seeks" (John Muir).

Transition smoothly from your attention getter to your background information. This may require the addition of one or two sentences.

Background

Tell your reader what the subject of the composition is about but do not say anything similar to "*This composition is about ... .*" Simply make a general statement about the subject. Then provide background information you think would be interesting or important. The background information should flow into the introduction of the topics.

Topics

End your introduction by listing the topics you wrote about in your body paragraphs in the same order they appear in the body of the paper. You can write a sentence about each topic or simply list the topics in one sentence. Highlight or bold the topic key words.

Sample

Key Word Outline for Introduction

I.   Attention getter   *quote by Harriet Tubman*

    Background   *desire, extraordinary, things*

                               👤 👤*, dreams, lofty, impossible*

                                 my, dreams, doable

    Topic A: *hope, travel, Amer. parks*

    Topic B: *hope, teacher, elementary*

Highlight or bold the topic key words in your paragraph.

Sample Paragraphs

Introduction

[Attention getter] "Every great dream begins with a dreamer. Always remember, you have within you the strength, the patience, and the passion to reach for the stars to change the world" (Harriet Tubman). [Background] [3] Surely, we all desire to do extraordinary things. Some people's dreams <u>strike</u> us as a bit lofty and <u>practically</u> impossible. [6] My dreams, though, are doable. [Topics] [5] Because I love to travel and love to be outdoors, I want to **travel** across America and camp, hike, and backpack in as many of our scenic national parks as possible. [2] After that, when it is time to settle into a career, I hope to become a **teacher** <u>because</u> I desire to be an <u>exemplary</u> role model for children, <u>who</u> learn by example.

Conclusion

[Restate the topics] [2] In the not-too-far future, I hope to pack an RV and **trek** through America's <u>stunning</u> national parks with my family. [5] When I finish college, I hope to <u>powerfully</u> impact the lives of children by working as a **teacher**. [1] These hopes and dreams, <u>which</u> give me things to aspire towards as I think of my future, excite me. [6] They <u>motivate</u> me. [Most significant] [3] Most importantly, I know of no reason I cannot accomplish both [Why] <u>because</u> with a little work and determination anything is possible. [4] Desiring to experience new adventures, I will never be afraid to set another goal or dream a new dream.

The #5 clausal opener and the *www.asia.b* dress-up are formed exactly the same way. The only difference is the position in the sentence. Openers begin sentences; dress-ups do not.

Teach students the comma rules: *adverb clause, main clause (AC, MC)* and *main clause no comma adverb clause (MC AC)*.

New Style

#5 Clausal Opener

In this lesson you will learn another sentence opener: the #5 clausal opener.

The clausal opener is an adverb clause placed at the beginning of a sentence. The clausal opener begins with one of these words: *when, while, where, as, since, if, although, because.*

This should look familiar. The *because* clause dress-up and the *www.asia* clause dress-up will now be combined into one dress-up called the *www.asia.b* clause dress-up.

> [5] When I grow up, I plan to be a nurse.
>
> I plan to be a nurse <u>when</u> I grow up.

www.asia.b
when
while
where
as
since
if
although
because

Notice:

1. A *www.asia.b* clause that begins a sentence is called a clausal opener. Label it with a 5 in the left margin or place a [5] right before the sentence.

2. A *www.asia.b* clause placed in the middle or end of the sentence is called a *www.asia.b* dress-up. Mark it by underlining the first word of the clause.

3. A *www.asia.b* clause contains a subject and a verb.

   > [5] When *I grow* up, I plan to be a nurse.
   >
   > I plan to be a nurse <u>when</u> *I grow* up.

4. A *www.asia.b* clause is added to a sentence that is already complete.

   > [5] When I grow up, *I plan to be a nurse.*
   >
   > *I plan to be a nurse* <u>when</u> I grow up.

❦ If the *www.asia.b* clause is at the beginning of the sentence, follow the entire clause with a comma. We do not usually put a comma before a *www.asia.b* clause.

Practice

Write a sentence with a #5 clausal opener. Remember to insert a comma. Label it with a [5].

[5] While I attend school, I can study and prepare for my career.

 From now on, include two *www.asia.b* clauses—a clausal opener and a *www.asia.b* dress-up in each paragraph you write. Label the opener with a 5 in the margin or place a [5] before the sentence. Underline the dress-up. There are now five, not six, dress-ups on the checklist.

Style Practice

Sentence Openers

The checklist will require that you include all of the sentence openers you have been introduced to thus far. Write sentences that can be used in your introduction or conclusion.

1. #2 prepositional opener *[2] With hard word and resolve, I will realize my dream.*

    _____

2. #3 -ly adverb opener *[3] Earnestly I desire to help others.*

    _____

3. #5 clausal opener – *www.asia.b* *[5] As I think of my future, I imagine myself as an engineer.*

    _____

4. #6 vss opener, 2–5 words (This can be your attention getter.) *[6] Dreams motivate.*

    _____

Dress-Ups

Look at your KWO and consider where you can include various clauses as well as strong verbs, quality adjectives, and -ly adverbs. When you write your paper, follow your checklist!

Vocabulary Practice

Look at the vocabulary words for Lesson 21. Fill in the blanks with a word that makes sense.

1. I would be _____*elated*_____ if this dream came true.

2. If I am _____*persistent*_____ , I will achieve my goal of finishing a marathon.

Look at the vocabulary chart on pages 322–323. Try to use words from Lessons 1–21 in sentences or phrases that could be in your composition. Write at least two ideas below.

*I will **zealously** pursue my dream without **wavering**.*

*I can **persevere** through **adverse** circumstances to reach my goals.*

Unit 7 Composition Checklist

Inventive
Writing

Lesson 21: Hopes and Dreams, Part 2 introduction and conclusion

Name: _____

Institute for Excellence in Writing

STRUCTURE

☐ MLA format (see Appendix I)	_____	2 pts
☐ title centered	_____	2 pts
☐ checklist on top, final draft, rough draft, key word outline	_____	1 pt

Introduction

☐ introduction includes attention getter, background information, **and** states topics (bold or highlight)	_____	10 pts

Body

☐ insert body paragraphs	_____	2 pts

Conclusion

☐ conclusion restates topics (**bold** or highlight) and **indicates** most significant/why	_____	10 pts
☐ final sentence repeats 1–3 key words for the title	_____	2 pts

STYLE

¶1 ¶4 Dress-Ups (underline one of each)   (2 pts each)

☐	☐	-ly adverb	_____	4 pts
☐	☐	*who/which* clause	_____	4 pts
☐	☐	strong verb	_____	4 pts
☐	☐	quality adjective	_____	4 pts
☐	☐	*www.asia.b* clause	_____	4 pts

Sentence Openers (number; one of each as possible)   (2 pts each)

☐	☐	[2] prepositional	_____	4 pts
☐	☐	[3] -ly adverb	_____	4 pts
☐	☐	[5] clausal - *www.asia.b*	_____	4 pts
☐	☐	[6] vss	_____	4 pts

CHECK FOR BANNED WORDS (-1 pt for each use): go/went, say/said, good, bad, pretty, big, small   _____ pts

MECHANICS

☐ spelling, grammar, and punctuation (-1 pt per error)	_____	pts

VOCABULARY

☐ vocabulary words - label *(voc)* in left margin or after sentence	

Total:	_____	65 pts
Custom Total:	_____	pts

Teachers are free to adjust a checklist by requiring only the stylistic techniques that have become easy, plus one new one. EZ+1

UNIT 7: INVENTIVE WRITING

Intentionally blank so the checklist can be removed.

Institute for Excellence in Writing

Lesson 22: The Preamble to the Constitution, Part 1

Structure:	Unit 7: Inventive Writing body paragraphs
Style:	no new style
Writing Topic:	purpose and goals of the Preamble
Literature Suggestion:	*Journey to Topaz* by Yoshiko Uchida

Lesson 22: The Preamble to the Constitution, Part 1

UNIT 7: INVENTIVE WRITING

Lesson 22: The Preamble to the Constitution, Part 1

Goals

- to practice the Unit 7 structural model
- to create a KWO from a writing prompt
- to write the body paragraphs of a 5-paragraph composition
- to review vocabulary words

Assignment Schedule

Day 1

1. Play No-Noose Hangman.
2. Read Historical Information and the writing assignment prompt.
3. Read Structure—Notes from the Brain. Follow instructions to write a 3-paragraph KWO.

Day 2

1. Review your KWO from Day 1.
2. Complete Style Practice.
3. Complete Vocabulary Practice. There are no new words for this lesson.
4. Using your KWO as a guide, begin writing your 3-paragraph rough draft.
5. Go over the checklist. Put a check in the box for each requirement you have completed.

Day 3

1. Review all vocabulary words learned thus far.
2. Finish writing the three body paragraphs of your composition. Follow the topic-clincher rule.
3. Turn in your rough draft to your editor with the completed checklist attached.

Day 4

1. Write or type a final draft making any corrections your editor asked you to make.
2. Paperclip the checklist, final draft, rough draft, and KWO together. Hand them in.

Note: Next week you will write an introduction and a conclusion to add to the paragraphs written for this lesson.

Literature Suggestion

Begin reading *Journey to Topaz* by Yoshiko Uchida.

No-Noose Hangman

For this lesson use the following phrases and bonus questions:

TOPICS, MOST SIGNIFICANT, WHY

Bonus: What will these words help you write? *a conclusion paragraph*

What are the components of an introduction paragraph? *attention getter, background, state the topics*

Ask students if they remembered to bold or highlight the words that tell the topics in the introduction and conclusion for Lesson 21.

ASK YOURSELF QUESTIONS

Bonus: Why do you ask yourself questions? *To get ideas for details in your paragraphs.* What are some question starter words? *Starter words are listed on page 200.*

Historical Information

Prior to the writing of the U.S. Constitution, the Articles of Confederation loosely governed America. Under this government, people considered themselves citizens of their state, not really of the country. Each state had its own laws, which might differ from its neighboring state. The Articles of Confederation did not provide for a very strong union of the states.

The Constitution of the United States of America established a new government for the country that bound the states together more closely as one nation. It created three branches of government and protected the basic rights of all citizens in every state. When it was first written, it included seven articles. It now additionally contains twenty-six amendments.

At the beginning of the document, the founding fathers placed a sentence that explains the purpose and goals. This sentence, called the Preamble to the Constitution, is written in italics below. It has been formatted so that you can easily see the purpose and goals. An explanation for each goal found within the Preamble is provided in the right column.

The Preamble to the U.S. Constitution

We, the people of the United States,

in order to form a more perfect union,	in order to have a form of government that will better bind the states together
establish justice,	to be sure all people are treated fairly, with a way to punish wrong and uphold what is right (a court system)
ensure domestic tranquility,	to be sure there is peace among the people throughout the country
provide for the common defense,	to protect all the states from foreign enemies (to form a military)
promote the general welfare,	to do what is best for all the people, not just a few wealthy or ruling people (equal rights)
and secure the blessings of liberty to ourselves and our posterity,	to keep our freedom and be sure our children and their children have the same freedom

do ordain and establish this Constitution for the United States of America.

Students begin by choosing three goals of the Constitution as stated in the Preamble. The sample KWO provides questions you may ask to generate key words for the topic line. For this assignment, students may write one or two key words from the chosen phrase on page 216 on their KWO. When they write their topic sentence from those words, they may copy the entire phrase, but if they do, be sure they understand that they must place it in quotation marks. For example, *The Preamble states that one goal of the Constitution is "to provide for the common defense."*

Lesson 22: The Preamble to the Constitution, Part 1

Prompt

Choose three of the goals stated in the Preamble of the U.S. Constitution. Explain each and, if necessary, define key words. Provide your thoughts about the specific goal and why it is important.

Structure

Notes from the Brain

After reading a prompt, you must determine the subject and length of the assignment. How do you do this? Ask yourself questions about the prompt. Based on the prompt, what is the subject of this composition? Does the prompt provide a clue to how many body paragraphs you need to write to complete the assignment?

The prompt for this lesson assigned the subject of your paper—the Preamble of the U.S. Constitution. Because the prompt directs you to choose three goals, you will write three paragraphs. Each paragraph will be about a specific goal. Begin by writing your topics on the Roman numeral lines of the KWO. Follow this pattern:

Preamble (subject), topic, one more word about the topic.

if 1 topic = 1 paragraph

then 3 topics = 3 paragraphs

On the lines under the first Roman numeral, describe the first topic by asking yourself questions. Brain-helping questions are listed on the KWO. These helpful questions include:

What is the definition of the important word or words of your topic?

Why is this goal important?

When or where is it most important?

What would happen if the goal were not accomplished?

What are some examples from history to support what you say?

What are some current examples to support what you say?

What are some personal examples to support what you say?

The answers to your questions become the details for the outline. As you answer a question, place two or three key words on the KWO. Use symbols, numbers, and abbreviations when possible. You do not have to answer every question or ask in the order they are written. Keep your answers brief. You can add more details when you write your composition.

Repeat this process for the second and third topics.

Examples to support points are important. Explain and give sample ideas.

For Historical Examples

For "establish justice," you might ask *Can you think of a time when a country did not have a fair justice system?* Possible answers could include *countries ruled by dictators, such as Germany under Hitler. What was that like?*

For Current Examples

For "promote the general welfare," you could ask, *How do all citizens benefit from the rights given in the Constitution?* An answer could be that *because discrimination is illegal, anyone can succeed.*

For Personal Examples

For "secure the blessings of liberty ... to our posterity," you could ask, *What does that mean for you personally?* Answers could include *freedom to attend church and worship without fear.*

The key to the process is asking questions. Here are the questions asked that resulted in the sample KWO.

Topic A

What is the subject? (*Preamble*)

What is your specific topic for this paragraph? Which goal stated in the Preamble will you write about? (*justice*)

What about justice will you focus on? (*the Constitution established it*)

1. What does *justice* mean? (See the chart on page 216.)

2. How did the Constitution establish justice?

3. How does a court system ensure all are treated fairly?

4. What might happen without a justice system?

5. What is an example in history of a country without justice? (notes 5–6)

6. Why won't that happen in America?

Topic B

What is the subject? (*Preamble*)

What is your specific topic for this paragraph? Which goal stated in the Preamble will you write about? (*defense*)

What about defense will you focus on? (*the Constitution provides*)

1. What does "*provide for the common defense*" mean?

2. How did the Constitution do this?

3. What is our military composed of?

4. How do they defend us?

5. How does our military compare to those of other countries?

6. Why is this important? (notes 6–7)

Sample

Key Word Outline

II. Topic A: Preamble, justice, establish, Const.
  1. j, = fair, all, + punish, 👮
  2. Const., formed, court, system
  3. accused, X jail, w/o, trial
  4. w/o ppl, jailed, X reason
  5. ex, Hitler, tyrannical, dictator
  (6.) persecuted, Jews, "undesirables"
  (7.) Amer, X dictator, ruled, Constitution
  Clincher

III. Topic B: Preamble, defense, provide
  1. safe, foreign, enemies
  2. Const., established, military
  3. Army, Air Force, Navy, Marines
  4. ready, fight, 24-7
  5. 1, strongest, world
  (6.) few, dare, attack
  (7.) live, peace, security
  Clincher

IV. Topic C: Preamble, liberty, preserve
  1. liberty= freedom, choose
  2. live, work, worship, ...
  3. brother, started, business
  4. Flikboard, toy, teens
  5. designed, printed, 3-D printer
  (6.) advertised, website, Instagram
  (7.) 6 mos, sold, >1000, learned, entreprenuership
  Clincher

?

who?

what?

when?

where?

why?

how?

how feel?

problems?

solutions?

best thing?

worst thing?

value?

significance?

meaning?

examples?

description?

Institute for Excellence in Writing

Style Practice

Sentence Openers

The checklist will require that you include all of the sentence openers you have been introduced to thus far. Write sentences that can be used in your body paragraphs.

1. #2 prepositional opener _____

    [2] In order to ensure justice for all, the Constitution formed a court system.

2. #3 -ly adverb opener _____

    [3] Thankfully, American citizens enjoy liberty today.

3. #5 clausal opener – *www.asia.b* _____

    [5] When enemies threaten, the American military is prepared to fight.

4. #6 vss opener, 2–5 words _____

    [6] America offers opportunity.

Dress-Ups

Write ideas for various dress-up you could use in your body paragraphs. Use a thesaurus or your vocabulary words.

1. strong verbs *create a strong government, uphold rights for all, safeguard the*

    *country, guarantee liberty, **affirm** the ideals of liberty and justice, foster peace,*

    *strive to offer opportunity and **prosperity** to all*

2. -ly adverbs ____ ***innovatively**, boldly, **diligently**, clearly, explicitly*

    _____

3. quality adjectives *equitable, impartial, unbiased, **formidable, prosperous***

    _____

To generate ideas ask, *What does the Preamble say the Constitution should do? Think especially about your topics.*

Let students answer in phrases. See the sample answers after strong verbs.

UNIT 7: INVENTIVE WRITING

Vocabulary Practice

Look at the vocabulary chart on pages 322–323. Try to use words from Lessons 1–21 in sentences or phrases that could be in your composition. Write at least two ideas below.

A **formidable** military is **imperative** for the safety of the people.

The Constitution **affirms** the rights of all men, not just **prominent** men.

Unit 7 Composition Checklist
Lesson 22: The Preamble, Part 1 body paragraphs

Inventive
Writing

Institute for
Excellence in
Writing

Name: _____

STRUCTURE

☐ MLA format (see Appendix I)	_____	3 pts
☐ checklist on top, final draft, rough draft, key word outline	_____	3 pts

Body

☐ topic-clincher sentences repeat or reflect 2–3 key words (highlight or bold)	_____	5 pts
☐ facts stay on topic	_____	5 pts

STYLE

¶2 ¶3 ¶4 Dress-Ups (underline one of each)   (2 pts each)

☐ ☐ ☐	-ly adverb		_____	6 pts
☐ ☐ ☐	who/which clause		_____	6 pts
☐ ☐ ☐	strong verb		_____	6 pts
☐ ☐ ☐	quality adjective		_____	6 pts
☐ ☐ ☐	www.asia.b clause		_____	6 pts

Sentence Openers (number; one of each as possible)   (2 pts each)

☐ ☐ ☐	[2] prepositional	_____	6 pts
☐ ☐ ☐	[3] -ly adverb	_____	6 pts
☐ ☐ ☐	[5] clausal - www.asia.b	_____	6 pts
☐ ☐ ☐	[6] vss	_____	6 pts

CHECK FOR BANNED WORDS (-1 pt for each use): go/went, say/said, good, bad,   _____   pts
pretty, big, small

MECHANICS

☐ spelling, grammar, and punctuation (-1 pt per error)	_____	pts

VOCABULARY

☐ vocabulary words - label *(voc)* in left margin or after sentence		

Total: _____   70 pts

Custom Total: _____   pts

Teachers are free to adjust a checklist by requiring only the stylistic techniques that have become easy, plus one new one. EZ+1

UNIT 7: INVENTIVE WRITING

Intentionally blank so the checklist can be removed.

Lesson 23: The Preamble to the Constitution, Part 2

Structure: Unit 7: Inventive Writing
                           introduction and conclusion

Style: no new style

Writing Topic: purpose and goals of the Preamble

Literature Suggestion: *Journey to Topaz* by Yoshiko Uchida

Lesson 23: The Preamble to the Constitution, Part 2

UNIT 7: INVENTIVE WRITING

Lesson 23: The Preamble to the Constitution, Part 2

Goals

- to practice the Unit 7 structural model
- to create KWOs for an introduction and a conclusion paragraph
- to write an introduction and a conclusion paragraph
- to complete a 5-paragraph composition
- to review vocabulary words

Assignment Schedule

Day 1

1. Play Vocabulary Pictionary.
2. Write a KWO for a conclusion and then a KWO for an introduction.

Day 2

1. Review both KWOs from Day 1.
2. Complete Style Practice.
3. Complete Vocabulary Practice. There are no new words for this lesson.
4. Using your conclusion KWO as a guide, write your conclusion.
5. Go over the checklist. Put a check in the box for each requirement you have completed.

Day 3

1. Review all vocabulary words learned thus far.
2. Using your introduction KWO as a guide, write your introduction.
3. Turn in your rough draft to your editor with the completed checklist attached.

Day 4

1. Write or type a final draft making any corrections your editor asked you to make. Add the introduction and the conclusion to the final draft body paragraphs written in Lesson 22.
2. Paperclip the checklist, final draft, rough drafts, and KWOs together. Hand them in.
3. If you are making a Magnum Opus Notebook, revise your Hopes and Dreams composition from Lessons 20–21.

Literature Suggestion

Continue reading *Journey to Topaz* by Yoshiko Uchida.

Key Word Outline—Conclusion

Restate the Topics

Write a sentence or two about each topic. Try to convey the main idea of each body paragraph. Highlight or bold the topic key words.

Most Significant and Why

What is the most important, most interesting, or most significant thing to remember about all that you wrote and why? Think about what the Preamble reveals about the Constitution and the men who wrote it. Consider why the Constitution is necessary, important, significant, or special. Tell what you believe the overriding desire of the founding fathers was when they wrote the Constitution or what the Preamble shows about the nation. You may choose one of your topics and tell why it is the most significant, or you may choose something that tells the importance of the entire subject.

Final Sentence

End with a sentence from which you can create a title. Be sure that your paper sounds complete.

Sample

Key Word Outline for Conclusion

V.   Topic A: _____ *Preamble, justice, establish, Const.* _____

Topic B: _____ *Preamble, defense, provide* _____

Topic C: _____ *Preamble, liberty, preserve* _____

Most significant _____ *founding fathers, succeeded, w/ ++ goals* _____

Why? _____ *Constitution, ➜ Amer, powerful, nation* _____

_____ *prosperous, "land, opportunity"* _____

Title repeats 1–3 key words from final sentence.

Highlight or bold the topic key words in your paragraph.

Key Word Outline—Introduction

Attention Getter

Start your introduction with a sentence that encourages your reader to continue reading. Create three different attention getters. When you are done, choose the one you like the best.

1. Ask your reader a question.

    Example: *Why did the founding fathers of America write the Constitution?*

    Write a question that you might use to begin your introduction:

    What has made America one of the greatest nations in the world?

2. Write a very short sentence (#6 vss).

    Example: *America still stands strong.*

    Write a very short sentence that you might use to begin your introduction:

    America needed a new government.

3. State a famous quote or fact. (If you do not know one, search on the Internet for a quote about the U.S. Constitution, government, or America.)

    Example: *"To live under the American Constitution is the greatest political privilege that was ever accorded to the human race" (Calvin Coolidge).*

    Write a quote or fact that you might use to begin your introduction:

    "We, the people of the United States of America, ... " begins the U.S. Constitution.

Transition smoothly from your attention getter to your background information. This may require the addition of one or two sentences.

Background

Make a general statement about the subject (goals stated in the Preamble of the Constitution). Then, provide background information you think would be interesting or important. The background information should help you flow into introducing your topics. You may use key facts found in Lesson 22 Historical Information, or you may use your own thoughts and ideas about the U.S. Constitution.

Topics

End your introduction by listing the topics you wrote about in your body paragraphs in the same order they appear in the body of the paper. You can write a sentence about each topic or simply list the topics in one sentence. Highlight or bold the topic key words.

Sample

Key Word Outline for Introduction

I.   Attention getter   *What, America, great ?*

Background   *US Constitution, created, innovative, gov't*

grants, rights, opportunity, ppl

Preamble, lists, goals, Const.

Topic A: *Preamble, justice, establish, Const.*

Topic B: *Preamble, defense, provide*

Topic C: *Preamble, liberty, preserve*

Highlight or bold the topic key words in your paragraph.

Style Practice

Sentence Openers

The checklist will require that you include all of the sentence openers you have been introduced to thus far. Write sentences that can be used in your introduction or conclusion.

1. #2 prepositional opener _____

   [2] In the Preamble the founding fathers stated the goals of the Constitution.

2. #3 -ly adverb opener _____

   [3] Clearly the Constitution formed one of the greatest governments ever.

3. #5 clausal opener – _www.asia.b_ _____

   [5] When they wrote the Constitution, the founding fathers desired a strong, fair government.

4. #6 vss opener, 2–5 words (This can be your attention getter.)_____

   [6] America grants rights to all.

Dress-Ups

Look at your KWO and consider where you can include various clauses as well as strong verbs, quality adjectives, and -ly adverbs. When you write your paper, follow your checklist!

Vocabulary Practice

Look at the vocabulary chart on pages 322–323. Try to use words from Lessons 1–21 in sentences or phrases that could be in your composition. Write at least two ideas below.

The founding fathers **aspired** to **lofty** goals and **espoused** the ideals of liberty and

justice for all when they **drafted** the Constitution.

Lesson 23: The Preamble to the Constitution, Part 2

Unit 7 Composition Checklist

Inventive Writing

Lesson 23: The Preamble, Part 2 introduction and conclusion

Name: _____

Institute for **Excellence** in **Writing**
Listen. Speak. Read. Write. Think!

STRUCTURE

☐ MLA format (see Appendix I) _____ 2 pts

☐ title centered _____ 2 pts

☐ checklist on top, final draft, rough draft, key word outline _____ 1 pt

Introduction

☐ introduction includes attention getter, background information, and states topics (bold or highlight) _____ 10 pts

Body

☐ insert body paragraphs _____ 2 pts

Conclusion

☐ conclusion restates topics (**bold or highlight**) and indicates most significant/why _____ 10 pts

☐ final sentence repeats 1–3 key words for the title _____ 2 pts

STYLE

¶1   ¶5 Dress-Ups (underline one of each)   (2 pts each)

☐ ☐ -ly adverb _____ 4 pts

☐ ☐ *who/which* clause _____ 4 pts

☐ ☐ strong verb _____ 4 pts

☐ ☐ quality adjective _____ 4 pts

☐ ☐ *www.asia.b* clause _____ 4 pts

Sentence Openers (number; one of each as possible)   (2 pts each)

☐ ☐ [2] prepositional _____ 4 pts

☐ ☐ [3] -ly adverb _____ 4 pts

☐ ☐ [5] clausal - *www.asia.b* _____ 4 pts

☐ ☐ [6] vss _____ 4 pts

CHECK FOR BANNED WORDS (-1 pt for each use): go/went, say/said, good, bad, pretty, big, small _____ pts

MECHANICS

☐ spelling, grammar, and punctuation (-1 pt per error) _____ pts

VOCABULARY

☐ vocabulary words - label *(voc)* in left margin or after sentence

Total: _____ 65 pts

Custom Total: _____ pts

Teachers are free to adjust a checklist by requiring only the stylistic techniques that have become easy, plus one new one. EZ+1

Intentionally blank so the checklist can be removed.

Lesson 24: The American Flag

Structure: Unit 7: Inventive Writing
Style: #1 subject opener, #4 -ing opener
Writing Topic: first person narrative of the flag
Literature Suggestion: *Journey to Topaz* by Yoshiko Uchida

UNIT 7: INVENTIVE WRITING

Lesson 24: The American Flag

Goals

- to practice the Unit 7 structural model
- to create a KWO from a writing prompt
- to write a 2-paragraph first person narrative
- to correctly add a new sentence opener: #4 -ing opener
- to understand the #1 subject sentence opener
- to review vocabulary words

Assignment Schedule

Day 1

1. Play the Question Game.
2. Read Historical Information and the writing assignment prompt.
3. Read Structure—Notes from the Brain. Follow instructions to write a 2-paragraph KWO.

Day 2

1. Review your KWO from Day 1.
2. Read New Style and complete Style Practice.
3. Complete Vocabulary Practice. There are no new words for this lesson.
4. Using your KWO as a guide, begin writing your 2-paragraph rough draft. Write in the first person as if you are the flag.
5. Go over the checklist. Put a check in the box for each requirement you have completed.

Day 3

1. Review all vocabulary words learned thus far.
2. Finish writing your 2-paragraph composition. Follow the topic-clincher rule.
3. Turn in your rough draft to your editor with the completed checklist attached.

Day 4

1. Write or type a final draft making any corrections your editor asked you to make.
2. Paperclip the checklist, final draft, rough draft, and KWO together. Hand them in.

Literature Suggestion

Continue reading *Journey to Topaz* by Yoshiko Uchida.

In this lesson students write two paragraphs as if they are the flag. They will write in the first person using pronouns *I*, *me*, *my*.

The two paragraphs students write this week will be the complete composition. Students will neither add an introduction nor a conclusion paragraph to the assignment.

Question Game

See Appendix VII for game directions.

Choose from the questions on pages 347–349. Be sure to include questions 24–29.

Historical Information

The years following WWI were times of great nationalism. The leaders of Germany, Italy, and Japan believed their nations were superior to other nations and tried to take over the world. This began World War II. During this war the German Nazi flag became despised and feared all across Europe. The Japanese flag represented aggression in Asia.

One of the most prominent and emotional victories of WWII occurred when the Americans and their Allies furiously fought the battle for Iwo Jima. The famous statue of American marines placing the U.S. flag on the island captures the memory of this victory. The American flag stands for victory and liberty. The flag is a revered symbol of a great country.

Prompt

Pretend you are the American flag. You do not have to be at Iwo Jima. You may be on the moon, waving in the wind during a parade, flying from a historic building or national monument, raised after an Olympic victory, or draped over a veteran's casket. Write two paragraphs about two places you have been. You may include what you have seen and what you have meant to the people who see you. Write in the first person. (Use *I* not *you*.)

Sample Paragraph and Key Word Outline

Position at the Post Office

[1] I am the United States **flag** that flies above a local **post office**. [2] From morning until evening, I <u>flutter</u> high in the breeze, and at night a postal worker lowers me and tucks me away until the next day. [3] Constantly I watch people bring <u>mysterious</u> letters and packages, <u>which</u> will be sent all over the world. [1] I have been told that postal workers stuff mail in numerous little boxes. [1] People seem eager to collect their mail, but lots of junk mail ends up in the big trash cans. [4] Bustling busily, many people laugh and talk <u>as</u> they get their mail, so they do not notice me watching silently. [6] Mail carriers tote big bags. [5] If someone important dies, a postal worker lowers me to half mast. [5] When a national holiday comes, I fly more <u>briskly</u>—proud to be an American flag. [1] I love my position as the United States **flag** at the United States **post office**.

I.   *flag, local, PO*

   1.   *flutter, breeze, ★, ☾, lowers*

   2.   *mysterious, mail, world*

   3.   *workers, stuff, ++☐*

   4.   *junk, mail, trash*

   5.   *laugh, talk, X ◉◉*

   6.   *carriers, carry, bags*

   7.   *dies, lower, ½ mast*

   8.   *national, holiday, proud*

Clincher

Structure

Notes from the Brain

How do you come up with content? Ask yourself questions about the prompt. Based on the prompt, what is the subject of this composition? Does the prompt provide a clue to how many body paragraphs you need to write to complete the assignment?

The prompt for this lesson begins *Pretend you are the American flag*. The subject of your paper is the American flag. Because the prompt directs you to write about two places you have been, you will write two paragraphs. As you choose your topics, consider where you (the flag) have been located (on a specific building, the moon, a veteran's casket, a float in a parade). Each paragraph will be about a specific place. Begin by writing your topics on the Roman numeral lines of the KWO. Follow this pattern:

flag (subject), topic, one more word *about the topic.*

if 1 topic = 1 paragraph

then 2 topics = 2 paragraphs

On the lines under the first Roman numeral, describe the first topic by asking yourself questions. Brain-helping questions are listed on the KWO. These helpful questions include:

Where were you?

Who sees you?

What do you mean to them?

How do they feel?

How do you feel?

What is the scene like?

What do you **see**? **think**? **feel**?

The answers to your questions become the details for the outline. As you answer a question, place two or three key words on the KWO. Use symbols, numbers, and abbreviations when possible. You do not have to answer every question or ask in the order they are written. Keep your answers brief. You can add more details when you write your composition.

Repeat this process for the second topic.

The key to the process is asking questions. Here are the questions asked that resulted in the sample KWO.

Topic A

What is the subject? (*flag*)

Where are you? (*house*)

When? (*July 4*)

1. What do you see?

2. What do you symbolize?

3. How do you feel?

4. What do you see, smell?

5. What do you hear?

6. What do you think?

Topic B

What is the subject? (*flag*)

Where are you? (*Olympics*)

When? (*US athlete receives gold medal*)

1. Who is with you?

2. What do you hear?

3. What do you see?

4. How do you and others feel?

5. What do the people do when anthem ends?

6. What do you do?

Sample

Key Word Outline

I.   Topic A: *flag, house, July 4*

   1.   👀, *parade, children's bikes*

   2.   *represent, freedom, opportunity*

   3.   *feel, honored, proud*

   4.   *BBQ, sizzling, laughter*

   5.   🎵, *nat'l anthem,* 🌙, *fireworks, pop*

 (6.)   *think, Amer., great, nation*

 (7.)

Clincher

II.   Topic B: *flag, Olympics, US, gold*

   1.   *w/ 2, flags, all,* 👀, *ppl, watch* ⬆

   2.   *I, highest, nat'l anthem* 🎵

   3.   *Americans, hands,* ❤, *honor*

   4.   *tears, pride, country*

   5.   🎵, *ends, cheers, celebrating*

 (6.)   *wait, hope,* ⬆, *again*

 (7.)

Clincher

who?

what?

when?

where?

why?

how?

how feel?

problems?

solutions?

best thing?

worst thing?

value?

significance?

meaning?

examples?

description?

Institute for Excellence in Writing

New Style

#4 -ing Opener

In this lesson you will learn another sentence opener: the #4 -ing opener.

The -ing opener is a participial opener placed at the beginning of a sentence. It follows the pattern: -ing word/phrase + comma + subject of sentence.

> [4] Flying above the capitol, the flag symbolizes freedom in America.

Notice:

1. The sentence must begin with an action word that ends in -ing. This is called a participle.

   [4] *Flying* above the capitol, the flag symbolizes freedom in America.

2. The -ing word/phrase and comma must be followed by a complete sentence.

   [4] Flying above the capitol, *the flag symbolizes freedom in America.*

3. The thing (subject of sentence) after the comma must be the thing doing the inging.

   [4] Flying above the capitol, the *flag* symbolizes freedom in America.

   What was flying? The flag. The noun *flag* follows the comma.

4. To indicate that a sentence begins with an -ing opener, label it with a 4 in the left margin or place a [4] right before the sentence.

The thing after the comma must be the thing doing the inging.

Warning:

1. Beware of the illegal #4, which is grammatically incorrect. If the thing after the comma is not the thing doing the inging, the sentence does not make sense. This is known as a *dangling modifier*.

   [4] Flying above the capitol, he saw the flags.

   What was flying high above the capitol? *He* was. This is incorrect because *he* cannot fly above the capitol.

2. Beware of two imposter #4s, which begin with an -ing word but do not follow the pattern.

   [1] Flying the flag shows my patriotism.

   This is a #1 subject opener. There is neither a comma nor a subject doing the inging.

   [2] During a fireworks show, the flag is surrounded by bursting colors.

   This is a #2 prepositional opener. *The flag* (the subject) is not doing the *during*. Prepositions ending in -ing include *according to, concerning, regarding, during.*

#1 Subject Opener

The sixth and final opener is the subject opener.

The subject opener is simply a sentence that begins with its subject. This is the kind of sentence you most naturally write if you do not purposely try to use one of the other sentence openers.

> [1] Fireworks light up the sky.

> [1] The American flag symbolizes freedom and independence.

Notice:

1. A subject opener begins with the subject of the sentence.

   In the second example there are adjectives (the American) in front of the subject, but that does not change the sentence structure. It is still a #1 subject opener.

2. To indicate that a sentence begins with a subject opener, label it with a 1 in the left margin or place a [1] right before the sentence.

Practice

Write a sentence with a #4 -ing opener: -ing word/phrase + comma + subject of sentence. Label it with a [4].

   [4] Placing their hands over their hearts, the crowd sings along with the national anthem.

Write a sentence with a #1 subject opener. Label it with a [1].

   [1] I proudly represent the United States.

Congratulations! You have learned all of the different sentence openers! Your literary toolbox is filling up. To continue practicing and using them appropriately, here is a new rule for you to follow.

Each sentence opener should be in every paragraph as possible. No more than two of the same in a row.

 From now on, label each sentence in every paragraph, using no more than two of the same sentence opener in a row. If you are unsure what a particular sentence is, mark it as a #1 subject opener.

Style Practice

Sentence Openers

Write sentences that can be used in your composition. As you write your sentences, write in the first person as if you are the flag.

1. #1 subject opener _____ *[1] I am red, white, and blue.* _____

2. #2 prepositional opener *[2] On the Fourth of July, I hang on front porches across the nation.*

3. #3 -ly adverb opener _____ *[3] Proudly I represent America's most skilled athletes.*

4. #4 -ing participial opener *[4] Noticing me at half mast, people remember the fallen.*

5. #5 clausal opener – *www.asia.b* *[5] While I am flying, Americans know they are free.*

6. #6 vss opener, 2–5 words *[6] Fireworks explode with colors.*

Dress-Ups

Dress-ups are particularly helpful in a descriptive paragraph, so thoughtfully consider how you will dress-up your composition as you complete the practice below and on the following page.

Who/Which Clause Dress-Up

Add a *who/which* clause to the sentence below. Punctuate and mark correctly.

On the Fourth of July, fireworks, <u>which</u> *fill the sky with shimmering colors,*

_____ stir up pride and patriotism.

Strong Verb Dress-Up and -ly Adverb Dress-Up

What might you, the flag, do? Think of strong verbs with -ly adverbs you could use in phrases in your composition.

Examples: fly majestically over public buildings; proudly declare freedom

strong verbs   *symbolize, inspire, comfort, remind, wave*

-ly adverbs   *boldly, continually, compassionately, tenderly, gently, confidently*

Quality Adjective Dress-Up

What adjectives describe you? Consider what you look like or feel like in various settings.

Examples: bright, proud

*stately, solemn, confident, honored, **audacious**, empowering, **lofty**, noble, glorious*

What adjectives could describe people who see you in various settings?

Examples: at the Olympics: proud, determined

*patriotic, unified, grateful, humbled, **reverent**, emboldened, passionate, teary-eyed, **enthralled***

Vocabulary Practice

Look at the vocabulary chart on pages 322–323. Try to use words from Lessons 1–21 in sentences or phrases that could be in your composition. Write at least two ideas below.

*I symbolize the **profound** ideals **espoused** by America's founding fathers.*

*When America **encounters adversity**, I am there, a **stirring emblem** of their **resolve**.*

To generate ideas ask, *What does the flag do for Americans and people around the world?*

What -ly adverbs would go with the strong verbs?

Unit 7 Composition Checklist
Lesson 24: The American Flag

Inventive
Writing

Name: _____

STRUCTURE

☐ MLA format (see Appendix I)	_____	1 pt
☐ title centered and repeats 1–3 key words from final sentence	_____	3 pts
☐ topic-clincher sentences repeat or reflect 2–3 key words (highlight or bold)	_____	6 pts
☐ checklist on top, final draft, rough draft, key word outline	_____	1 pt

STYLE

¶1 ¶2 Dress-Ups (underline one of each)   (2 pts each)

☐ ☐ -ly adverb	_____	4 pts
☐ ☐ *who/which* clause	_____	4 pts
☐ ☐ strong verb	_____	4 pts
☐ ☐ quality adjective	_____	4 pts
☐ ☐ *www.asia.b* clause	_____	4 pts

Sentence Openers (number; one of each as possible)   (2 pts each)

☐ ☐ [1] subject	_____	4 pts
☐ ☐ [2] prepositional	_____	4 pts
☐ ☐ [3] -ly adverb	_____	4 pts
☐ ☐ [4] -ing	_____	4 pts
☐ ☐ [5] clausal - *www.asia.b*	_____	4 pts
☐ ☐ [6] vss	_____	4 pts

CHECK FOR BANNED WORDS (-1 pt for each use): go/went, say/said, good, bad, pretty, big, small   _____ pts

MECHANICS

☐ spelling, grammar, and punctuation (-1 pt per error)	_____	pts

VOCABULARY

☐ vocabulary words - label *(voc)* in left margin or after sentence		

Total: _____   55 pts
Custom Total: _____   pts

Teachers are free to adjust a checklist by requiring only the stylistic techniques that have become easy, plus one new one. EZ+1

UNIT 7: INVENTIVE WRITING

Intentionally blank so the checklist can be removed.

Institute for Excellence in Writing

Lesson 25: Transportation Milestones, Part 3

Teaching Writing: Structure and Style

Structure: Unit 8: Formal Essay Models
                    introduction and conclusion

Style: no new style

Writing Topic: transportation in America

Literature Suggestion: *Journey to Topaz* by Yoshiko Uchida

Watch the sections for Unit 8: Formal Essay Models. At IEW.com/twss-help reference the TWSS Viewing Guides.

UNIT 8: FORMAL ESSAY MODELS

Lesson 25: Transportation Milestones, Part 3

Goals

- to learn the Unit 8 Formal Essay structural model
- to review the components of an introduction and a conclusion paragraph
- to create KWOs for an introduction and a conclusion paragraph
- to write an introduction and a conclusion paragraph
- to complete a 5-paragraph essay with a bibliography
- to correctly use new vocabulary words: *achievement*, *flourish*, *transformation*, *efficient*

Assignment Schedule

Day 1

1. Complete the Review.
2. Using the three paragraphs you wrote in Unit 6 as your body paragraphs, you will write an introduction and a conclusion to form a 5-paragraph essay about transportation milestones in America. Read New Structure—Basic Essay Model: Introduction and Conclusion.
3. Read the three paragraphs you wrote in Lessons 17–18 to refresh your memory of the topics.
4. Write a KWO for a conclusion and then write a KWO for an introduction.

Day 2

1. Review both KWOs from Day 1.
2. Complete Style Practice.
3. Look at the vocabulary cards for Lesson 25. Discuss the definitions and complete Vocabulary Practice.
4. Using your conclusion KWO as a guide, write your conclusion. Highlight or bold the topic key words.
5. Go over the checklist. Put a check in the box for each requirement you have completed.

Day 3

1. Review all vocabulary words learned thus far.
2. Using your introduction KWO as a guide, write your introduction. Highlight or bold the key topic words.
3. Turn in your rough draft to your editor with the completed checklist attached.

In this lesson students craft an essay about transportation milestones in America by adding an introduction and conclusion to the topic/body paragraphs written in Lessons 17–18. Remind students that both the introduction and conclusion paragraphs follow their own unique structure.

Day 4

1. Write or type a final draft making any corrections your editor asked you to make. Add the introduction and the conclusion to the final draft body paragraphs written in Lessons 17–18. Include the bibliography written in Lesson 18 as the final page.

2. Paperclip the checklist, final draft, rough drafts, and KWOs together. Hand them in.

3. If you are making a Magnum Opus Notebook, revise your Preamble composition from Lessons 22–23.

In Lessons 26–27 you will write a report about a prominent American of the mid to late twentieth century. In preparation for Lesson 26, you must find three fairly short, simple sources either from the library or the Internet. There is a list of possible subjects on page 253.

Literature Suggestion

Finish reading *Journey to Topaz* by Yoshiko Uchida.

Acquire *Cheaper by the Dozen* by Frank B. Gilbreth Jr. and Ernestine Gilbreth Carey to read for Lessons 26–29.

Review

Fill in the pattern for a #4 -ing opener:

-ing word/phrase + _____ + _____

Label each sentence. Only 2 sentences will be labeled as a #4 -ing opener.

_____ Stretching all across the country, railroads became the chief form of transportation in the late 1800s.

_____ During the early 1900s the Wright brothers began the Age of Flight.

_____ Hoping to make the automobile available to middle-class Americans, Ford significantly lowered the cost of production.

_____ Constructing the transcontinental railroad was a major feat.

Review

-ing word/phrase + comma + subject of sentence

[4] The subject *railroads* is doing the *stretching*.

[2] *During* is a preposition.

[4] The subject *Ford* is doing the *hoping*.

[1] *Nothing* is doing the *constructing*. This sentence does not follow the #4 -ing opener pattern. There is no comma after the -ing word/phrase. In this case, *Constructing* is the subject of the sentence.

New Structure

Basic Essay Model: Introduction and Conclusion

Unit 8 Formal Essay Models teaches various types of essays. Essays begin with an introduction and end with a conclusion. The essays you will write in this book follow the basic essay model, which looks like this:

I.   Introduction   *attention getter, background, state topics*

      Body Paragraphs

V.   Conclusion   *restate topics, most significant/why, last sentence ➜ title*

The model can be adapted by simply changing the number of body paragraphs. You have already used this structure to write compositions in Unit 7. In this lesson you will use the same structure to complete the Unit 6 report you wrote about transportation milestones in Lessons 17–18. To complete your essay, you will simply add an introduction and a conclusion to the three body paragraphs that you have already written. This will allow you to understand the structure of the basic essay model as you continue to practice writing introductory and concluding paragraphs.

Review the information in the three the body paragraphs you wrote in Lessons 17 and 18 so that the details are fresh on your mind. Even though the conclusion will be placed last, you will outline and write it before the introduction.

Key Word Outline—Conclusion

Restate the Topics

> Write a sentence or two about each topic. Try to convey the main idea of each body paragraph. Highlight or bold the topic key words.

Most significant and why

> What is the most important, most interesting, or most significant thing to remember about all that you wrote and why? You may choose one of your topics and tell why it is the most significant, or you may choose something that tells the importance of the entire subject. The background information in the source texts on pages 161–166 may be helpful.

> As you consider what to write, ask yourself questions. Why is the transportation of people and goods important? How did better transportation impact the lives of Americans and the economy of the country? What does the development of better transportation systems indicate about America's ability to meet challenges and solve problems?

Final sentence

> End with a sentence from which you can create a title. Be sure that your paper sounds complete.

Sample

Key Word Outline for Conclusion

V.   Topic A: _____ *Erie Canal, 1st transportation, milestone, Amer.*

Topic B: _____ *TRR, ++ significant, accomplishment, 1800s*

Topic C: _____ *automobile, transformed, America*

Most significant _____ *transport, ppl, goods, resources*

Why? _____ *helped, US, grow, prosper*

➔ *strong, thriving, country*

Title repeats 1–3 key words from final sentence.

Highlight or bold the topic key words in your paragraph.

Key Word Outline—Introduction

Attention Getter

Start your introduction with a sentence that encourages your reader to continue reading. Create three different attention getters. When you are done, choose the one you like the best.

1. Ask your reader a question.

   Example: *What would daily life look like without cars?*

   Write a question that you might use to begin your introduction:

   Would you want to travel across the country in a covered wagon?

2. Write a very short sentence (#6 vss).

   Example: *People depend on transportation.*

   Write a very short sentence that you might use to begin your introduction:

   Transportation moves America.

3. State a famous quote or fact. (If you do not know one, search on the Internet for a quote about transportation, trains, the Transcontinental Railroad, or cars.)

   Example: *On the famous Golden Spike that completed the Transcontinental Railroad, David Hewes engraved these words: "May God continue the unity of our Country as this Railroad unites the two great Oceans of the world."*

   Write a quote or fact that you might use to begin your introduction:

   "Transportation is the center of our world. It is the glue of our daily lives" (Robin Chase).

Background

Tell your reader what the subject of the composition is about but do not say anything similar to *"This composition is about ... ."* Simply make a general statement about the subject. Then provide background information you think would be interesting or important. The background information should flow into the introduction of the topics.

Each of the source texts on pages 161–166 begins with background information. You may read this information and choose some facts to include in your background, or you may write your own ideas.

Topics

End your introduction by listing the topics you wrote about in your body paragraphs in the same order they appear in the body of the paper. You can write a sentence about each topic or simply list the topics in one sentence. Highlight or bold the topic key words.

Sample

Key Word Outline for Introduction

I.   Attention getter   *want, across, US, wagon?*

   Background   *1800s, few, other, options*

   travel, E, long, dangerous

   realized, need, better

   Topic A: *Erie Canal, 1st transportation, milestone, Amer.*

   Topic B: *TRR, ++ significant, accomplishment, 1800s*

   Topic C: *automobile, transformed, America*

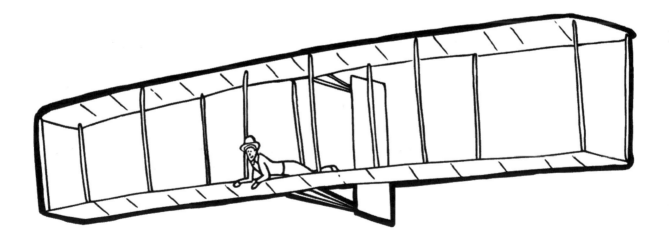

Style Practice

Sentence Openers

Write sentences that can be used in your introduction or conclusion.

1. #1 subject opener _____ *[1] Goods and resources needed to be moved across the country.*

2. #2 prepositional opener _____ *[2] During the 1800s traveling long distances was difficult.*

3. #3 -ly adverb opener _____ *[3] Inevitably the nation built a transcontinental railroad.*

4. #4 -ing participial opener _____

   [4] Transporting people, resources, and goods, the railroad helped build America.

5. #5 clausal opener – *www.asia.b* _____

   [5] When Ford made cars affordable, the American way of life changed drastically.

6. #6 vss opener, 2–5 words (This can be your attention getter.) _____

   [6] America prospered.

Dress-Ups

Look at your KWO and consider where you can include various clauses as well as strong verbs, quality adjectives, and -ly adverbs. When you write your paper, follow your checklist!

Vocabulary Practice

Look at the vocabulary words for Lesson 25. Fill in the blanks with a word that makes sense.

1. Henry Ford developed a more _____*efficient*_____ way of manufacturing motor cars.

2. Cities were able to *flourish.*_____

Look at the vocabulary chart on pages 322–323. Try to use words from Lessons 1–25 in sentences or phrases that could be in your composition. Write at least two ideas below.

*__**Innovative** advances in transportation had a **profound** impact on America.__*

*__New modes of transportation caused a **transformation** in American life.__*

Unit 8 Composition Checklist
Lesson 25: Transportation Milestones, Part 3

Formal
Essay
Models

Name: _____

Institute for
Excellence in
Writing

STRUCTURE

- ☐ MLA format (see Appendix I) _____ 2 pts
- ☐ title centered _____ 2 pts
- ☐ bibliography entries in proper format _____ 2 pts
- ☐ checklist on top, final draft, rough draft, key word outline _____ 1 pt

Introduction

- ☐ introduction includes attention getter, background information, and states topics (bold or highlight) _____ 10 pts

Body

- ☐ insert body paragraphs _____ 2 pts

Conclusion

- ☐ conclusion restates topics (**bold** or highlight) and indicates most significant/why _____ 10 pts
- ☐ final sentence repeats 1–3 key words for the title _____ 2 pts

STYLE

¶1 ¶5 Dress-Ups (underline one of each)   (2 pts each)

- ☐ ☐ -ly adverb _____ 4 pts
- ☐ ☐ *who/which* clause _____ 4 pts
- ☐ ☐ strong verb _____ 4 pts
- ☐ ☐ quality adjective _____ 4 pts
- ☐ ☐ *www.asia.b* clause _____ 4 pts

Sentence Openers (number; one of each as possible)   (2 pts each)

- ☐ ☐ [1] subject _____ 4 pts
- ☐ ☐ [2] prepositional _____ 4 pts
- ☐ ☐ [3] -ly adverb _____ 4 pts
- ☐ ☐ [4] -ing _____ 4 pts
- ☐ ☐ [5] clausal - *www.asia.b* _____ 4 pts
- ☐ ☐ [6] vss _____ 4 pts

CHECK FOR BANNED WORDS (-1 pt for each use): go/went, say/said, good, bad, pretty, big, small _____ pts

MECHANICS

- ☐ spelling, grammar, and punctuation (-1 pt per error) _____ pts

VOCABULARY

- ☐ vocabulary words - label *(voc)* in left margin or after sentence _____

Total: _____ 75 pts

Custom Total: _____ pts

Teachers are free to adjust a checklist by requiring only the stylistic techniques that have become easy, plus one new one. EZ+1

UNIT 8: FORMAL ESSAY MODELS

Intentionally blank so the checklist can be removed.

Lesson 26: A Prominent American, Part 1

Structure:	Unit 8: Formal Essay Models
	body paragraphs
Style:	no new style
Writing Topic:	a prominent American
Literature Suggestion:	*Cheaper by the Dozen* by Frank B. Gilbreth Jr. and Ernestine Gilbreth Carey

UNIT 8: FORMAL ESSAY MODELS

Lesson 26: A Prominent American, Part 1

Goals

- to practice the Unit 8 structural model
- to practice scanning multiple sources to determine three topics for an essay
- to create source outlines from multiple sources
- to create three fused outlines about three different topics
- to write the body paragraphs of a 5-paragraph essay
- to review vocabulary words

Assignment Schedule

Day 1

1. Play Vocabulary Pictionary.

2. In Lessons 26–27 you will use more than one source of information to write an essay about a prominent American of the mid to late twentieth century. You will write the body paragraphs in this lesson.

3. Read New Structure—Basic Essay Model: Body Paragraphs.

4. After you choose an individual to write about (the subject of your essay), find sources and choose three topics.

5. For your first body paragraph, choose a topic that is covered in two or three sources. Write the topic on the topic line on page 254. Complete the source outlines. Using notes from your source outlines, write a fused outline.

6. For your second body paragraph, choose another topic that is covered in two or three sources. Write the topic on the topic line on page 256. Complete the source outlines. Using notes from your source outlines, write a fused outline.

Day 2

1. For your third body paragraph, choose a third topic that is covered in two or three sources. Write the topic on the topic line on page 258. Complete the source outlines. Using notes from your source outlines, write a fused outline.

2. Complete Style Practice.

3. Complete Vocabulary Practice. There are no new words for this lesson.

4. Using your fused outline as a guide, begin writing your rough draft.

5. Go over the checklist. Put a check in the box for each requirement you have completed.

This lesson requires students to research and write about three topics by making source outlines and fused outlines. This process takes some time, so you may want to consider allowing two weeks to complete it. If your schedule does not accommodate an added week, consider assigning Topic C with Lesson 27 when students complete the essay by adding an introduction an conclusion. The introduction and conclusion do not require source and fused outlines, so they are not as time consuming.

Day 3

1. Review all vocabulary words learned thus far.

2. Finish writing your three body paragraphs. Follow the topic-clincher rule.

3. Turn in your rough draft to your editor with the completed checklist attached.

Day 4

1. Write or type a final draft making any corrections your editor asked you to make.

2. Paperclip the checklist, final draft, rough draft, and KWO together. Hand them in.

3. If you are making a Magnum Opus Notebook, revise your American flag composition from Lesson 24.

Literature Suggestion

Begin reading *Cheaper by the Dozen* by Frank B. Gilbreth Jr. and Ernestine Gilbreth Carey.

New Structure

Basic Essay Model: Body Paragraphs

In Lessons 26–27 you will write a 5-paragraph essay. Consider again the Basic Essay Model.

I.   Introduction   *attention getter, background, state topics*

Body Paragraphs

II.   Topic A   *topic, 5–7 details, clincher*

III.   Topic B   *topic, 5–7 details, clincher*

IV.   Topic C   *topic, 5–7 details, clincher*

V.   Conclusion   *restate topics, most significant/why, last sentence ➜ title*

An essay is a multiple-paragraph composition written about one subject. Once you know what the subject of the composition is, you determine how many body paragraphs to write. Once you know the number of body paragraphs, you determine the topics. Each body paragraph equals one topic. Remember, the model can be adapted by simply changing the number of body paragraphs. When you follow this model, write from the inside out beginning with the body paragraphs.

This should sound familiar. You followed this same structure to write your Unit 7 composition about hopes and dreams. In Unit 7 you asked yourself questions to create your KWO. Because this essay requires research, look at your sources to determine the topics of your body paragraphs. For each topic that you choose, you will take notes using source outlines and fuse those notes using a fused outline approach.

Assignment

Write a 5-paragraph research essay about a prominent American of the mid to late twentieth century. You may choose an individual listed below or you may conduct your own research and choose any notable American from that time period in history.

Possibilities

Astronauts such as Neil Armstrong, Sally Ride, Jim Lovell

Civil Rights leaders such as Martin Luther King, Jr., Rosa Parks

American presidents such as Dwight D. Eisenhower, John F. Kennedy, Ronald Reagan

Leaders in technology such as Bill Gates

Others such as Jonas Salk for the polio vaccine, Billy Graham the evangelist

Find Sources

Once you determine the subject you will research, find at least three sources of information about it. History textbooks, Internet articles (especially those labeled "for kids"), encyclopedia articles, and short children's books make the best sources. Choose short, easy sources.

Choose Topics

Identify various topics that you might write about by skimming your sources. Look at the table of contents, chapter titles, and headings. For a five-paragraph paper, you must choose three topics.

if 1 paragraph = 1 topic

then 3 paragraphs = 3 topics

When writing about famous people, your three topics may include young life, what work or idea made the person famous, and later years. If you are writing about an individual who is famous for a variety of accomplishments, consider writing about three different accomplishments.

After you have chosen three topics to write about, you are ready to research each topic in more detail using source outlines. Remember to follow this pattern for the topic lines of your KWO: *subject, topic,* one more word *about the topic.*

After reading this section with the students, review the process of writing reports.

Choose a subject.

Find sources.

Look for possible topics (things about the subject) in the sources.

Choose the number of topics needed. Three paragraphs require three topics.

Write the key words on the topic line following the pattern: subject, topic, another word about the topic.

Write source and then fused KWOs.

Write the research report using the fused KWOs.

Refer to the checklist.

The subject of the report is the entire thing being written about. In this case it the prominent American.

The topics are the divisions—the things within the subject. As students write their topic lines, they should follow this pattern: *subject, topic,* one more word *about the topic.* (i.e. Reagan, lifeguard, high school. In this example, students would look for interesting, important, and relevant facts from sources about Reagan as a lifeguard in high school.)

Sample
Source Outlines

Write the name of the first topic you will research on the line below.

First Topic: _____*subject, topic, another word about the topic*_____

Choose your first source. Write the title on the Source line. Using key words, write the topic on the Roman numeral line. Complete the source outline by noting three to five interesting facts about the topic. Repeat the process with the second source and, if applicable, with the third.

Source A: _____*Write the title of one of the sources from the library or the Internet.*_____

II. Topic: _____*The topic lines of the source outlines and the fused outline must be the same.*_____

   1. _____*Each student's outline will be different because they are writing about different*_____

   2. _____*subjects, topics, and using different sources.*_____

   3. _____

  (4.) _____

  (5.) _____

Source B: _____*Write the title of one of the sources from the library or the Internet.*_____

II. Topic: _____

   1. _____

   2. _____

   3. _____

  (4.) _____

  (5.) _____

Source C: _____

II. Topic: _____*Write the title of one of the sources from the library or the Internet.*_____

   1. _____

   2. _____

   3. _____

  (4.) _____

  (5.) _____

Institute for Excellence in Writing

Sample

Fused Outline

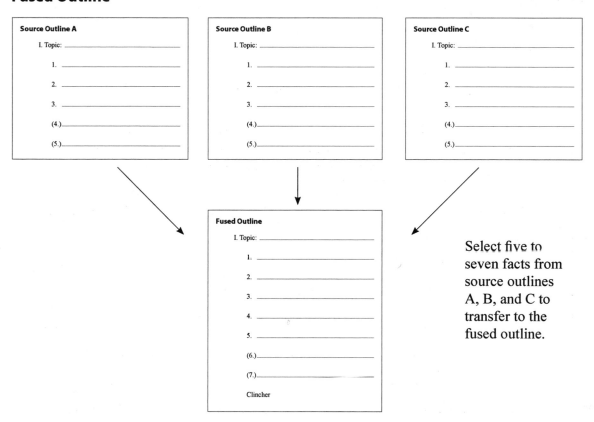

Select five to seven facts from source outlines A, B, and C to transfer to the fused outline.

Using key words, write the topic on the Roman numeral line. This should be the same topic that you placed on the source outlines.

II. Topic: _____

   1. _____ *Students choose facts from their source outlines to place onto their fused outline.* _____

   2. _____

   3. _____

   4. _____

   5. _____

  (6.) _____

  (7.) _____

Clincher

The subject of the second paragraph of the report is the same as the subject of the first paragraph. In this case it the prominent American. The topic, however, changes. As students write their topic lines, they should follow this pattern: *subject, topic,* one more word *about the topic.* (i.e. Reagan, radio, sportscaster. In this example, students would look for interesting, important, and relevant facts from sources about Reagan as a radio sportscaster.)

Sample

Source Outlines

Write the name of the second topic you will research on the line below.

Second Topic: *subject, topic, another word about the topic*

Choose your first source. Write the title on the Source line. Using key words, write the topic on the Roman numeral line. Complete the source outline by noting three to five interesting facts about the topic. Repeat the process with the second source and, if applicable, with the third.

Source A: *Write the title of one of the sources from the library or the Internet.*

III. Topic: *The topic lines of the source outlines and the fused outline must be the same.*

   1.   *Each student's outline will be different because they are writing about different*

   2.   *subjects, topics, and using different sources.*

   3. _____

   (4.) _____

   (5.) _____

Source B: *Write the title of one of the sources from the library or the Internet.*

III. Topic: _____

   1. _____

   2. _____

   3. _____

   (4.) _____

   (5.) _____

Source C: _____

III. Topic: *Write the title of one of the sources from the library or the Internet.*

   1. _____

   2. _____

   3. _____

   (4.) _____

   (5.) _____

Sample

Fused Outline

Using key words, write the topic on the Roman numeral line. This should be the same topic that you placed on the source outlines. Select five to seven facts from the source outlines to transfer to the fused outline.

III. Topic: _____

1. _____ *Students choose facts from their source outlines to place onto their fused outline.*

2. _____

3. _____

4. _____

5. _____

(6.) _____

(7.) _____

Clincher

The subject of the third paragraph of the report is the same as the subject of the first and second paragraphs. In this case it the prominent American. The topic, however, changes. As students write their topic lines, they should follow this pattern: *subject, topic,* one more word *about the topic.* (i.e. Reagan, Hollywood, actor. In this example, students would look for interesting, important, and relevant facts from sources about Reagan as an actor in Hollywood.)

Sample

Source Outlines

Write the name of the third topic you will research on the line below.

Third Topic: *subject, topic, another word about the topic*

Choose your first source. Write the title on the Source line. Using key words, write the topic on the Roman numeral line. Complete the source outline by noting three to five interesting facts about the topic. Repeat the process with the second source and, if applicable, with the third.

Source A: *Write the title of one of the sources from the library or the Internet.*

IV. Topic: *The topic lines of the source outlines and the fused outline must be the same.*

1.   *Each student's outline will be different because they are writing about different*

2.   *subjects, topics, and using different sources.*

3.   _____

(4.)   _____

(5.)   _____

Source B: *Write the title of one of the sources from the library or the Internet.*

IV. Topic: _____

1.   _____

2.   _____

3.   _____

(4.)   _____

(5.)   _____

Source C: _____

IV. Topic: *Write the title of one of the sources from the library or the Internet.*

1.   _____

2.   _____

3.   _____

(4.)   _____

(5.)   _____

Sample

Fused Outline

Using key words, write the topic on the Roman numeral line. This should be the same topic that you placed on the source outlines. Select five to seven facts from the source outlines to transfer to the fused outline.

IV. Topic: _____

1. _____ *Students choose facts from their source outlines to place onto their fused outline.*

2. _____

3. _____

4. _____

5. _____

(6.) _____

(7.) _____

Clincher

Style Practice

#2 Prepositional Opener

Prepositional openers add variety to your sentences. List some prepositional phrases that you could possibly add to a sentence.

Ideas will depend upon students' chosen subjects.

Dress-Ups

Write ideas for various dress-up you could use in your body paragraphs. Use a thesaurus or your vocabulary words.

1. strong verbs *Encourage students to look at their fused outlines and consider words to include in their composition.*

2. -ly adverbs

3. quality adjectives

Vocabulary Practice

Look at the vocabulary chart on pages 322–323. Try to use words from Lessons 1–25 in sentences or phrases that could be in your composition. Write at least two ideas below.

Unit 8 Composition Checklist

Formal
Essay
Models

Lesson 26: A Prominent American, Part 1 body paragraphs

Name: _____

IEW Institute for Excellence in Writing

STRUCTURE

☐ MLA format (see Appendix I) _____ 2 pts

☐ checklist on top, final draft, rough draft, key word outline _____ 2 pts

Body

☐ topic-clincher sentences repeat or reflect 2–3 key words (highlight or bold) _____ 4 pts

☐ facts stay on topic _____ 4 pts

STYLE

¶2 ¶3 ¶4 Dress-Ups (underline one of each) (1 pt each)

☐ ☐ ☐ -ly adverb _____ 3 pts

☐ ☐ ☐ *who/which* clause _____ 3 pts

☐ ☐ ☐ strong verb _____ 3 pts

☐ ☐ ☐ quality adjective _____ 3 pts

☐ ☐ ☐ *www.asia.b* clause _____ 3 pts

Sentence Openers (number; one of each as possible) (1 pt each)

☐ ☐ ☐ [1] subject _____ 3 pts

☐ ☐ ☐ [2] prepositional _____ 3 pts

☐ ☐ ☐ [3] -ly adverb _____ 3 pts

☐ ☐ ☐ [4] -ing _____ 3 pts

☐ ☐ ☐ [5] clausal - *www.asia.b* _____ 3 pts

☐ ☐ ☐ [6] vss _____ 3 pts

CHECK FOR BANNED WORDS (-1 pt for each use): go/went, say/said, good, bad, pretty, big, small _____ pts

MECHANICS

☐ spelling, grammar, and punctuation (-1 pt per error) _____ pts

VOCABULARY

☐ vocabulary words - label *(voc)* in left margin or after sentence

Total: _____ 45 pts

Custom Total: _____ pts

Teachers are free to adjust a checklist by requiring only the stylistic techniques that have become easy, plus one new one. EZ+1

UNIT 8: FORMAL ESSAY MODELS

Intentionally blank so the checklist can be removed.

Lesson 27: A Prominent American, Part 2

Structure:	Unit 8: Formal Essay Models
	introduction and conclusion
Style:	no new style
Writing Topic:	a prominent American
Literature Suggestion:	*Cheaper by the Dozen* by Frank B. Gilbreth Jr. and Ernestine Gilbreth Carey

Lesson 27: A Prominent American, Part 2

UNIT 8: FORMAL ESSAY MODELS

Lesson 27: A Prominent American, Part 2

Goals

- to practice the Unit 8 structural model
- to create KWOs for an introduction and a conclusion paragraph
- to write an introduction and a conclusion paragraph
- to complete a 5-paragraph essay with a bibliography
- to review vocabulary words

Assignment Schedule

Day 1

1. Play the Question Game.
2. Write a KWO for a conclusion and then write a KWO for an introduction.

Day 2

1. Review your KWOs from Day 1.
2. Complete Style Practice.
3. Complete Vocabulary Practice. There are no new words for this lesson.
4. Using your conclusion KWO as a guide, write your conclusion.
5. Go over the checklist. Put a check in the box for each requirement you have completed.

Day 3

1. Review all vocabulary words learned thus far.
2. Using your introduction KWO as a guide, write your introduction.
3. Write a bibliography that includes all the sources you used. Follow the format on page 177.
4. Turn in your rough draft to your editor with the completed checklist attached.

Day 4

1. Write or type a final draft making any corrections your editor asked you to make. Add the introduction and conclusion to the final draft body paragraphs written in Lesson 26. Include the bibliography.
2. Paperclip the checklist, final draft, rough drafts, and KWOs together. Hand them in.
3. If you are making a Magnum Opus Notebook, revise your Transportation Milestones composition from Lesson 25.

Literature Suggestion

Continue reading *Cheaper by the Dozen* by Frank B. Gilbreth Jr. and Ernestine Gilbreth Carey.

Question Game

See Appendix VII for game directions. Choose from the questions on pages 347–349. Be sure to include questions 21–23 and 26–29. Renumber them.

Sample

Key Word Outline—Conclusion

Restate the Topics

Write a sentence or two about each topic you wrote about in Lesson 26.

Most Significant and Why

Why is the person you researched remembered and studied in history? How did he or she influence or impact others? What admirable character traits does he or she possess?

Do not use the word "I" when stating what is most important or significant. When you use "I," it limits the impact your statement has on your reader. Consider these two statements:

I think Sally Ride is most significant for inspiring and encouraging young women to seek careers in science.

Sally Ride is most significant for inspiring and encouraging young women to seek careers in science.

The second is clearly stronger and more persuasive.

Final Sentence

End with a sentence from which you can create a title. Be sure that your paper sounds complete.

Sample

Key Word Outline for Conclusion

V.   Topic A: _____   *Ride, career, NASA advertisement* _____

Topic B: _____   *1st, woman, space* _____

Topic C: _____   *retired, NASA, cont. science* _____

Most significant   _____   *determination, persistence → goals* _____

Why?   _____   *milestone, space, prog.* _____

_____   *+ role model, ♀, inspirational* _____

Title repeats 1–3 key words from final sentence.

Highlight or bold the topic key words in your paragraph.

Institute for Excellence in Writing

Key Word Outline—Introduction

Attention Getter

>   Start your introduction with a sentence that encourages your reader to continue reading. Begin with a question, a very short sentence, or a famous quote or fact.

Background

>   Tell your reader what the subject of the composition is about by making a general statement about the subject. Then provide background information you think would be interesting or important. The background information should flow into the introduction of the topics.

Topics

>   End your introduction by listing the topics you wrote about in your body paragraphs in the same order they appear in the body of the paper. Highlight or bold the topic key words.

Sample

Key Word Outline for Introduction

I.	Attention getter	*Sally Ride, American, 1st*
	Background	*born, May 26, 1951, Encino, CA*
		bright, student, ♥, science
		1973–1978, study, Stanford U
	Topic A:	*Ride, career, NASA, advertisement*
	Topic B:	*1st, woman, space*
	Topic C:	*retired, NASA, cont. science*

Highlight or bold the topic key words in your paragraph.

This sample outline is for an essay about Sally Ride. Each student will outline a similar introduction for his or her chosen subject.

Ideas will depend upon students' chosen subjects. The sample ideas are general enough to be used with any chosen subject of a prominent American.

UNIT 8: FORMAL ESSAY MODELS

Style Practice

Sentence Openers

Write sentences that can be used in your introduction or conclusion.

1. #1 subject opener _____ *[1] Great people have made America great.*

2. #2 prepositional opener _____ *[2] With resolve and diligence, anything is possible.*

3. #3 -ly adverb opener _____ *[3] Fondly America will remember this hero.*

4. #4 -ing participial opener _____

   [4] Striving unwaveringly for excellence, such men become esteemed leaders.

5. #5 clausal opener – *www.asia.b* _____

   [5] When adversity struck, he remained resolved.

6. #6 vss opener, 2–5 words (This can be your attention getter.) _____

   [6] America remembers its heroes.

Dress-Ups

Look at your KWO and consider where you can include various clauses as well as strong verbs, quality adjectives, and -ly adverbs. When you write your paper, follow your checklist!

Vocabulary Practice

Look at the vocabulary chart on pages 322–323. Try to use words from Lessons 1–25 in sentences or phrases that could be in your composition. Write at least two ideas below.

*Our nation **thrives** because such men work **incessantly** against **formidable adversity***

*in order to succeed. His **innovative achievement** has **enthralled** the nation for decades.*

Institute for Excellence in Writing

Unit 8 Composition Checklist

Formal
Essay
Models

Lesson 27: A Prominent American, Part 2 introduction and conclusion

Name: _____

Institute for
Excellence in
Writing

STRUCTURE

☐ MLA format (see Appendix I) _____ 1 pt

☐ bibliography entries in proper format _____ 2 pts

☐ checklist on top, final draft, rough draft, key word outline _____ 1 pt

Introduction

☐ introduction includes attention getter, background information, and states topics (bold or highlight) _____ 10 pts

Body

☐ insert body paragraphs _____ 2 pts

Conclusion

☐ conclusion restates topics (bold or highlight) and indicates most significant/why _____ 10 pts

☐ final sentence repeats 1–3 key words for the title _____ 2 pts

STYLE

¶1 ¶5 Dress-Ups (underline one of each) (1 pt each)

☐ ☐ -ly adverb _____ 2 pts

☐ ☐ *who/which* clause _____ 2 pts

☐ ☐ strong verb _____ 2 pts

☐ ☐ quality adjective _____ 2 pts

☐ ☐ *www.asia.b* clause _____ 2 pts

Sentence Openers (number; one of each as possible) (1 pt each)

☐ ☐ [1] subject _____ 2 pts

☐ ☐ [2] prepositional _____ 2 pts

☐ ☐ [3] -ly adverb _____ 2 pts

☐ ☐ [4] -ing _____ 2 pts

☐ ☐ [5] clausal - *www.asia.b* _____ 2 pts

☐ ☐ [6] vss _____ 2 pts

CHECK FOR BANNED WORDS (-1 pt for each use): go/went, say/said, good, bad, pretty, big, small _____ pts

MECHANICS

☐ spelling, grammar, and punctuation (-1 pt per error) _____ pts

VOCABULARY

☐ vocabulary words - label *(voc)* in left margin or after sentence

Total: _____ 50 pts

Custom Total: _____ pts

Teachers are free to adjust a checklist by requiring only the stylistic techniques that have become easy, plus one new one. EZ+1

UNIT 8: FORMAL ESSAY MODELS

Intentionally blank so the checklist can be removed.

Lesson 28: Davy Crockett, Part 1

Structure: Unit 9: Formal Critique
body paragraphs

Style: no new style

Writing Topic: Davy Crockett

Literature Suggestion: *Cheaper by the Dozen* by Frank B. Gilbreth Jr. and Ernestine Gilbreth Carey

Teaching Writing: Structure and Style

Watch the sections for Unit 9: Formal Critique. At IEW.com/twss-help reference the TWSS Viewing Guides.

UNIT 9: FORMAL CRITIQUE AND RESPONSE TO LITERATURE

Lesson 28: Davy Crockett, Part 1

Goals

- to learn the Unit 9 Formal Critique structural model
- to create a KWO
- to write the body paragraphs of a short story critique
- to learn and practice using some critique vocabulary
- to correctly use new vocabulary words: *narrative, intrigue, recount, triumph*

Assignment Schedule

Day 1

1. Play a vocabulary game such as Vocabulary Lightning.
2. Read Historical Information.
3. Read New Structure—Formal Critique Model: Body Paragraphs.
4. Read "Davy Crockett Saves the Day." Then write a KWO by answering the Story Sequence Chart questions.

Day 2

1. Review your KWO from Day 1.
2. Complete Style Practice.
3. Look at the vocabulary cards for Lesson 28. Discuss the definitions and complete Vocabulary Practice.
4. Using your KWO as a guide, begin writing a rough draft.
5. Go over the checklist. Put a check in the box for each requirement you have completed.

Day 3

1. Review all vocabulary words learned thus far.
2. Finish writing your three body paragraphs.
3. Turn in your rough draft to your editor with the completed checklist attached.

Day 4

1. Write or type a final draft making any corrections your editor asked you to make.
2. Paperclip the checklist, final draft, rough draft, and KWO together. Hand them in.

Study for the Final Vocabulary Quiz. It will cover words from Lessons 1–28.

In Lessons 28–29 students write a 5-paragraph formal critique. They begin by forming the body paragraphs based on the Story Sequence Chart. Help students focus on writing about the story rather than simply telling the story. Using words from the Critique Thesaurus will help. *The protagonist of the story ...*

Remind students that these paragraphs do not contain topic or clincher sentences.

Literature Suggestion

Continue reading *Cheaper by the Dozen* by Frank B. Gilbreth Jr. and Ernestine Gilbreth Carey.

Historical Information

Davy Crockett was born in the mountains of Tennessee in 1786. A skilled woodsman, Crockett was famous for his coonskin cap. He liked to boast and tell tall tales. In fact, he once declared, "I'm that same David Crockett, fresh from the backwoods, half-horse, half-alligator, a little touched with the snapping turtle; can wade the Mississippi, leap the Ohio, ride upon a streak of lightning, and slip without a scratch down a honey locust." He wrote almanacs filled with tall tales and eventually became a celebrity. People of his day loved him. When he ran for political office, the citizens elected him to the Tennessee legislature and later to the U.S. Congress. Sadly, Crockett died in the Battle of the Alamo when the men there refused to surrender despite overwhelming odds. After his death, people continued to tell tall tales about Crockett out of admiration. In fact, Walt Disney created a television series and a movie about Crockett. In Tennessee Ernie Ford's theme song "The Ballad of Davy Crockett," Crockett is referred to as "the king of the wild frontier."

New Structure

Formal Critique Model: Body Paragraphs

In Unit 9 you will write critiques of literature. Do this by combining your knowledge of how to retell narrative stories (Unit 3) with how to write introduction and conclusion paragraphs (Units 7 and 8). You may follow this model to critique short stories, movies, novels, plays, and television shows.

The model contains an introduction, three body paragraphs, and a conclusion. The body paragraphs follow the Story Sequence Chart. The elements required in the introduction and conclusion are specific to critiques. Notice the paragraphs in this model do not contain topic or clincher sentences.

	I.	Introduction	*attention getter, background*
Story	II.	Characters and Setting	
Sequence	III.	Conflict or Problem	
Chart	IV.	Climax and Resolution	
	V.	Conclusion	*your opinion/why, message/moral, last sentence ➜ title*

Like other 5-paragraph compositions, write from the inside out beginning with the body paragraphs. When you write a critique, it is not necessary to relate every character or detail of the story. Instead, provide a brief summary of different parts of the story in order to give your opinion about those specific parts. To do this, use the Story Sequence Chart.

Although Unit 9 does not contain topic or clincher sentences, each body paragraph may begin with the focus of the paragraph. For example, the first body paragraph may begin "Davy Crockett Saves the Day" *is set in* ___. In this paragraph you will explain the setting and indicate the characters of the story.

The second body paragraph may begin *The problem is* ___. In this paragraph indicate the primary conflict or problem of the story and how the characters attempt to solve the problem.

The third body paragraph may begin *The climax occurs* ___. After indicating the climax of the story, the rest of the paragraph explains how the author brought the story to an end. When applicable, this paragraph may tell the message or moral of the story.

Critique Thesaurus

Use vocabulary words on the Critique Thesaurus in Appendix IV to enhance your critique. In the body paragraphs, use words that describe the *setting, characters, conflict, climax,* and *resolution.*

UNIT 9: FORMAL CRITIQUE AND RESPONSE TO LITERATURE

Source Text

Davy Crockett Saves the Day

Retold by Lori Verstegen

Let me tell you about an American legend from the backwoods of the great state of Tennessee. His name is Davy Crockett. As a youngster, Davy spent all his time roaming the wilderness. He delighted in chasing bears, and it is known everywhere east of the Mississippi that he killed his first grizzly when he was only three. He excelled at hunting, too, and I'll prove to you just what I mean. One day while hunting, Davy spotted a flock of geese in the sky and a buck in the meadow. Since he had a double-barreled shot gun, he aimed it so that with one pull of the trigger he hit both. The force of the shot was so great that he fell back into the river where his pockets filled with all kinds of flopping fish. Being so weighted down, his shirt pulled at its buttons. Two of them popped off with enormous force, like bullets. One hit and killed a nearby squirrel and the other a bear. Davy headed home with enough food to last a month—all from one shot!

Davy liked to brag, too. Sometimes his boasting got him into trouble, though. One such time occurred in a thunderstorm in the middle of a dense forest. He had been hiking for miles and miles, so he was mighty hungry. *Well*, he thought, *I'll just have to find me a meal*. He began poking and prodding around the forest when he spotted two big bright eyeballs glaring at him out of the pitch-black darkness. "Hello, there," he bellowed, "I'm Davy Crockett, the greatest hunter in the land. I'm real hungry, so that's bad news for you!"

Just then a lightning bolt revealed that the eyes belonged to an enormous panther surrounded by piles of bones. He was licking his lips because he too was hungry. Davy backed up and attempted to beg the beast's pardon, but the panther growled, ground its teeth, and raised its razor-sharp claws. It leapt at Davy. Well, a whirlwind of a fight erupted and grew into a hurricane of a fight until Davy grabbed the beast by the tail and hurled it at the ground over and over again. The cat begged for mercy, but Davy could not leave it to menace the forest animals. He decided to take it home, civilize it, and make it his pet.

Well, eventually Davy grew up. He was so loved by the people of Tennessee that they elected him to the United States House of Representatives. He rode all the way to Washington D.C. on the back of a massive bear. He hoped to impress the highfalutin society folks in the capital city. He got his chance because everyone there was in a panic.

"We'll all be killed!" a woman screamed.

"There's no hope," a man despaired.

"Somebody must do something!"

They were staring at the sky. Davy looked up, too. What do you suppose he spotted? A monstrous comet with a long, icy tail was zooming straight for the earth! A collision would be disastrous.

Davy knew just what to do. He skedaddled up the nearest mountain and leapt into the sky. He grabbed that comet by the tail. Then, with all of his might, he twirled it 'round and 'round and 'round over his head like a lasso. Then, he let it loose. It sailed far into outer space where it belonged. The town was saved! Davy was a hero!

These are just a few of the stupendous feats of Davy Crockett. He did many more, too many to tell in this short tale. But suffice it to say that Davy Crockett is an esteemed American legend.

I. Characters and Setting

Students give opinion of Davy, the lengthy background information, and the setting. Do not retell the details of Davy's hunt or his encounter with the panther. Instead, tell only the details that help describe Davy.

II. Conflict or Problem

In this paragraph, students critique the main problem—a comet is headed towards earth and causing everyone to panic.

III. Climax and Resolution

In the final paragraph begin with the climax. Davy's spotting the comet is the climax. The resolution starts with Davy grabbing the comet and spinning it. The people admire the man.

Sample

Key Word Outline—Story Sequence Chart

Identify the Story Sequence Chart elements. Use words such as *setting, characters, conflict, climax, resolution*, and their synonyms found on the Critique Thesaurus in Appendix IV.

Characters and Setting

When and where does the story occur? This is the *setting*.

Name and describe each main character.

II. _____ set, backwoods, Tennessee _____
1. _____ Davy Crockett, Amer., legend _____
2. _____ young, grew, ↑, wilderness _____
3. _____ ♥, chasing, bears _____
4. _____ expert, hunter _____
(5.) _____ fights, tames, panther _____

Conflict or Problem

What does the main character want or need? This is the *conflict*.

Tell what the main characters do, say, and think in order to solve the problem.

Tell how they feel as they try to solve the problem.

III. _____ problem, comet, ↓, earth _____
1. _____ Davy, arrives, Washington D.C. _____
2. _____ ppl, panicking, 👀, ↑, sky _____
3. _____ world, end ? _____
4. _____ X know, what, do _____
(5.) _____

Climax and Resolution

What event in the story reveals how the conflict will work out (whether the problem will be solved or not)? This is the *climax*.

What is the outcome for the main characters at the end of the story? This is the *resolution*.

IV. _____ climax, D.C., 👀, comet, knows _____
1. _____ climbs, 🏔, grabs, tail _____
2. _____ twirls, like, lasso _____
3. _____ flings, outer, space _____
4. _____ world, saved, D.C., hero _____
(5.) _____

These paragraphs do not contain topic-clincher sentences.

The stylistic and vocabulary exercises in Unit 9 are written in present tense because literature critiques are most commonly written in present tense. The narrator says, not said.

Style Practice

Quality Adjective Dress-Up

When you critique a story, you do not tell the story. Rather you tell about the story. Next to each noun write ideas for adjectives that will help you tell about the story.

1. the legend _beloved, renowned, enduring, unforgettable_

2. the wilderness _wild, untamed, expansive, **extensive**, fierce_

3. the problem _imminent, **looming**, startling, ghastly, dreadful_

4. the climax _outlandish, sensational, humorous, dramatic, incredible_

Strong Verb Dress-Up and -ly Adverb Dress-Up

On the first line under each sentence, write strong verbs that could replace the italicized banned verb. On the second line under each sentence, write ideas for -ly adverbs that you could use with the strong verbs. Use a thesaurus or your vocabulary words.

1. The narrator _says_ that "Davy Crockett is an esteemed American legend."

   strong verbs _declares, remarks, reminds us, claims_

   -ly adverbs _affectionately, boldly, heartily_

2. The problem occurs when Davy Crockett _goes_ to Washington D.C.

   strong verbs _travels, treks, rides, struts_

   -ly adverbs _eventually, confidently, arrogantly, **loftily**_

3. Davy lets _go_ of the comet.

   strong verbs _hurls, flings, launches, casts_

   -ly adverbs _triumphantly, vigorously, determinedly, readily_

Vocabulary Practice

Look at the vocabulary words for Lesson 28. Fill in the blanks with a word that makes sense.

1. The story _____ *recounts* _____ some of the adventures of Davy Crockett.

2. His_____ *triumph* _____ over the comet earns him fame as a hero in Washington D.C.

Look at the critique vocabulary chart in Appendix IV. Try to use words from this chart in sentences or phrases that could be in your critique. Write at least two ideas below.

*The **tale** of Davy Crockett...*

*The **central character** is obviously Davy Crockett.*

*The **setting** is in the **wild frontier**.*

*In the **sequence of events** in this **narrative**, Davy treks to the capital.*

*The **inevitable conclusion** to this dilemma is that Davy Crockett will save the day.*

Unit 9 Composition Checklist
Lesson 28: Davy Crockett, Part 1 body paragraphs

Formal Critique

Name: _____

Institute for Excellence in Writing
Listen. Speak. Read. Write. Think!

STRUCTURE

☐ MLA format (see Appendix I) _____ 1 pt

☐ checklist on top, final draft, rough draft, key word outline _____ 1 pt

Body

☐ Unit 9: 3 paragraphs follow Story Sequence Chart (Unit 3) and include words from the Critique Thesaurus page in each paragraph _____ 15 pts

STYLE

¶2 ¶3 ¶4 **Dress-Ups** (underline one of each2)   (1 pt each)

☐ ☐ ☐ -ly adverb _____ 3 pts

☐ ☐ ☐ *who/which* clause _____ 3 pts

☐ ☐ ☐ strong verb _____ 3 pts

☐ ☐ ☐ *www.asia.b* clause _____ 3 pts

☐ ☐ ☐ quality adjective _____ 3 pts

Sentence Openers (number; one of each as possible)   (1 pt each)

☐ ☐ ☐ [1] subject _____ 3 pts

☐ ☐ ☐ [2] prepositional _____ 3 pts

☐ ☐ ☐ [3] -ly adverb _____ 3 pts

☐ ☐ ☐ [4] -ing _____ 3 pts

☐ ☐ ☐ [5] clausal - *www.asia.b* _____ 3 pts

☐ ☐ ☐ [6] vss _____ 3 pts

CHECK FOR BANNED WORDS (-1 pt for each use): go/went, say/said, good, bad, pretty, big, small _____ pts

MECHANICS

☐ spelling, grammar, and punctuation (-1 pt per error) _____ pts

VOCABULARY

☐ vocabulary words - label *(voc)* in left margin or after sentence

Total: _____ 50 pts

Custom Total: _____ pts

Teachers are free to adjust a checklist by requiring only the stylistic techniques that have become easy, plus one new one. EZ+1

UNIT 9: FORMAL CRITIQUE AND RESPONSE TO LITERATURE

Intentionally blank so the checklist can be removed.

Lesson 29: Davy Crockett, Part 2

Structure:	Unit 9: Formal Critique introduction and conclusion
Style:	no new style
Writing Topic:	Davy Crockett
Literature Suggestion:	*Cheaper by the Dozen* by Frank B. Gilbreth Jr. and Ernestine Gilbreth Carey

Lesson 29: Davy Crockett, Part 2

UNIT 9: FORMAL CRITIQUE AND RESPONSE TO LITERATURE

Lesson 29: Davy Crockett, Part 2

Goals

- to practice the Unit 9 structural model
- to create KWOs for an introduction and a conclusion paragraph
- to add an introduction and a conclusion paragraph to the short story critique
- to take the Final Vocabulary Quiz

Assignment Schedule

Day 1

1. Take the Final Vocabulary Quiz.
2. Complete the Review.
3. Read New Structure—Formal Critique Model: Introduction and Conclusion.
4. Write a KWO for a conclusion and then write a KWO for an introduction.

Day 2

1. Complete Style Practice.
2. Complete Vocabulary Practice. There are no new words for this lesson.
3. Using your conclusion KWO as a guide, write your conclusion.
4. Go over the checklist. Put a check in the box for each requirement you have completed.

Day 3

1. Review all vocabulary words learned thus far.
2. Using your introduction KWO as a guide, write your introduction.
3. Turn in your rough draft to your editor with the completed checklist attached.

Day 4

1. Write or type a final draft making any corrections your editor asked you to make. Add the introduction and the conclusion to the final draft body paragraphs written in lesson 28.
2. Paperclip the checklist, final draft, rough drafts, and KWOs together. Hand them in.
3. If you are making a Magnum Opus Notebook, revise your Prominent American essay from Lessons 26–27.

Literature Suggestion

Finish reading *Cheaper by the Dozen* by Frank B. Gilbreth Jr. and Ernestine Gilbreth Carey.

Students complete the formal critique begun in the last lesson by adding an introduction and conclusion. The structures of the introduction and conclusion paragraphs are unique to this unit. Help students recognize and incorporate each important element.

Review

Explain the structure of a basic five-paragraph critique by writing the purpose of each paragraph.

I.   *Introduction (attention getter, background)*

II.   *Characters and Setting*

III.   *Conflict or Problem*

IV.   *Climax and Resolution*

V.   *Conclusion (your opinion/why, message/moral, last sentence)*

New Structure

Formal Critique Model: Introduction and Conclusion

Now that you have completed the body paragraphs, you are ready to add the introduction and conclusion. Look at the model below and notice the components that make up the introduction and conclusion. In the critique model, these two paragraphs follow their own unique structure.

I.   Introduction   *attention getter, background*

      Body Paragraphs

V.   Conclusion   *your opinion/why, message/moral, last sentence ➜ title*

The introduction must get the readers' attention by enticing readers to keep reading. This paragraph must also introduce the story to the reader. This is where you write the title of the story, tell when it was written, and provide details about the author and/or publisher.

The conclusion is where you tell if you like or do not like the story and why. This paragraph must indicate your opinion of the story, which is the purpose of a critique. For this reason, the conclusion is the most important paragraph of the critique and often the longest. Because the conclusion must flow smoothly from the final body paragraph, you will outline and write the conclusion before you write the introduction.

Key Word Outline—Conclusion

In the conclusion do not use *I*, *my*, *we*, *us*, or *you*. Consider these statements:

> In my opinion, this story symbolizes Crockett's strength and tenacity.

> This story symbolizes Crockett's strength and tenacity.

The second is clearly stronger and more persuasive.

Your opinion

Begin the conclusion with your overall impression of the story. The conclusion may begin like this: "Davy Crockett Saves the Day" is a _____ story that _____. Do not use vague adjectives like *good*, *bad*, *interesting*, or *wonderful*. Use specific adjectives like *suspenseful*, *predictable*, *engrossing*, *boring*, *tragic*, *powerful*, *thought-provoking*, *captivating*, *wild*.

> "Davy Crockett Saves the Day" is a wild tall tale that entertains through exaggeration.

Why

Support your opinion by telling a few things you like or do not like in the story. You may mention the style of writing, the best or worst aspect of the story, how realistic the characters appear, how much action the story contains, what makes the conflict exciting or boring, what makes the climax suspenseful or predictable, and if the story ends well.

Message/moral

Indicate if there is a message or moral found within the story and what that message's overall effect has upon the reader.

Final sentence

Make sure your final sentence makes the paper sound complete and contains words you can use to create a title.

Sample

Key Word Outline for Conclusion

V.	Your opinion	*rip-roaring, sure, laugh*
	Why?	*DC, impossible, feats*
		ex, tames, panther, flings, 🔥
	Message/moral	*obviously, exaggerated, = fun*
		legends, endear, DC, ➜, Amer, ppl

Title repeats 1–3 key words from final sentence.

Never use *I*, *my*, *we*, *us*, *you*.

Key Word Outline—Introduction

Attention Getter

> Begin with something intriguing that will make your reader want to read more. Consider using a quote about the author or from the story.

Background

> In this section of the introduction, provide basic information specific to the author and the story including the title, type of story, and publisher. It would be appropriate to mention facts from Historical Information on page 270. In addition to mentioning where the story is found, you could mention the historical time of the story and any events that parallel the story. You could also indicate some information about the story's author.

Sample

Key Word Outline for Introduction

I.   Attention getter   _"King, wild, frontier"_

    Background   _DC Saves the Day, Lori Verstegen, pub., IEW, 2020_

                    DC real ♂ born, 1786, TN

                    woodsman, brag, lightheartedly

                    Amer ♥ elected, Congress

                    XX, Alamo, legends, continued

Style Practice

Dress-Ups and Sentence Openers

Look at your KWO and consider where you can include various clauses as well as strong verbs, quality adjectives, -ly adverbs, and sentence openers. When you write your paper, follow your checklist!

Vocabulary Practice

Look at the critique vocabulary chart in Appendix VI. Try to use words from this chart in sentences or phrases that could be in your critique. Write at least two ideas below.

The **hero** is **adventurous** and **comic** at the same time.

The **narrative** has almost a **mythical** feel.

Unit 9 Composition Checklist

Formal Critique

Lesson 29: Davy Crockett, Part 2 introduction and conclusion

Name: _____

Institute for Excellence in Writing
Listen. Speak. Read. Write. Think!

STRUCTURE

☐ MLA format (see Appendix I)	_____	1 pt
☐ checklist on top, final draft, rough draft, key word outline	_____	1 pt

Introduction

☐ Unit 9: introduction includes attention getter, background information (title, author, publisher, type of story, awards)	_____	10 pts

Body

☐ insert body paragraphs	_____	2 pts

Conclusion

☐ Unit 9: your opinion of the story: well written or not, like/dislike and why, may also discuss character development, conflict, message, effect of story on reader	_____	10 pts
☐ no "I," "my," "we," "us," "you"	_____	3 pts
☐ final sentence repeats 1–3 key words for the title	_____	1 pt

STYLE

¶1 ¶5 Dress-Ups (underline one of each)   (1 pt each)

☐ ☐ -ly adverb		_____	2 pts
☐ ☐ *who/which* clause		_____	2 pts
☐ ☐ strong verb		_____	2 pts
☐ ☐ *www.asia.b* clause		_____	2 pts
☐ ☐ quality adjective		_____	2 pts

Sentence Openers (number; one of each as possible)   (1 pt each)

☐ ☐ [1] subject		_____	2 pts
☐ ☐ [2] prepositional		_____	2 pts
☐ ☐ [3] -ly adverb		_____	2 pts
☐ ☐ [4] -ing		_____	2 pts
☐ ☐ [5] clausal - *www.asia.b*		_____	2 pts
☐ ☐ [6] vss			2 pts

CHECK FOR BANNED WORDS (-1 pt for each use): go/went, say/said, good, bad, pretty, big, small   _____ pts

MECHANICS

☐ spelling, grammar, and punctuation (-1 pt per error)	_____	pts

VOCABULARY

☐ vocabulary words - label *(voc)* in left margin or after sentence		

Total:	_____	50 pts
Custom Total:	_____	pts

> Teachers are free to adjust a checklist by requiring only the stylistic techniques that have become easy, plus one new one. EZ+1

UNIT 9: FORMAL CRITIQUE AND RESPONSE TO LITERATURE

Intentionally blank so the checklist can be removed.

Institute for Excellence in Writing

Lesson 30: John Henry

Structure:	Unit 9: Formal Critique and Response to Literature character analysis
Style:	no new style
Writing Topic:	John Henry
Literature Suggestion:	*Cheaper by the Dozen* by Frank B. Gilbreth Jr. and Ernestine Gilbreth Carey

Lesson 30: John Henry

UNIT 9: FORMAL CRITIQUE AND RESPONSE TO LITERATURE

Lesson 30: John Henry

Goals

- to learn a variation of the Unit 9 structural model: Response to Literature
- to correctly write a character analysis
- to learn the TRIAC technique for developing a paragraph supporting an opinion
- to review vocabulary words

Assignment Schedule

Day 1

1. Play a vocabulary game such as Around the World.
2. Read Historical Information.
3. Read New Structure—Character Analysis.
4. Read "John Henry."
5. Follow the Story Sequence Chart to outline and write paragraph II. This paragraph does not have a topic or clincher sentence.
6. Go over the checklist. Put a check in the box for each requirement you have completed.

Day 2

1. Complete Style Practice and Vocabulary Practice.
2. Follow the TRIAC model to outline and write paragraph III. This paragraph does have a topic and clincher sentence.
3. Go over the checklist. Put a check in the box for each requirement you have completed.

Day 3

1. Review all vocabulary words learned thus far.
2. Write a KWO for a conclusion and then write a KWO for an introduction.
3. Using your KWOs as a guide, write your conclusion and then write your introduction.
4. Highlight or bold the topic key words in each paragraph.
5. Turn in your 4-paragraph critique to your editor with the completed checklist attached.

Day 4

1. Write or type a final draft making any corrections your editor asked you to make.
2. Paperclip the checklist, final draft, rough draft, and KWO together. Hand them in.

In this lesson instead of writing a critique on the entire story, students are taught to analyze a particular aspect of the literature. The first body paragraph, a summary of the entire story, is formed by following a modified version of the critique model. The second body paragraph, an analysis paragraph, is formed by using the TRIAC model.

The key word outlines guide the students in the process. For additional information on the TRIAC model, see pages 162–164 of *Teaching Writing Structure and Style Seminar Workbook.*

Historical Information

John Henry, like Davy Crockett, was a real man. However, the many legends about him, which are all sung as ballads, make it difficult to separate fact from fiction. We know that the real John Henry was born a slave. A large man for his day, he was six feet tall and two hundred pounds. After the Civil War he became a free man. A railroad company hired him as a steel driver, a hammer man. As a hammer man, he drove holes into rock by hammering a thick spike into it. Each hammer man had a helper called a shaker, who rotated the spike after each blow. Another employee, the blaster, placed explosives into the holes. When a mountain stood in their way, it is said that John Henry used a fourteen-pound hammer and cleared ten to twenty feet a day.

According to legend, a salesman approached the camp one day with a steam-powered machine, boasting that his machine could out drill any man. John Henry, who would not be outdone by a machine, challenged the man and his machine to a race. After hours of pounding, Henry won the race by driving fourteen feet to the machine's nine. Shortly thereafter, John Henry died. He was immortalized and came to symbolize the strength and dignity of man in an age when machines were replacing men in the workforce.

New Structure

Character Analysis

In this lesson you will use a variation of Unit 9 to analyze a particular aspect of literature. Rather than write a critique on the entire story, you will critique one aspect of one character. Notice that the first body paragraph contains all of the elements of the Story Sequence Chart, and the second body paragraph follows the TRIAC model. The elements required in the introduction and conclusion are specific to this type of critique.

I.	Introduction	*attention getter, background, state main focus*
II.	Story Summary	*characters and setting, conflict or problem, climax and resolution*
III.	Character Analysis	*topic, restriction, illustration, analysis, clincher*
IV.	Conclusion	*restate main focus, personal feelings/significance, most significant/why, last sentence ➔ title*

Critique Thesaurus

Use vocabulary words on the Critique Thesaurus in Appendix IV to enhance your critique.

Sample Paragraphs

These sample paragraphs are about Davy Crockett, whom we read about in Lessons 28–29.

Character Analysis

[Topic] [1] Davy **Crockett** is a bit of a **braggart** and **show** off [Restriction] <u>who</u> enjoys astonishing others with his <u>lofty</u> antics. [Illustration] [4] Being elected to the U.S. Congress, he <u>ostentatiously</u> heads for Washington D.C. on the back of a bear. [1] The narrator states, "He hoped to impress the highfalutin society folk of the capital city." [Analysis] [3] Clearly, his thoughts were not on how he could help or serve his country <u>although</u> he did do just that. [2] In that moment his thoughts and desires were on how he could <u>gain</u> more glory. [6] He focuses on himself. [Clincher] [5] Although Davy **Crockett** appears to **exalt** himself, his purpose was to amuse and **entertain**; therefore, it is difficult to fault him.

Conclusion

[Main Focus] [1] Davy Crockett enjoys the attention his **boasting** and adventures bring him. [Personal feelings/significance] [5] Although bragging and showing off typically offend, Crockett <u>manages</u> to endear readers to himself. [1] Perhaps that is <u>because</u> the tales are so <u>outlandish</u> that no one would actually believe them. [6] They entertain. [Most significant] [3] Most significantly, tall tales about Davy Crockett have captivated readers of all ages for decades. [Why] [2] In every way Crockett is a likable character. [4] Being remembered <u>fondly</u> as a legendary American frontiersman <u>who</u> turned politician, Davy Crockett truly remains "king of the wild frontier."

Source Text

John Henry, Steel Driving Man

Blankenship Version

John Henry was a railroad man,
He worked from six 'till five,
"Raise 'em up bullies and let 'em drop down,
I'll beat you to the bottom or die, lord, lord."
I'll beat you to the bottom or die."

John Henry said to his captain
"You are nothing but a common man,
Before that steam drill shall beat me down,
I'll die with my hammer in my hand."

John Henry said to the Shakers
"You must listen to my call,
Before that steam drill shall beat me down,
I'll jar these mountains till they fall."

John Henry's captain said to him
"I believe these mountains are caving in."
John Henry said to his captain: "Oh, Lord!"
"That's my hammer you hear in the wind."

John Henry, he said to his captain
"Your money is getting mighty slim,
When I hammer through this old mountain,
Oh Captain will you walk in?"

John Henry's captain came to him
With fifty dollars in his hand,
He laid his hand on his shoulder and said,
"This belongs to a steel driving man."

John Henry was hammering on the right side,
The big steam drill on the left,
Before that steam drill could beat him down,
He hammered his fool self to death.

They carried John Henry to the mountains,
From his shoulder his hammer would ring,
She caught on fire by a little blue blaze
I believe these old mountains are caving in.

John Henry was lying on his death bed,
He turned over on his side,
And these were the last words John Henry said
"Bring me a cool drink of water before I die."

John Henry had a little woman,
Her name was Pollie Ann,
He hugged and kissed her just before he died,
Saying, "Pollie, do the very best you can."

John Henry's woman heard he was dead,
She could not rest on her bed,
She got up at midnight, caught that No. 4 train,
"I am going where John Henry fell dead."

They carried John Henry to that new burying ground
His wife all dressed in blue,
She laid her hand on John Henry's cold face,
"John Henry I've been true to you."

Lesson 30: John Henry

Key Word Outline—Story Summary

Follow the Story Sequence Chart to outline and write paragraph II. Use the elements listed in the chart to provide a brief overview of the entire story of John Henry in one paragraph. To be successful, you must limit the details, giving only key elements the reader must have to understand the main points of the story.

Sample

Key Word Outline for Story Summary

II.   Characters and Setting

set, near, , RR, construction

character, John Henry, hammerman

Conflict or Problem

prob., begins, w/ steam drill

JH, challenges, dig,

Climax and Resolution

climax, JH, wins

dies, soon, after

This paragraph does not contain a topic or clincher sentence.

Key Word Outline—Character Analysis

Follow the TRIAC model to outline and write paragraph III. This differs from the formal critique because in this assignment you focus on one aspect of one character. This is the most important paragraph of this composition because it is where you give your personal critique.

Because the illustration should include at least one quotation from the source text, it is often easier to build your paragraph around a quote by or about a character than to awkwardly fit a quote into something you have already written.

For example, this is John Henry's response to the steam drill: "Before that steam drill shall beat me down, / I'll die with my hammer in my hand."

Topic

    State the topic. Choose one character in the story and make a statement about a quality, motive, effect, change, or something the character learned.

    If you decided to use the quote above, the topic will highlight the character John Henry and his proud, tenacious spirit. The key words for the topic line may be *JH, tenacity, X surrender, machine*. Using those words, the topic sentence might be *John Henry's proud, tenacious spirit would not allow him to surrender to a machine.*

Restriction

    Make a statement or claim about the topic, focusing the paragraph.

Illustration

    Give an example illustrating the statement or claim. This must be a quotation from the original story.

Analysis

    Explain the illustration.

Clincher

    Repeat or reflect two or three key words from the topic sentence.

Sample

Key Word Outline for Character Analysis

III. **T**opic   _JH, pride, X surrender, machine._

    Restriction   _challenges, steam, drill,_

                             JH, blinded, w/ determination

    Illustration   _"Before that steam drill..._

                             I'll die w/ ... my hand."

    Analysis   _J.H., pride, ➜, do, impossible_

                             won, comp, XX, ➜, ?, gain

    Clincher   _J.H., pride, ➜, grave_

Highlight or bold 2–3 key words that repeat or reflect in the topic and clincher sentences.

Key Word Outline—Conclusion

The Response to Literature conclusion is structured differently than the other conclusions.

Restate the Main Focus

The character analysis topic in paragraph III is the main focus of the composition. Begin the conclusion by stating the topic and explaining its importance.

Personal Feelings/Significance

Your opinion regarding the topic is very important. For that reason, include a sentence with the phrase *This story demonstrates ... or teaches ...* or *This story reminds one of ...* or *This story changes the reader ...* or *causes the audience to think ...* . Use this as a way to make a personal connection with the story.

Most Significant and Why

Similar to other conclusions you have written, tell what is significant, moving, or important about this narrative. Then explain why.

Final Sentence

Make sure your final sentence makes the paper sound complete and contains words you can use to create a title.

Sample

Key Word Outline for Conclusion

IV.   Main focus (state ¶ III topic) _____ *JH, pride, X surrender, machine*

Personal feelings/ _____ *demonstrates, ppl, need, valued*
significance

_____ *+ > feats, prove, worth*

Most significant _____ *J.H., symbolized, resolve, ♀, soul*

Why? _____ *b/c, willing, die, dignity, ♀*

_____ *tragedy = legend, inspires*

Title repeats 1–3 key words from final sentence.

Highlight or bold the topic in your paragraph.

Never use *I, me, we, us, you.*

Key Word Outline—Introduction

The structure for the Response to Literature introduction should look familiar. It begins just like the formal critique introduction. The only difference is that this introduction has an additional element.

Attention Getter

> Begin with something intriguing that will make your reader want to read more. Consider using a quote about the author or from the story.

Background

> In this section of the introduction, provide basic information specific to the author and the story including the title, type of story, and publisher. It would be appropriate to mention facts from Historical Information on page 286. In addition to mentioning where the story is found, you could mention the historical time of the story and any events that parallel the story.

State Main Focus

> The character analysis topic in paragraph III is the main focus of the composition. Introduce that topic by ending the introductory paragraph with a sentence that reflects the clincher sentence of paragraph III.

Sample

Key Word Outline for Introduction

I.   Attention getter   _____ *"I'll, XX, w/ hammer, hand"* _____

    Background   _____ *words, J.H., "J.H., Steel Driving Man"* _____

          _____ *Blankenship version, ballad, pub., IEW, 2020* _____

          _____ *based, real, RR, ⋏ mid 1800s* _____

          _____ *machines, replacing, ⋏ build, RR* _____

    Main focus (state ¶ III topic) _____ *JH, pride, X surrender, machine* _____

Highlight or bold the topic in your paragraph.

Style Practice

Dress-Ups and Sentence Openers

Look at your KWO and consider where you can include various clauses as well as strong verbs, quality adjectives, -ly adverbs, and sentence openers. When you write your paper, follow your checklist!

Vocabulary Practice

Look at the critique vocabulary chart in Appendix IV. Try to use words from this chart in sentences or phrases that could be in your critique. Write at least two ideas below.

_____ The **legendary ballad** of John Henry is a **tragedy**.

_____ The **protagonist** is a **victim** of his own pride.

_____ John Henry's statement at the start of the poem is a **foreboding** of his **tragic** end.

_____ The **conflict** is **initiated** by the invention of the steam drill and **heightened** by Henry's pride.

Unit 9 Composition Checklist
Lesson 30: John Henry

Formal
Critique

Name: _____

IEW Institute for Excellence in Writing

STRUCTURE

☐ MLA format (see Appendix I) _____ 1 pt

☐ checklist on top, final draft, rough draft, key word outline _____ 1 pt

Introduction

☐ attention getter, background, main focus _____ 5 pts

Body

☐ body ¶1 follows Story Sequence Chart (Unit 3) _____ 5 pts

☐ body ¶2 follows TRIAC Model _____ 5 pts

Conclusion

☐ conclusion restates topic (bold or highlight) and indicates most significant/why _____ 5 pts

☐ no "I," "my," "we," "us," "you" _____ 2 pts

☐ final sentence repeats 1–3 **key words** for the title _____ 2 pts

STYLE

¶1 ¶2 ¶3 ¶4 Dress-Ups (underline one of each)   (1 pt each)

☐ ☐ ☐ ☐ -ly adverb _____ 4 pts

☐ ☐ ☐ ☐ *who/which* clause _____ 4 pts

☐ ☐ ☐ ☐ strong verb _____ 4 pts

☐ ☐ ☐ ☐ *www.asia.b* clause _____ 4 pts

☐ ☐ ☐ ☐ quality adjective _____ 4 pts

Sentence Openers (number; one of each as possible)   (1 pt each)

☐ ☐ ☐ ☐ [1] subject _____ 4 pts

☐ ☐ ☐ ☐ [2] prepositional _____ 4 pts

☐ ☐ ☐ ☐ [3] -ly adverb _____ 4 pts

☐ ☐ ☐ ☐ [4] -ing _____ 4 pts

☐ ☐ ☐ ☐ [5] clausal - *www.asia.b* _____ 4 pts

☐ ☐ ☐ ☐ [6] vss _____ 4 pts

CHECK FOR BANNED WORDS (-1 pt for each use): go/went, say/said, good, bad, pretty, big, small _____ pts

MECHANICS

☐ spelling, grammar, and punctuation (-1 pt per error) _____ pts

VOCABULARY

☐ vocabulary words - label *(voc)* in left margin or after sentence

Total: _____ 70 pts

Custom Total: _____ pts

Teachers are free to adjust a checklist by requiring only the stylistic techniques that have become easy, plus one new one. EZ+1

UNIT 9: FORMAL CRITIQUE AND RESPONSE TO LITERATURE

Intentionally blank so the checklist can be removed.

Bonus Lesson: Vocabulary Story

Writing Topic: Familiar Story of Choice

JUST FOR FUN

Bonus Lesson: Vocabulary Story

Goals

- to master the use of the vocabulary words
- to write an original version of a familiar story or to borrow a conflict to write an original story

Assignment Schedule

Day 1

1. Complete the Review.

2. Read New Structure—Vocabulary Story and Borrowing a Conflict.

3. Complete Structure Practice.

Day 2

1. Write a KWO by answering the Story Sequence Chart questions.

2. Using your KWO as a guide, begin writing your story. Include as many vocabulary words as possible.

Day 3

1. Complete your story.

2. Bold each vocabulary word that you used. (There is no checklist for this lesson.)

3. Turn in your story to your editor.

Day 4

1. Write or type a final draft, making the corrections your editor asked you to make.

2. Hand your paper in.

3. If you are making a Magnum Opus Notebook, revise your Davy Crockett critique from Lessons 28–29.

Review

What is the structure of a formal critique?

What is the structure of a 4-paragraph character analysis?

What does each letter of TRIAC stand for?

New Structure

Vocabulary Story

This last lesson is a "just for fun" assignment. Writing a vocabulary story is not only a fun way to end the year, but it serves as a great review of the vocabulary words that you have learned.

The instructions are simple: Write a story using as many vocabulary words as you can. You may write a familiar story (such as an Aesop fable, a children's story, or a fairy tale), or you may make up your own story by borrowing a conflict from a familiar story. Borrowing a conflict is explained below.

Here are the rules:

1. Words must be used correctly and fit naturally.

2. You may not put more than three adjectives in front of one noun. (For example, you may not say something like this: the zealous, awestruck, appalled, prominent monster)

There is no checklist for this assignment, but tickets will be given as follows:

*   One ticket is given for each vocabulary word used well and bolded.

*   If you use at least fifty vocabulary words, you earn 100 tickets. (Repeated words do not count.)

Read the sample at the end of this lesson.

Borrowing a Conflict

It is difficult to come up with a completely original story; however, it is not as difficult to borrow a conflict in order to create your own story. Borrowing a conflict means that you take the basic "problem" of a story and change the characters and setting.

For example, the conflict of "The Tortoise and the Hare" is that one character (the hare) is proud and makes fun of another character (the tortoise) because he believes he is not as good at something (running). But the second character challenges the first to a contest and wins. How could we borrow this basic conflict and set the story in America with different characters?

How about an arrogant British redcoat who constantly makes fun of the American militia until one of the Americans challenges him to shooting contest. Something related to his arrogance must cause the redcoat to miss the target. For example, maybe he did not take enough time to prepare his gun because he was overconfident, or maybe he was distracted by a pretty lady he desired to impress.

Structure Practice

1. Below, list at least five children's stories. If you would like to try to change the setting and characters of your story, write an idea for doing so below each. Since this is a U.S. history-based course, try to set your story in America. Remember, it is not required that you change the characters and setting. You may write any story and simply add many vocabulary words to it.

    The Lion and the Mouse

    The Tortoise and the Hare

    The Three Little Pigs

    The Ugly Duckling

    Little Red Riding Hood

    Little Red Hen

    Goldilocks and the Three Bears

    Jack and the Beanstalk

    The Goose that Laid the Golden Egg

    The Gingerbread Boy

    The Milkmaid and Her Pail

    Cinderella

2. Now open to your chart of vocabulary words on pages 322–323. For each story you listed, see if you can quickly think of ways to use several of the vocabulary words in your story. If you cannot do so for one story idea, you should probably choose another to write.

    Answers will vary depending upon the stories chosen.

You may want to host a class party. Encourage students to read the vocabulary story or a favorite composition from Unit 5 or Unit 7. Consider having an auction in which students can use their tickets to buy prizes. (See Appendix VII for details about the auction.) If you prefer not to do an auction, consider a final review game such as simplified Jeopardy, also explained in Appendix VII.

Outlines will vary because each student will choose a different story. Remind students to begin their stories by taking time to describe the setting and introduce the characters. Next, they should introduce a conflict; then, of course, they must find a way to solve that conflict. Outlining before they write will help them remember to do these things.

JUST FOR FUN

Key Word Outline—Story Sequence Chart

Characters and Setting

When does the story happen?	
Who is in the story?	
What are they like?	
Where do they live or go?	

I. _____

1. _____

2. _____

3. _____

4. _____

(5.) _____

Conflict or Problem

What does the main character want or need?
What do the main characters do, say, think, and feel?
What happens before the climax?

II. _____

1. _____

2. _____

3. _____

4. _____

(5.) _____

Climax and Resolution

What leads to the conflict being solved (the climax)?
What happens as a result?
What is learned? (message, moral)

III. _____

1. _____

2. _____

3. _____

4. _____

(5.) _____

Title repeats 1–3 key words from final sentence.

Institute for Excellence in Writing

Sample Vocabulary Story

Nathan E.

Lesson 30

30 April 2019

Build Your House on the Rock

Once upon a time, three little piggies resided with their mother. Outside the safety of their neighborhood, **cunning** and deplorable wolves prowled the forest, each **aspiring** to lure a plump, juicy pig into his jaws. The most **prominent** of these **hostile** predators was a **formidable** creature named Warrick W. Wolf. **Tyrannically**, he ruled the forest, **compelling** many pigs to leave the land.

One day, the mother of the three little pigs called them all into the kitchen.

"My precious porkers," their mother began, "you have lived here all your life. Now, it is **imperative** that you **endeavor** to be **prosperous** and **flourish** in this **adverse** world. So pack your things and travel away. But be warned! Warrick W. Wolf is **innovative** and **persistent**."

Laden with their possessions, the **audacious** pigs **ventured** out on their **quest**. Presently, the road split into three parts, each leading through the **perilous** wood. Piggies Number One and Two waltzed carelessly down their own roads. As he skipped along, Piggy Number One **encountered** a straw-dealer. Immediately the **adroit** dealer sold him a crate of straw. **Presuming** all would be well, the naïve pig **imprudently** threw up a house of flimsy straw on meadow grass. He then **squandered** the rest of the day playing **stirring** tunes on his flute, **enthralled** by his own music.

Piggy Number Two **resolved** to build his house out of twigs on a convenient sandy riverbank so that he could then play with his ball the rest of the day.

Meanwhile, Piggy Number Three soon reached a clearing flanked by trees. He looked **warily** about. He was **elated** at the discovery of a broad, flat rock for the foundation of his abode. He **drafted** blueprints. He seemed **destined** for success. **Diligently** he purchased the supplies and sped back to the clearing. Piggy Number Three began constructing his **exemplary** house. It was **grueling** work, but he **persevered**.

Danger was **looming** right around the corner for the pigs. **Inevitably**, Warrick W. Wolf was slinking about the secluded forest when he met Piggy Number One. The pig let out a squeal of fright and dashed into his house.

"Little pig, little pig," growled Warrick, "let me come in." The villain hoped that his charisma would **transfix** the pig.

With **trepidation**, Piggy Number One squealed, "Not by the hair on my chinny chin chin!" Gaining courage, he added **indignantly**, "I'll not let you come in!"

"Then I'll blow your house down!" howled the wolf. **Vehemently**, Warrick blew with such a **stupendous** force that the **onrush** of wind lifted the straw house off its weak foundation. The piggy was **distraught**. He took off towards his brother's house. Piggy Number Two was **confronted** with the **appalling** scene of his brother dashing away from the snapping, **eerie** jaws of Warrick. Acting quickly, Piggy Number Two sheltered his brother.

"Little pigs, little pigs," Warrick growled, "let me come in."

But Piggy Number Two stated **obstinately**, "Not by the hair on my chiny chin chin! I'll not let you come in!"

"Then I'll blow your house down!"

The wolf's tempestuous wind did not **subside** until the whole house was tipped off its puny foundation and **diminished** into a pile of sticks. The pigs were frightened at the power of Warrick W. Wolf. Seeing him advancing, the frightened porkers scampered speedily off to Piggy Number Three's house. Just as Piggy Number Three **efficiently** laid the last brick onto his wonderful house, he was amazed to spot both his brothers running at top speed towards him. But he did not **waver** in the least. He flung the door open and let his brothers rush in. Then he spotted Warrick.

Warrick let out his **incessant** call, "Little pigs, little pigs, let me come in!"

"Not by the hair on my chiny chin chin! I'll not let you in!" answered Piggy Number Three.

"Then I'll blow your house down!" bellowed the wolf.

The wolf blew with all his might, but the **lofty** house stood firm. The pigs then worked **zealously** to station a pot of boiling water under the chimney. They were none too soon; the wolf was **provoked** to rage. He clambered up to the roof and leapt down the chimney into the house. When he fell into the pot of water, he screeched in pain and crashed through the window. The pigs squealed in **triumph**! And that was the last anyone ever laid eyes on Warrick W. Wolf.

Now, Piggies Number One and Two **affirm** the **profound** philosophy **espoused** by the third pig: "Build your house on the rock," and often **recount** their adventure in a **narrative esteemed** by all their fellow piggies.

Contents

Appendices

APPENDICES

Institute for Excellence in Writing

If your students are handwriting their assignments, disregard the MLA requirement on the checklist.

Appendix I: Modified MLA Format

Format your paper in the following manner:

1. Double-space the entire composition, including the heading and title. Set 1-inch margins all the way around.

2. Only the first page should have the heading in the upper left corner with your name, lesson number, and the date.

3. If your paper is more than one page, every page (including the first) must have a header in the top right corner with your last name and page number. Look at the example below.

4. The text should be left justified. Use 12 pt Times New Roman or similar serif font. Paragraphs should be indented half an inch. There should only be one space after end punctuation to separate sentences.

Your essay should use the format shown below at 3/4 scale.

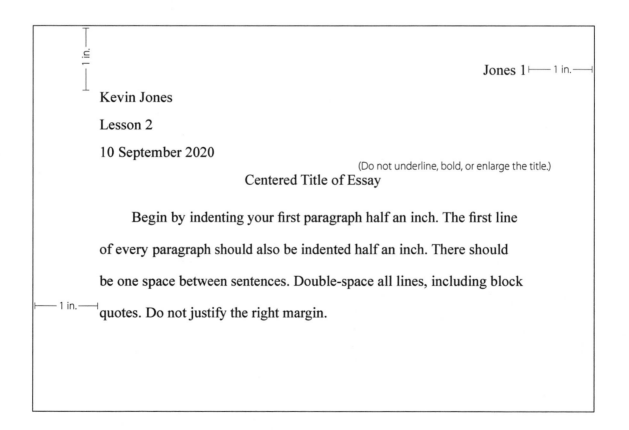

APPENDICES

Institute for Excellence in Writing

Appendix II: Magnum Opus Notebook and Keepsake

If you choose to make a Magnum Opus Notebook, students should make the corrections noted by the teacher. Parents should help their students understand the reason for each correction. This last draft should have the stylistic technique markings removed.

The following page is the checklist that should be attached to each Magnum Opus draft if teachers require them to be turned in. To check, teachers simply make sure that each correction marked on the final draft has been made and that a picture has been added if desired.

Once returned, the Magnum Opus drafts should be kept in a half-inch binder in clear sheet protectors *with the original, labeled final drafts hidden behind the first page of each Magnum Opus draft*. At the end of the year, students will have a fine collection of a variety of types of compositions that move through major themes in U.S. history.

Each student also may do an "About the Author" page as his title page. This can either be a paragraph about himself or an acrostic poem. For the poem option, each student writes his name in large, bold letters in a column down the page. He then uses each of the letters of his name as the first letter of each line of the poem describing himself. With either option, students may include a picture of themselves.

Another fun idea is to make a picture collage of the class for each of the students to put in the front of their notebooks. The students also sign one another's books on blank paper placed at the end of the notebook (like a yearbook) in a clear sheet protector. All these things make the Magnum Opus Notebook a wonderful keepsake of the year.

In a class setting, the teacher may display the Magnum Opus Notebooks at the end of the year at a Parent Day party.

Make copies of this page. You will need one checklist for each lesson.

Magnum Opus Draft Checklist

Each item is worth 5 points.

- ☐ Magnum Opus draft is in clear sheet protector(s) with the original final draft and checklist hidden behind the first page.

- ☐ Composition is neat and double-spaced.

- ☐ Elements of style missing on final draft have been added.

- ☐ Grammar and spelling corrections have been made.

    Picture is added. (Optional)
    (You may draw, or you may cut and paste from the Internet.)

    Note: Magnum Opus drafts do not have to be relabeled.

Total _____ /20

Magnum Opus Draft Checklist

Each item is worth 5 points.

- ☐ Magnum Opus draft is in clear sheet protector(s) with the original final draft and checklist hidden behind the first page.

- ☐ Composition is neat and double-spaced.

- ☐ Elements of style missing on final draft have been added.

- ☐ Grammar and spelling corrections have been made.

    Picture is added. (Optional)
    (You may draw, or you may cut and paste from the Internet.)

    Note: Magnum Opus drafts do not have to be relabeled.

Total _____ /20

Appendix III: Mechanics

Well-written compositions are not only written with structure and style, but they also contain correctly spelled words and proper punctuation. This list represents all of the directions that address correct mechanics or writing which are included within various lessons.

Numbers

Occasionally you will need to incorporate numbers into your writing. Here are rules to keep in mind.

1. Spell out numbers that can be expressed in one or two words.

   twenty, fifty-three, three hundred

2. Use numerals for numbers that are three or more words.

   123, 204

3. Spell out ordinal numbers.

   the seventh city, the first settlement

4. Use numerals with dates. Do not include st, nd, rd or th.

   January 1, 1400

   December 25 not December 25th

5. Never begin a sentence with a numeral.

   1492 is a famous year in history. (incorrect)

   The year 1492 is a famous year in history. (correct)

Names

Names of adults are referenced by their first and last name the first time they are mentioned. After the first time, they are only referenced by their last name.

One of the first attempts was by a group led by John White. (first mention)

White left over a hundred settlers there. (second mention)

Names of ships, aircraft, and spacecraft are italicized. If a report is handwritten, the names of these vessels are underlined.

In 1620 Goodman John Howland boarded an old, creaky merchant ship called the *Mayflower* with a group of Englishmen seeking religious freedom.

Direct Quotes

When characters talk in a story, use quotation marks to indicate the exact words that the characters say.

The Patriots rushed at White yelling, "Kill him! Kill him!"

Separate the speaking verb (*yelling*) from the direct quote with a comma. If the direct quote is an exclamation or question, follow it with an exclamation mark or question mark. Follow the patterns:

| speaking verb, "quote." | speaking verb, "quote!" | speaking verb, "quote?" |
| "quote," speaking verb | "quote!" speaking verb | "quote?" speaking verb |

Commas and periods always go inside the closing quotations. Exclamation marks and question marks go inside closing quotations when they are part of the material quoted; otherwise, they go outside.

Hyphens and Adjectives

Use hyphens when an age comes in front of a noun. Do not use hyphens when the age is after the noun.

Ten-year-old Paul watched the ships in the harbor.

Paul was ten years old.

Titles

Titles of official documents are capitalized. They do not require quotation marks or italics.

In 1776 Benjamin Franklin signed the Declaration of Independence.

Contractions

Contractions are not used in academic writing.

Washington did not want one man to have too much power. (correct)

Washington didn't want one man to have too much power. (incorrect)

Dates, Locations, Directions

When a date includes the month, day, and year, place a comma between the day and year. If the date is placed in the middle of a sentence, place a comma on both sides of the year.

On April 22, 1889, right at noon, over 50,000 people rushed into Oklahoma Territory.

Separate a city and state with a comma. When a city and state are placed in the middle of a sentence, place a comma on both sides of the state.

The day after the rush, Oklahoma City, Oklahoma, became an official city.

Capitalize *north*, *south*, *east*, and *west* when they refer to a region or proper name. Do not capitalize these words when they indicate direction. Do not capitalize the words *northern*, *southern*, *eastern*, or *western*.

People were discovering that the West had valuable resources that could be used by factories in the East.

Many people settled on the western side of the country.

APPENDICES

Appendix IV: Critique Thesaurus

Introduction

Story tale, saga, narrative, epic, legend, mystery, tragedy, comedy, romance, novel, yarn, anecdote, myth

Type sad, nature, science fiction, love, adventure, historical, horror, folk, fairy, animal, moral, space, descriptive

Characters players, actors, heroes, personae, participants, figures, villain, victim, protagonist, antagonist, foil

Role main, central, leading, major, minor, subordinate, lesser, supporting, shadowy, background, secondary, foil

Types adventurous, tragic, comic, bumbling, retiring, extroverted, pliant, scheming, sordid, acquisitive, inquisitive, impulsive, sinister

Analysis well- or poorly-drawn, convincing, fully or underdeveloped, consistent, lifeless, too perfect, overly evil, idyllic, static, dynamic, flat, round

Setting

Time long ago, ancient or biblical times, Middle Ages or medieval, modern, contemporary, futuristic, mythical

Place rural, urban, small town, frontier, pioneer, war, space, slums, ghetto, exotic

Mood mysterious, foreboding, tragic, bland, comic, violent, suspenseful, compelling, sad, supernatural, emotional

Conflict

Stages initiated, promoted, continued, expanded, resolved

Intensity exacerbated, heightened, lessened

Analysis over- or under-played, realistic or unrealistic, convincing, contrived, stretched, sketchy

Plot plan, conspiracy, scheme, intrigue, subplot, sequence of events, action, narrative, episode, unfolds

Climax turning point, most exciting moment, dramatic event, high point, crisis, anticlimactic, inevitable conclusion

Theme message, moral, lesson, topic, sub-theme, matter, subject

Literary Techniques foreshadowing, symbolism, quality of language, short sentences, repetition, revelation of subplot to the narrative, suspense

APPENDICES

Appendix V: Adding Literature

Great literature will be a valuable addition to these lessons. There are many great books set in U.S. history. The books below are suggested because their stories provide background to the compositions students will write in lessons. Many of them make good read-aloud stories. Teachers should read the books before assigning them to their students.

Lessons	Books
1–2	*Squanto, Friend of the Pilgrims*, retold by Clyde Robert Bulla

This is the story of the life of the Wampanoag Indian best known for befriending and helping the Pilgrims. His life was filled with surprising adventure on both sides of the Atlantic that highlight the struggles between Native Americans and Europeans who desired to settle their land. Written for young readers, the story is simply but engagingly told.

3–5

For elementary students: *A Lion to Guard Us* by Clyde Robert Bulla

This is the story of three children who, after the death of their mother, set out on their own from England to America to find their father. It is a classic, inspiring story of "faith, courage, and a great deal of grit" that *The New Yorker* called "An exciting tale. Top-notch writing."

For junior and senior high students: *Night Journeys* by Avi

In 1768, when Peter York loses his parents, he is taken in by a deeply religious Quaker. Peter does not understand this man's ways and longs to break away. But when he crosses paths with a runaway indentured servant, he is faced with a difficult choice that will change his life and his views. This book is written in the powerful, adventure-filled style of Avi, a much-loved writer of more than sixty books for children and teens, three of which are Newbury Award and Honor books.

6–9

For elementary students: *Ben and Me* by Robert Lawson

This is a beloved classic story. It is humorously told by a mouse named Amos who boldly claims to be the mastermind behind Franklin's many inventions and other successes. Kids will grow to love Amos as they laugh their way through the events of one of America's most significant time periods.

For junior and senior high students: *Give Me Liberty* by L.M. Elliot

Nathaniel is an indentured servant in Virginia just prior to the Revolutionary War when Basil, a kind schoolmaster, takes him in. Basil exposes him to music, books, and new philosophies about equality and liberty for all. When war breaks out, both Nathaniel and Basil are swept into it. L.M. Elliot does an excellent job of weaving historical events and people into this story that ALA *Booklist* says is "filled with action, well-drawn characters, and a sympathetic understanding of many points of view." It is a lengthy book (384 pages), but well worth the read.

10–11	For girls: *Tolliver's Secret* by Esther Wood Brady

When her grandfather is injured, ten-year-old Ellen Tolliver must deliver a secret message hidden in a loaf of bread to General Washington. To do so, she must disguise herself as a boy and cross New York Harbor all by herself. Though she meets many unexpected difficulties along the way, she eventually succeeds. Even though this is marked "for girls," boys will enjoy the story, too.

For boys: *Guns for General Washington* by Seymour Reit

This is the true story of how Henry and Will Knox led a group of American soldiers in doing what all the other officers thought was impossible. They transported 183 cannons across three hundred miles of dangerous terrain in the dead of winter to bring them to General Washington in Boston just before the British were to attack.

12–14	*By the Great Horn Spoon!* by Sid Fleischman

This is a fun, humorous tale of a young boy named Jack and his butler, Praiseworthy, who head to California to strike it rich in the gold rush. Their journey begins on a ship sailing from Boston, which must sail all the way around South America. All kinds of adventures meet them both on the ship and once they reach California. The story is jam-packed with IEW dress-ups and decorations.

15–17	For elementary students: *Mr. Lincoln's Drummer* by G. Clifton Wisler

Willie Johnston is only ten years old, but when his father joins the Union Army during the Civil War, Willie decides to join as a drummer boy. The story is based on the real experiences of the real Willie Johnston, the youngest soldier ever to receive the Medal of Honor.

Warning: This book is about war. There are two places that contain fairly graphic depictions of death. One is in the middle of chapter 7 when Willie's friend is shot in the chest. The other is at the end of chapter 10 when the narrator describes the dying and amputated men in the hospital.

For junior and senior high students: *Behind Rebel Lines* by Seymour Reit

Emma Edmonds is a woman who did not want to sit on the sidelines during the Civil War. She disguised herself as a man, joined the Union army, and became an expert spy and master of disguises. This book is based on an unbelievable but true story filled with suspense, danger, and intrigue. Although it is recommended for junior and senior high, elementary students will enjoy this tale as well.

18–21   *Hattie Big Sky* by Kirby Larson

Orphaned sixteen-year-old Hattie has been bounced around from one distant relative to another. She longs for a home of her own, and the opportunity comes when an uncle leaves her a homesteading claim in Montana. The story is set in 1918 and is filled with insight into the challenges of those times, including homesteading, WWI, the discrimination against Germans in America, the Spanish influenza, and more.

22–25   *Journey to Topaz* by Yoshiko Uchida

Yuki and her family are Japanese Americans who live in California when Pearl Harbor is bombed. Her father is suddenly whisked away, and she is moved to an internment camp with the rest of her family. This story is based on the real experiences of the author. It gives much insight into a tragic time for the Japanese in America that is too often overlooked when studying WWII.

26–29   *Cheaper by the Dozen* by Frank B. Gilbreth Jr. and Ernestine Gilbreth Carey

This is a humorous, heartwarming story of a family with twelve children. The parents are both industrial engineers. Father is an efficiency expert, helping assembly-line factories run more smoothly. Mother factors in human emotions. They apply their skills to running their household, which leads to unique, entertaining ways of educating and nurturing their children. Book Rags says, "The book is filled with delightful adventures and lessons learned in this loving household."

Weekly Literature Response Sheet

As you read, do the following:

1. Circle unfamiliar words or words that you particularly like and might want to use in your own writing.

2. Highlight or underline a few elements of style that you particularly like, such as dress-ups and decorations that you have learned and vivid descriptions. *(If you are not allowed to mark in your book, use sticky notes.)*

After you finish reading each section, do the following:

At the top of a paper, under your name and date, write the book title and the chapter numbers you read. Then format your paper like this:

Vocabulary

Under this heading, write two of the words you circled. Follow each with its definition and the sentence and page number in which it was used in the book.

Dress-Ups

Under this heading, write one of the dress-ups you highlighted or underlined. Write the entire sentence in which it occurs and underline the dress-up.

Summary

Write the most significant events of each chapter you read. Write three to five sentences per chapter.

When you finish the entire book, fill out the Final Literature Response Sheet instead of doing the above.

Institute for Excellence in Writing

Final Literature Response Sheet

After you finish a book, use your own paper to answer the following questions.

1. What is the title and author of the book?

2. What is the setting of the book? Describe it.

3. Describe each main character (no more than four).

4. What is the main conflict of the story? (What is the main problem, want, or need of the main character?) Write in complete sentences, but be brief.

5. Are there other important conflicts?

6. What is the climax of the main conflict? (What event leads to the conflict being solved?)

7. What is the resolution? (How do things work out in the end?)

8. Is there a message in the story? If so, what did the main character learn, or what should you, as the reader, have learned?

9. What is your favorite part of the story? Why?

10. What other things do you like or not like about the story?

APPENDICES

Appendix VI: Vocabulary

Most of the lessons have a sheet of four vocabulary cards. In lessons that have cards, you will be instructed to cut them out and place them in a plastic bag or pencil pouch for easy reference. Each week you should study the words for the current lesson and continue to review words from previous lessons. Try to use the vocabulary words in your compositions. For this purpose, you may use any of the words, even from lessons you have not yet had if you would like to look ahead.

For convenience, the following chart shows the words that go with each lesson and where quizzes fall. Quizzes are cumulative and cover all the words listed above them.

Quizzes can be found after the chart. Teachers who do not want students to see the quizzes ahead of time may ask you to tear them from your books and turn them in at the beginning of the school year. This is at the discretion of your teacher.

APPENDICES

Vocabulary at a Glance

Lesson 1	reverently	with deep respect
	presume	to take for granted or suppose
	transfixed	motionless with amazement or terror
	hostile	not friendly; unfavorable to one's well-being
Lesson 2	zealously	with enthusiastic devotion or diligence
	futilely	uselessly or unsuccessfully
	prosperity	successful or thriving condition
	quest	a pursuit to find or obtain something
Quiz 1		
Lesson 3	audaciously	boldly or daringly
	inevitably	unavoidably
	endeavor	an effort or attempt (noun); to make a major effort or attempt (verb)
	eerily	uncomfortably strange in a fearful way
Lesson 4	perilously	involving grave risk or danger
	imprudently	lacking caution or good judgment
	subside	to become less violent or intense
	vehemently	intensely, strongly, or violently
Lesson 5	animosity	strong dislike that shows in action
	adroitly	skillfully or cleverly
	onrush	a strong, fast movement forward
	warily	watchfully and cautiously; looking out for danger
Lesson 6	confront	to face in hostility or defiance
	provoke	to anger; to arouse to action or feeling
	obstinately	firmly holding a purpose or opinion; stubbornly
	indignantly	with strong displeasure at injustice or insult
Quiz 2		
Lesson 7	squander	to waste recklessly
	waver	to be uncertain or unsteady; to swing back and forth
	cunningly	cleverly or slyly
	venture	to boldly go somewhere or do something risky
Lesson 8	persevere	to endure despite difficulty
	compel	to force, drive, or urge
	destined	determined ahead of time
	appalled	filled with horror or dismay
Lesson 9	draft	to write the first form of something (verb); a drawing, sketch, or design (noun)
	diligently	with much care and effort
	acknowledge	to admit to be real or true
	resolve	to make a firm decision; to settle or find a solution
Lesson 10	exemplary	worthy of imitation
	esteemed	highly respected
	prominent	leading or well-known; standing out
	conceive	to form a notion or idea

Quiz 3			
Lesson 11	stirring	rousing, exciting, or lively	
	affirm	to confirm or state positively	
	tyrant	a cruel or brutal ruler	
	adept	very skilled or proficient	
Lesson 12	grueling	exhausting and demanding	
	stupendous	astounding or marvelous	
	extensive	far-reaching or great in amount	
	formidable	having qualities that cause fear, dread, or awe	
Lesson 13	laden	burdened or loaded down	
	fathom	to understand the depth of something	
	incessant	unceasing; continuing without interruption	
	trepidation	fear or agitation	
Lesson 14	deplorable	terrible or disgraceful	
	loom	to appear in a threatening form	
	imperative	absolutely necessary or required	
	distraught	deeply upset or agitated	
Quiz 4	No new words for Lessons 16, 17, and 19		
Lesson 15	diminish	to lessen	
	awestruck	filled with wonder, amazement, or dread	
	solemn	serious or earnest	
	encounter	to come upon unexpectedly or in conflict	
Lesson 18	milestone	a significant event or step in life or in progress	
	thrive	to grow vigorously; to gain in wealth	
	innovative	creative; able to think of new ideas and methods	
	profound	of deep meaning or significance	
Lesson 20	espouse	to support or adopt a cause or theory	
	adverse	unfavorable or opposing one's desires	
	aspire	to long or aim for ambitiously	
	lofty	exalted or superior	
Quiz 5	No new words for Lessons 22–24, 26–27		
Lesson 21	enthrall	to captivate or charm	
	persistent	not giving up	
	emblem	a sign or object that represents something	
	elated	filled with joy and pride	
Lesson 25	achievement	something accomplished by great courage or effort	
	flourish	to achieve success; to thrive	
	transformation	a change	
	efficient	working well with little waste	
Lesson 28	narrative	a story or account of events	
	intrigue	to arouse curiosity by the unusual	
	recount	to give the facts or details in order	
	triumph	a victory	
Final Quiz	No new words for Lessons 29–30		

APPENDICES

Vocabulary Quiz 1 *Answer Key*

futilely	presume	quest	transfixed
hostile	prosperity	reverently	zealously

Fill in the blanks with the appropriate word. Be sure to spell correctly.

1. with deep respect

    1. *reverently*

2. to take for granted or suppose

    2. *presume*

3. motionless with amazement or terror

    3. *transfixed*

4. with enthusiastic devotion or diligence

    4. *zealously*

5. uselessly or unsuccessfully

    5. *futilely*

6. not friendly

    6. *hostile*

7. a pursuit to find or obtain something

    7. *quest*

8. successful or thriving condition

    8. *prosperity*

APPENDICES

Vocabulary Quiz 2 *Answer Key*

adroitly	eerie	indignantly	perilously	subside
audaciously	endeavor	inevitably	provoke	vehemently
confront	futilely	obstinately	reverently	warily

Fill in the blanks with the appropriate word. Be sure to spell correctly.

1. with deep respect   1.   *reverently*

2. unavoidably   2.   *inevitably*

3. uncomfortably strange in a fearful way   3.   *eerie*

4. with strong displeasure at injustice or insult   4.   *indignantly*

5. involving grave risk or danger   5.   *perilously*

6. to anger; to arouse to action or feeling   6.   *provoke*

7. uselessly or unsuccessfully   7.   *futilely*

8   to become less violent or intense   8.   *subside*

9. watchfully and cautiously   9.   *warily*

10. an effort or attempt   10. *endeavor*

11. skillfully or cleverly   11. *adroitly*

12. stubbornly   12. *obstinately*

13. intensely, strongly, or violently   13. *vehemently*

14. to face in hostility or defiance   14. *confront*

15. boldly or daringly   15. *audaciously*

APPENDICES

Vocabulary Quiz 3 *Answer Key*

acknowledge	cunningly	draft	persevere	venture
appalled	destined	exemplary	resolve	waver
compel	diligently	imprudently	squander	zealously

Fill in the blanks with the appropriate word. Be sure to spell correctly.

1. with enthusiastic devotion or diligence

2. lacking caution or good judgment

3. to waste recklessly

4. to be uncertain or unsteady

5. cleverly or slyly

6. to boldly go somewhere or do something risky

7. to endure despite difficulty

8. to force, drive, or urge

9. determined ahead of time

10. filled with horror or dismay

11. to write the first form of something

12. with much care and effort

13. to admit to be real or true

14. to make a firm decision

15. worthy of imitation

1. *zealously*

2. *imprudently*

3. *squander*

4. *waver*

5. *cunningly*

6. *venture*

7. *persevere*

8. *compel*

9. *destined*

10. *appalled*

11. *draft*

12. *diligently*

13. *acknowledge*

14. *resolve*

15. *exemplary*

APPENDICES

Institute for Excellence in Writing

Vocabulary Quiz 4 *Answer Key*

adept	extensive	incessant	onrush	trepidation
affirm	formidable	inevitably	prominent	tyrant
conceive	grueling	laden	quest	waver

Fill in the blanks with the appropriate word. Be sure to spell correctly.

1. a pursuit to find or obtain something
2. a strong, fast movement forward
3. unavoidably
4. to be uncertain or unsteady
5. having qualities that cause fear, dread, or awe
6. to form a notion or idea
7. unceasing; continuing without interruption
8. a cruel or brutal ruler
9. very skilled or proficient
10. fear or agitation
11. leading or well-known; standing out
12. exhausting and demanding
13. to confirm or state positively
14. far-reaching or great in amount
15. burdened or loaded down

1. *quest*
2. *onrush*
3. *inevitably*
4. *waver*
5. *formidable*
6. *conceive*
7. *incessant*
8. *tyrant*
9. *adept*
10. *trepidation*
11. *prominent*
12. *grueling*
13. *affirm*
14. *extensive*
15. *laden*

APPENDICES

Vocabulary Quiz 5 *Answer Key*

adverse	destined	espouse	innovative	obstinately
aspire	diminish	esteemed	lofty	profound
awestruck	distraught	grueling	loom	squander
deplorable	encounter	incessant	milestone	thrive

Fill in the blanks with the appropriate word. Be sure to spell correctly.

1. exalted or superior   1. *lofty*

2. to long or aim for ambitiously   2. *aspire*

3. unfavorable or opposing one's desires   3. *adverse*

4. to support or adopt a cause or theory   4. *espouse*

5. to grow vigorously; to gain in wealth   5. *thrive*

6. of deep meaning or significance   6. *profound*

7. creative; able to think of new ideas and methods   7. *innovative*

8. a significant event or step in life or in progress   8. *milestone*

9. to come upon unexpectedly or in conflict   9. *encounter*

10. terrible or disgraceful   10. *deplorable*

11. filled with wonder, amazement, or dread   11. *awestruck*

12. unceasing   12. *incessant*

13. to lessen   13. *diminish*

14. deeply upset or agitated   14. *distraught*

15. to appear in a threatening form   15. *loom*

16. highly respected   16. *esteemed*

17. exhausting and demanding   17. *grueling*

18. determined ahead of time   18. *destined*

19. to waste recklessly   19. *squander*

20. stubbornly   20. *obstinately*

APPENDICES

Institute for Excellence in Writing

Final Vocabulary Quiz *Answer Key*

animosity	elated	imperative	persistent	transfixed
audaciously	emblem	intrigue	profound	transformation
compel	enthrall	narrative	recount	triumph
efficient	flourish	perilously	solemn	zealously

1. motionless with amazement or terror
2. strong dislike that shows in action
3. serious or earnest
4. boldly or daringly
5. to achieve success; to thrive
6. a change
7. working well with little waste
8. a story or account of events
9. to arouse curiosity by the unusual
10. absolutely necessary or required
11. to give the facts or details in order
12. a victory
13. with enthusiastic devotion or diligence
14. involving grave risk or danger
15. to force, drive, or urge
16. filled with joy and pride
17. to captivate or charm
18. not giving up
19. a sign or object that represents something
20. of deep meaning or significance

1. *transfixed*
2. *animosity*
3. *solemn*
4. *audaciously*
5. *flourish*
6. *transformation*
7. *efficient*
8. *narrative*
9. *intrigue*
10. *imperative*
11. *recount*
12. *triumph*
13. *zealously*
14. *perilously*
15. *compel*
16. *elated*
17. *enthrall*
18. *persistent*
19. *emblem*
20. *profound*

Appendix VII: Review Games

Earning Tickets for the Auction (a semester-long game) ⸻⸻⸻⸻⸻
Gather

raffle tickets (5-, 10-, 25-point tickets printed on colored paper)

Play

Because positive reinforcement is a wonderful motivator, throughout the year allow students opportunities to earn tickets that they can use at an auction conducted at the end of each semester. Give tickets when students win games, incorporate vocabulary words or advanced additions in their writing, and when they do something particularly well. Periodically offer contests for tickets such as "Best Title" or the best of each type of dress-up. Many of the games explained in this appendix include directions for giving tickets.

The Auction (a game to play the last day of each semester) ⸻⸻⸻⸻⸻
Gather

items for auction
a whiteboard and marker
an envelope for each student

Prepare

At the end of the semester, ask students to bring one to three items to auction to class. The items can be new or items from home. Students put their tickets in envelopes. Label each envelope with the student name and number of tickets. Write the students' names and number of tickets on a whiteboard in order from greatest to least. Instead of having students physically use tickets when they buy and sell, add and subtract from the totals written on the board.

Play

1. To begin the bidding, ask the student with the most tickets which item he or she would like to be auctioned first. Bids must begin at 25 tickets or higher. Students who would like the item continue to bid. The highest bidder receives the item, and the bid price is subtracted from his or her ticket total. Once a student has purchased an item, he or she may not bid on another item until everyone has bought one item.

2. Repeat this process, letting the second student listed on the board choose the next item. Then the third student, and so forth. This means the last person will get his or her pick of what is left for 25 tickets.

3. Once everyone has one item, it is open bidding for what is left.

Vocabulary Find the Card

Gather

twelve to sixteen index cards with vocabulary words written on each
a timer
pocket chart (optional for large class)

Play

1. Divide the class into three teams and spread the cards face up on a table. In a large class, display the cards in a pocket chart instead of laying on a table. Allow the students thirty seconds to study the cards.

2. Turn the cards face down.

3. Read the definition of one of the words. The first team must turn over one of the word cards, trying to find the word that matches the definition.

   ✔ If the word matches the definition, that team receives two points and the word card is returned to its spot on the table (face down) so that all word cards remain on the table the entire game. Play continues with the next team and the next definition.

   ✔ If the word card does not match the definition, the word card is returned and the next team attempts to find the correct word for the same definition. Now the correct word is worth three points. If missed again, the next team tries to find the correct word for the same definition for four points. Continue in this way until the correct word is found. Limit the point value to ten. *Variation*: When an incorrect word is turned over, award one point if the team that picked it can give its correct definition.

4. After the first word is found, repeat #3 with a new definition. Continue the process until all definitions have been used.

5. The player or team with the most points wins.

No-Noose Hangman

Gather

> a whiteboard and marker
> a die (optional)
> tickets

Play

1. Choose a phrase and place lines to represent the letters of the phrase on the board. The phrase may be a vocabulary definition or an IEW concept.

   Example Phrase

   > To remind students what can be written on a key word outline, use the phrase THREE KEY WORDS. On a whiteboard, write a blank for each letter in the phrase.
   >
   > ___ ___ ___ ___ ___   ___ ___ ___   ___ ___ ___ ___ ___

2. Students take turns guessing letters, one letter per turn. If the letter is in the puzzle, place it on the correct blank(s) and give the student a ticket for each time it is used. If the letter is not in the puzzle, write it on the bottom of the whiteboard so no one else will guess it. *Variation*: Let students roll a die and give tickets equal to the number rolled times how many times the letter is used.

3. When a student knows the phrase, he or she may solve the puzzle. It does not have to be his turn. If a student states the phrase correctly, he receives 10 tickets.

4. After a student states the phrase, ask a bonus question about the phrase. If the student answers the bonus question correctly, he receives 5 additional tickets.

   Example Question

   > In addition to two to three key words, what may you write on each line of a KWO?
   >
   > *symbols, numbers, and abbreviations*

5. Repeat with several puzzles.

Around the World

Gather

vocabulary cards
tickets

Play

1. Start with two students. Read a definition. The first to shout the correct vocabulary word receives a ticket and moves on to challenge the next student.

2. Continue in the same way. The winner always moves on to the next student. If one student makes it all the way "around the world" (beats everyone in the class), he receives 5 extra tickets.

Vocabulary Pictionary

Gather

two whiteboards (or one large one with a line sectioning it)
two whiteboard markers
a die

Play

1. Divide the class into two teams. Assign each a whiteboard. Call one person from each team to the front of the class. Have each drawer roll the die to determine the number of points his or her team will receive if he or she wins the round. Instruct the drawers to write the number rolled on the top of the whiteboards so it is not forgotten.

2. Show the drawers the vocabulary word you want them to draw. They will both draw the same word. Letters and numbers may not be used.

3. The first team to guess the word receives the number of points rolled on the die. Erase the boards and play again with two new drawers.

Vocabulary Lightning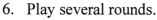

Gather

vocabulary cards
a timer

Play

1. Divide the class into two or three teams.

2. Choose one or two players from one of the teams to represent the team. Show the representative(s) the stack of vocabulary cards with the word sides up. He may not look at the back of the card to see the definition.

3. The representative(s) tries to get the team to say as many of the vocabulary words as possible in one minute. To do so, he or she looks at the first word and gives the team various clues by stating the definition, acting out the word, or describing the picture on the card. He or she may not say things such as what letter the word begins with or what it rhymes with. *Variation:* Do not allow talking—only acting.

4. As soon as someone from the team shouts the correct word, the teacher should place the card on a table and move to the next word. If the representative gets stuck on a word, he or she may "pass" it, resulting in losing a point. For ease in sorting, passed word cards should be placed in a separate stack from the word cards guessed correctly.

5. When the time is up, count the number of words the first team guessed. Subtract the number of words passed. That difference is that team's score for that round. Let other team(s) have a turn in the same way. The team with the highest score wins that round.

6. Play several rounds.

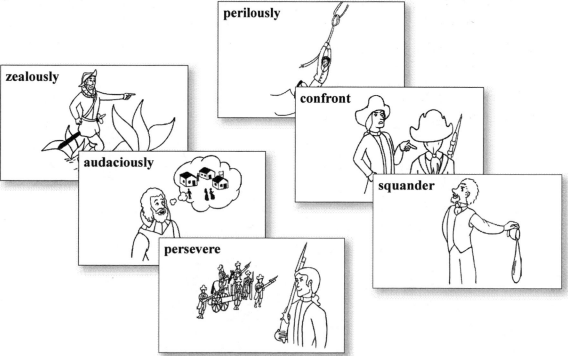

Question Game

Gather

a whiteboard and marker
a die
a list of questions (See suggested questions on pages 347–349.)
tickets

Play

1. Write numbers 1 through how many questions you will be using on a whiteboard and divide the class into three teams.

2. The first team chooses a number, and you read the corresponding question from your list.

    ✔ If the team answers correctly, one of the members rolls the die for points, and you erase the number from the board so that question will not be chosen again.

    ✔ If the team answers incorrectly, you circle the number. That team receives no points and another team may choose that circled number for double points on their turn.

    Three different ways to roll the die for points:

     The simple way is to roll the die once and receive the points indicated.

     A more challenging way is to let a team roll as many times as they choose, adding each roll to their total for that turn. So, if their first roll is a 4, and then they roll a 3, they are at 7 points. However, if they roll a 6 before they choose to stop rolling, they lose all the accumulated points for that turn. In other words, they must choose after each roll whether to roll again for more points or to stop before they roll a 6.

     As added fun, declare 2 means "Lose a turn" and 4 means "Free roll."

3. Play until most questions have been chosen and teams have had an equal number of turns. Each player on the team with the most points receives 5 tickets.

Tic-Tac-Toe

Gather

a list of questions (See suggested questions on pages 347–349.)
a whiteboard and marker
two dice

Prepare

Draw a Tic-Tac-Toe board and number the squares 1–9. Write the Special Moves on the whiteboard.

1	2	3
4	5	6
7	8	9

Special Moves

A total of 7	=	Take an extra turn.
Double 1, 2, or 3	=	Erase an opponent's mark.
Double 4, 5	=	Erase an opponent's mark and replace it with yours.
Double 6	=	WILD. Go anywhere. You may erase your opponent's mark if need be.

Play

1. Divide players into an X team and an O team.

2. The X team begins. Read a question. If the team answers correctly, place an X in the square of choice. The team then rolls two dice to determine whether they make special moves before the O team plays. If the team answers incorrectly, the O team plays.

3. The O team plays.

4. Play until one team has three in a row or all squares are filled.

5. Repeat until one team has won two out of three or three out of five games.

Two Strikes and You're Out

Gather

eleven index cards (Write strong verbs and quality adjectives on each. Include vocabulary words.)
five index cards (Write banned words students know on each, repeating words if necessary.)
tickets

Play

1. Place the cards in a pocket chart and cover them with numbers or lay the cards face down on a table.

2. Divide the class into three teams.

3. Teams take turns picking a card.

   ✔ If the card chosen is a strong verb or a quality adjective, team members must identify it as such and use it in a sentence. If it is a vocabulary word, they should give the definition. They keep the card.

   ✔ If the card chosen is a banned word, the team receives a strike. When a team has received two strikes, the team is out and may not take any more turns.

4. Play until two teams have been eliminated. The remaining team wins, and each member receives 10 tickets. In addition, give each player on all teams 5 tickets for each strong verb or quality adjective found.

Find the *www.asia* Clause Starters (a variation of the game above)

Gather

seven index cards with *when, while, where, as, since, if, although* written on each
    (After lesson 21, include *because*.)
six index cards with *who, what, why, is, and* written on each (After lesson 21, include *because of.*)
tickets

Play

1. Place the cards in a pocket chart and cover them with numbers or lay the cards face down on a table.

2. Divide the class into three teams.

3. Teams take turns picking a card.

   ✔ If the card chosen is an adverb clause starter, team members must identify it as such and use it in a sentence. They keep the card.

   ✔ If the card chosen is not an adverb clause starter, the team receives a strike. When a team has received two strikes, the team is out and may not take any more turns.

4. Play until two teams have been eliminated. The remaining team wins, and each member receives 10 tickets. In addition, give each player on all teams 5 tickets for each www.asia clause starter found.

Preposition Round Robin

Gather

a list of prepositions (A short list is on page 115. The *Portable Walls for Structure and Style® Students* and the IEW Writing Tools App contain longer lists.)
a whiteboard and marker
tickets
a timer

Play

1. Give students one minute to study the list of prepositions. Remove the list from sight.

2. In turn, allow each student ten seconds to name a preposition. As each preposition is named, write it on the whiteboard and let the student take a ticket.

3. Students who are successful remain standing; however, if a student cannot think of a preposition, says a word that is not a preposition, or says a preposition already on the whiteboard, he must sit down.

4. Continue until only one student remains standing. (If two or three students remain and none of them can say another preposition, they tie.)

5. The winner receives 10 additional tickets.

Prepositions

above

across

around

after

by

during

for

from

in

inside

into

...

Elimination

Gather

vocabulary cards
tickets

Play

1. Divide the class into groups of three or four students. Try to have an even number of groups.

2. Begin with the first group. Read a definition of a vocabulary word. The first student in that group to shout out the matching word gets a ticket. Continue with the first group until one student has 3 tickets. He or she is the winner and will advance. The rest of the group has been eliminated.

3. Repeat the process with the other groups.

4. Divide winners into two groups and repeat the process with both groups.

5. Finally, repeat the process with the two remaining students. The winner of the final round receives 5 additional tickets.

Simplified Jeopardy!® (an end-of-the-year game) _____

Gather

> prepared cards
> three dice
> a whiteboard and marker

Prepare

> Write several question index cards. Categorize the questions by *Structure, Style, Mechanics,* or *Vocabulary.* Rank the questions by level of difficulty (1 = easy; 2 = medium; 3 = difficult). Write a question on one side of each card and the category and level of difficulty on the other side.

Play

1. Lay the cards question side down as illustrated.

STRUCTURE 1	STYLE 1	MECHANICS 1	VOCABULARY 1
STRUCTURE 2	STYLE 2	MECHANICS 2	VOCABULARY 2
STRUCTURE 3	STYLE 3	MECHANICS 3	VOCABULARY 3

2. Divide the class into three teams. Teams take turns choosing a question by category and level of difficulty. If the team chooses a Level 1 (easy) question, they may roll one die to determine its point value. If they choose a Level 2, they roll two dice. If they choose a Level 3, they roll three dice.

   ✔ If the team answers the question correctly, they receive the points indicated on the dice. Keep track of points on the whiteboard.

   ✔ If they do not answer correctly, they do not get any points. The missed card should be placed face up as a jeopardy question. This means another team may choose it when it is their turn. Any team that can answer a previously missed question receives double the point value that they roll with two dice. However, if they miss it, they must subtract the points rolled (not doubled).

3. Jeopardy! If a team rolls a total of 5, the question becomes a jeopardy question. This means that if they miss it, 5 points will be subtracted from their point total. However, if they answer correctly, they receive double points, which will be 10 points.

4. Play until time runs out, ensuring each team has had the same number of questions.

? Questions (to use with the question games) _____

Style (Dress-Ups)

1. What dress-ups have we learned thus far? How should you label them? *(underline)*

2. If you take a *who/which* clause out of a sentence, what should be left? *(a complete sentence)*

3. What are the banned words? *(go/went, say/said, good, bad, pretty, big, small)*

4. Where does a comma go with a *because* clause (and *www.asia* clause)? *(after the entire www.asia.b clause)*

5. Improve this sentence by changing the banned word: *The minutemen went to Lexington Green to stop the redcoats. (Answers will vary.)*

6. Improve this sentence by changing the banned word and adding a *because* clause: *America is a good nation. (Answers will vary.)*

Structure (Units 2–4)

7. What do we call the time and place of a story? *(setting)*

8. What do we call the problem, want, or need of the main character of a story? *(conflict)*

9. What do we call the event that leads to the conflict being solved? *(climax)*

10. When summarizing a reference, what should each paragraph of a summary report begin with? *(topic sentence)*

11. What is the topic-clincher rule? *(The topic sentence and the clincher sentence must repeat or reflect two or three key words.)*

12. Do narrative story paragraphs have topic sentences? *(no)*

Style (Sentence Openers)

13. What sentence openers have you learned? How do you label them? *(number)*

14. How many -ly adverbs do you need at minimum in each paragraph? *(two: one as a dress-up and one as a #3 -ly adverb opener)*

15. Give six prepositions that can begin a #2 sentence. *(See page 115.)*

16. What is a #5 sentence opener? *(www.asia.b clause)* What do these letters stand for? *(when, while, where, as, since, if, although, because)*

17. With which is a comma always required, and where do you place the comma: #5 opener or *www.asia.b* dress-up? *(opener; comma goes after the entire clause)*

18. How many words may be in a #6 sentence? *(2–5)*

19. Give an example of a sentence with a #4 sentence opener. *(Answers will vary.)*

? **Questions** (to use with the question games) _____

Structure (Units 5–9)

20. When writing a three-paragraph story from three pictures, how should you begin each paragraph? *(with the central fact of each picture)*

21. When writing a research report (using more than one source text), after you have your sources, what must you do BEFORE you begin making key word outlines? *(choose topics)*

22. Should each note page for a research report have all the notes from the *same source* or all the notes for the *same topic*? *(same topic)*

23. What is a fused outline? *(the outline you make by picking notes from key word outlines you made from more than one source; it is the outline you use to write your paragraph)*

24. When you must write without a source text (your own thoughts), how can you get ideas for what to write? *(ask yourself questions)*

25. What are the brain-helping questions that can help you ask questions to think of more details to add to your writing? *(who, what, where, how, why, when, doing, thinking, feeling, saying, before, after, outside) (See page 200.)*

26. What is the structure of a basic five-paragraph essay? *(introduction, three body paragraphs, conclusion)*

27. What must an introduction paragraph include? *(attention getter, background, and the topics of the body paragraphs)*

28. What are some techniques for creating attention getters? *(ask a question, use a vss, use a quote, begin with an intriguing fact)*

29. What must a concluding paragraph include? *(restate the topics, tell what is most something (significant, interesting, ...) and why, end with a final sentence that repeats one to three words in the title)*

30. What is the purpose of a critique? *(to give and support an opinion about a story)*

31. What should you *not* say in a critique? *("I" or "my," as in "I think" or "in my opinion")*

32. What is the structure of a basic five-paragraph critique? *(introduction paragraph, paragraph for setting and characters, paragraph for conflict, paragraph for climax and resolution, conclusion paragraph that analyzes the story)*

? **Questions** (to use with the question games) _____

Mechanics

33. Which numbers should usually be spelled out rather than written as numerals? *(numbers that can be written in one or two words)*

34. When writing the names of ships, aircraft, or spacecraft, what should you do? *(italicize)*

35. When used with quotations, do periods and commas always go inside or outside of end quotation marks? *(inside)*

36. When must you hyphenate ages? *(When used in front of a noun: nine-year-old Mary)*

37. Must titles of official documents such as the U.S. Constitution be written in italics? *(no)*

38. Where must commas be placed in this sentence: *He was born May 15 1884 in London England on a bleak day. (before and after 1884 and before and after England: He was born May 15, 1884, in London, England, on a bleak day.)*

39. When must you capitalize direction words like north, south, east, west? *(when they refer to a region or proper name: The West was an exciting place of new growth.)*

Vocabulary

Use any definition and ask the student to give the vocabulary word.

What's next?

Always prepare yourself for each unit with our teacher-training course.

Teaching Writing: Structure and Style

This powerful and inspiring seminar will transform the way you teach writing to children (and perhaps your own writing as well)!

IEW.com/TWSS2

AND Choose a new theme-based book.
Continue with comparable source texts and lessons.

| SLIGHTLY EASIER FOR REVIEW | COMPARABLE FOR MORE PRACTICE | | | MORE CHALLENGING | |

     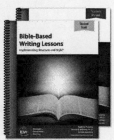

Ancient History-Based Writing Lessons
IEW.com/AHW-TS

Canadian History-Based Writing Lessons
IEW.com/CAH-TS

Medieval History-Based Writing Lessons
IEW.com/MHW-TS

Modern World History-Based Writing Lessons
IEW.com/WHB-TS

Following Narnia® Volume 1: The Lion's Song
IEW.com/FN1-TS

Bible-Based Writing Lessons
IEW.com/BBW-TS

OR Choose the video instruction method on the next page.

IEW
Listen. Speak. Read. Write. Think!

IEW.com
800.856.5815